Mastering the Amstrad PCW 8256/8512:
word processing and personal computing

by

John M. Hughes

SIGMA PRESS

ISBN 1 85058 052 9

Published by:

SIGMA PRESS
98A Water Lane
Wilmslow
Cheshire
U.K.

Distributed by:

U.K., Europe, Africa:
JOHN WILEY & SONS LIMITED
Baffins Lane, Chichester
West Sussex, England

Australia:
JOHN WILEY & SONS INC.
GPO Box 859, Brisbane
Queensland 40001
Australia

Acknowledgments

PCW 8256 and PCW 8512 are trademarks of Amstrad Consumer Electronics PLC, who also kindly provided the cover photographs for this book.
Locoscript is a trademark of Locomotive Software Ltd.

Printed in Great Britain by J. W. Arrowsmith Ltd,
Bristol

CONTENTS

PREFACE

The Amstrad PCW8256 Personal Computer and Word Processor is one of the most exciting aids to business for years. It offers, at an astonishingly low price, advanced word processing and computing facilities which must prove attractive to the first-time user and the computer expert alike.

With such an attractive machine available, there existed a need for a comprehensive but straightforward tutorial book which would focus on the beginning user, and introduce him to the PCW8256.

Taking a cue from the PCW8256 itself, and stressing simplicity and ease of use, this is a book for the user who is aware of the advantages the PCW8256 offers, but is uncertain of how best to make use of them.

It is an indication of the writer's familiarity with the PCW8256, as well as of the flexibility of the machine, that the greater part of this book was actually written using it as a word processor.

Although the book sets out first and foremost to provide a jargon-free introduction to the PCW8256, it also provides a guide to some of the hundreds of CP/M programs which will run on the machine.

We hope that 'Mastering the Amstrad PCW8256/8512' will give you a better understanding of what your computer can do, and of how best to use it. We believe that by the time you have read the book you will feel confident and completely at your ease with your Amstrad.

INTRODUCTION

Starting From Where You Are.

The book you have in your hand, a PCW8256 on your desk, and your natural curiosity and determination – these are all you need to set yourself on the road to easy word processing and personal computing.

What you certainly *don't* need is previous experience of computing, or any notion of how a computer or word processor works. You don't even need the sort of natural caution with which most people approach computers for the first time, for your PCW8256 is far more difficult to damage accidentally (unless you drop it or attack it with a hatchet!) than almost anything else.

There are two ways of looking at a personal computer. The first is to see it as a help in carrying out the same tasks as before, but in a better way.

Used as a word-processor, for example, it makes the typist's job easier; used for accounting, it enables you to make a more efficient job of keeping the same sort of records that you have always kept.

The other approach is more radical; with the PCW8256 you can not only do the old things better, but a multitude of new things too – things that would have been well-nigh impossible before.

Spreadsheets, for instance, enable you to prepare detailed financial projections for a vast range of eventualities; databases give you virtually instantaneous access to information that might otherwise have remained buried in the depths of your filing system, so that you can make rapid decisions based on accurate, up-to-the minute information.

No matter which approach you favour, the sure key to success is to take things a step at a time. If you hope to have a fully automated office within a week of installing your new PCW8256, then you will certainly be disappointed; better to familiarise yourself with the machine, remembering that a modest investment of time at the start will pay handsome dividends later.

1

That is why this book is designed to start you off gently with an introduction to LocoScript, the word processing program included with your PCW8256, and then gradually extend the frontiers of your experience as you become more confident and more familiar with what the machine can do.

As you work your way through the book, sooner or later you will come to some topic that doesn't interest you, or that you feel is beyond what you can cope with. When that happens, skip that section. One day, when your needs change or your confidence increases, you may come back to it; but if not, no matter.

Where to go from here.

If you are already familiar with computers, you may want to skip Chapter One and move straight on to word-processing with LocoScript in Chapter Two; if not, we suggest that you sit down with Chapter One open in front of you and with the computer on your desk.

To help you find your way around the book, each chapter starts with a short Preview of the material to be covered in that chapter, and ends with a brief Postscript.

Occasionally, if a particular topic is introduced in one part of the book, but dealt with in more detail somewhere else, the Preview will refer you to the other section as well.

As the various steps are outlined in the text, try them out; this is a far more effective way of learning than reading through the book first and then trying to remember everything it said.

When you reach the Postscript to each chapter, take time to check it over and make sure that you really are comfortable with the various items that you need to know; there is no advantage in racing on to the next section if you are not tolerably sure of what you have already read.

If you do get really stuck, perhaps you can find a friend who will be able to help. But if you take things gently, you will assuredly not get stuck very often.

An important note on LocoScript.

Like any other complicated modern product, **LocoScript**, the program which turns the PCW8256 into a convenient and fast word processor, is undergoing continuous development.

This book was written while Version 1.04 was being finalised, and an early copy of it was made available to the author.

This differed from Version 1.00 in that certain minor bugs had been eliminated; the most significant improvements were the correction of a fault which made page numbering difficult, and an offer to store files on drive M if drive A was using a read-only disc.

Later versions have since been released which offer further improvements in two areas. First, they enable text files to be created in ASCII format for access by spelling checker programs and the like; and second, they offer the facility of printing a selected page or pages from within a larger document.

This file is *not* meant for the beginner, and if you are new to word processing, it will be best to ignore it for the time being.

When in due course you feel ready to explore it, call it up like any other file. We suggest that you do not even consider looking at it until you have worked your way through the examples in Chapters One and Two.

One disc drive or two?

The PCW8256 is supplied complete with a single disc drive, Drive A. If you wish, a second drive, Drive B, can be fitted in the space underneath Drive A; among other things, this will facilitate making 'backup' copies of discs, to reduce the chances of accidental loss of your precious files.

It also appears likely that in the near future, a high-capacity 'fixed disc' (as opposed to the removable 'floppy discs' which are supplied as standard with the PCW8256) will become available.

In this book it is generally assumed that only the single Drive A is available, though a few hints are given about specific points that may need extra care if a second drive is installed.

Beyond the PCW8256

It is expected that the Amstrad PCW8512 will be launched just as this book appears. The PCW8512 should be similar to the PCW8256, except for a larger memory which, in any event, it is possible to add to an 8256.

The effects of this additional memory are two-fold. First, and most important, the storage capacity of the RAM-Disc (Drive M) is increased to bring it into line with the capacity of a real 3" floppy disc; this means that the duplicating of discs will be made much easier, as the entire contents of a floppy disc can now be copied onto Drive M (and thence to another real disc) in one move.

A second result of the increased capacity of the RAM-Disc is that the operation of programs which make use of **overlays** may be made faster by placing the overlays onto Drive M; the procedure is described in the body of the book.

The increased memory capacity of the machine will also enable much greater quantities of text to be stored and manipulated using the LocoScript word processor. This can only be beneficial.

However, the usual cautions about the length of any individual document still apply; long documents are especially vulnerable to loss in the event of power failure, and there are few benefits in creating them.

In the following chapters, everything which is described for the PCW8256 can also be carried out in exactly the same way on a larger machine; in those places where the extra memory of any newer machine (or an upgraded PCW8256) may be helpful, this has been remarked on in the text.

CHAPTER ONE

Getting Started

Preview.

In this chapter, we shall discuss the following topics:

> About word processing
> Settling in with the PCW8256
> The keyboard
> Starting up
> Setting up the printer
> Direct printing
> Copying discs – see Chapter 6 for more information
> Looking after discs

Starting off.

Computers aren't hard to master – witness the number of schoolchildren who use them – but many people do find them hard to get on with at first.

No doubt a lot of this is the fault of the experts who set out to popularise them. "See how easy it is," they say, performing some feat which leaves the onlookers in bewildered silence, "Look! No hands!"

In this chapter, we shall be taking a rather basic look at the How of word-processing on the PCW8256. To use an analogy from motoring, we shall not be discussing the operation of the carburettor and the exhaust manifold, but rather seeing what happens when you press the accelerator or brake pedals.

Looking at the machinery.

A computer like the PCW8256 is made up of a number of separate component parts, such as the printer, the screen, the disc drive and the processor (which is the part which actually does the work of word processing or whatever you are doing).

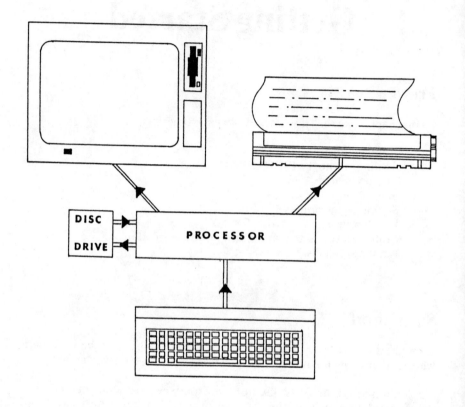

Fig. 1.1

The easiest way to think of it is as a series of inter-connected boxes – the screen, the printer, the disc drive, the keyboard and the processor and its memory – like Fig. 1.1.

(This doesn't correspond precisely with the actual component parts of the PCW8256, as the processor and the disc drives are physically housed in the screen unit, but in terms of what actually goes on in the machine, and the flow of data through the system, the diagram is accurate.)

For the most part, this information flows in one direction only, as shown by the arrows between the keyboard and the processor, between the processor and the screen, and between the processor and the printer.

When you switch on the computer, the processor's memory is, to all intents and purposes, empty. In this, the PCW8256 differs from most so-called 'home computers' which are ready to use as soon as they are turned on.

The first job of the user, therefore, is to put enough information into the processor to enable it to begin doing its job. This is extremely straight-forward, and involves no more than putting the appropriate disc into the disc drive. The process is described in detail a little further on.

You will see that information can travel in both directions between the processor and the disc; in Fig. 1.1 this is shown by the arrows pointing in both directions between the disc drive and the processor.

Once the information has been put into the processor, the PCW8256 is ready to work. Remember that the information which you have loaded in, like everything else that you will feed into the processor, will stay there only until you replace it with something else or you switch the computer off; next time you use it, you will have to repeat the procedure.

Two kinds of information can be fed into the processor. The first kind is a set of instructions for the processor to obey, which is called a **program** (note the un-British spelling, by the way); the second is **data**, such as the text of a letter or price-list that you are preparing.

An expression which is often used in computing circles as a sort of shorthand for 'programs' is **software**. A computing or word processing system can thus be said to consist of both hardware and software.

The first section of this book is about the powerful word processing program supplied with your PCW8256, **LocoScript**. It is loaded automatically into the computer when you load the first disc, as described below.

7

Once this has been done, you are ready to type in at the keyboard whatever text you wish. The processor will know what to do with it, because it will simply be following its program of instructions.

In the majority of cases, this will involve displaying on the screen the text you have entered; at the same time it will be stored in the memory – known in computer circles as **RAM**, standing for Random Access Memory.

Other instructions you could give might cause text to be deleted, or moved from one part of the document on which you are working to another.

When you are ready, the typed-in data can be passed from the processor to the printer, giving what is often called 'hard copy' or 'printout.'

In computer terms, the keyboard is an **input device**, and both the printer and the screen are **output devices**, on which the results of the processor's operations can be displayed.

We have already seen that when the computer is turned off, everything stored in it – data and program alike – will be lost. All computers therefore need some form of permanent 'external storage.'

On the PCW8256, this takes the form of discs which are fitted into the built-in disc-drive. Anything of which you want to keep a permanent copy can be recorded (**saved** is the usual computer jargon) onto a disc placed in the drive.

You will often hear computer discs referred to as 'floppy discs,' or even 'floppies,' and if you are not used to computers this term may surprise you, as those used with the PCW8256 are actually quite rigid.

The reason for this is that discs are available in a number of different sizes and types (though only 3" discs will fit the PCW8256). These 3" discs are enclosed in a strong plastic case for ease of use, but the larger 5 ¼" discs used by some computers do not have this protection, so that they are indeed 'floppy.'

3" discs are sometimes called 'compact discs,' but they have nothing in common with the 'compact discs' used for sound recording. They are also occasionally referred to as 'diskettes' but there is no special significance to the term.

This process of saving material on disc is an extremely rapid one, and even substantial amounts of data can be recorded in just a few seconds.

More important than the speed, perhaps, is the fact that you don't need to know anything at all about how or where information is stored on the disc; in this regard, recording material onto a disc is quite different from recording onto a video or audio cassette tape, where you have to advance the tape to the right place before recording to avoid erasing some other material.

All these details are automatically taken care of by the computer, and a simple instruction to save information onto the disc is all that is required – your PCW8256 will know exactly where on the disc it is best to store it, and how to find it again when the time comes.

When you need to gain access to that information in the future, you can simply 'read' it back into the memory off the same disc.

One disc drive, known as Drive A, is already fitted to the PCW8256, and there is room for an optional second drive (Drive B) to be fitted as well.

Although data can be transferred to and from the discs so quickly, short delays are inevitable. To overcome these, one portion of the PCW8256's memory is set aside as a sort of imaginary disc drive.

As far as the computer is concerned, this imaginary disc drive is treated exactly like a real one. It is known as Drive M.

Information can be stored on Drive M and recovered without even waiting for the few seconds needed by a real drive. It therefore makes an excellent scratch-pad for use during a writing session, for example.

Sometimes, the processor uses Drive M for this purpose without you even being aware of it; however, you can make deliberate use of Drive M yourself, if you wish.

Like everything else in the computer's memory, the contents of Drive M are lost when you switch the machine off, so anything you want to keep permanently has to be transferred from there to an actual disc. The way in which this is done is covered in Chapter Two.

Settling In.

Although your PCW8256 does not need the air-conditioned sterile environment which more old-fashioned computer equipment demanded, you will still not get the best out of it if you simply set it up on some convenient desk-top; however, the problems that will arise if you do this are more likely to affect you as a user than the reliability of the computer.

Some aspects of the installation of the PCW8256 are more or less firmly fixed by the physical layout of the computer itself; the short length of the ribbon cable joining the printer to the monitor, for example, may limit the number of ways in which the various units can be positioned.

Every so often there is press speculation about health hazards from the use of computer equipment. Most of these fears are probably very much over-stated, but there are some points which deserve attention.

In order to avoid back, wrist and shoulder strain, and to ensure that the operator is as comfortable as possible when using the machine for long periods, it is important to place the components at the right height.

The screen should be placed rather higher than the keyboard; the optimum height for the former is about 29" – 32" from the floor, and the latter should be about 6" lower.

Special desks can be obtained which have a raised area for this purpose; alternatively, 'plinths' or 'bridges' can be placed on ordinary desk tops to achieve a similar effect.

Eye-strain, leading to headaches and loss of concentration, may occur when the monitor is used continuously for long periods, but a few simple precautions can be taken which will help to reduce the problem.

The major requirement is to avoid glare, first by ensuring that the brightness control (on the bottom of the screen unit at the front right) is kept turned down to the lowest comfortable level, and second by positioning the unit so that there is no external reflection onto the screen.

A slight downward tilt to the monitor also helps, by eliminating reflections from overhead lighting. If discomfort persists, special polarising filters can be obtained, and when these are placed over the monitor screen they will eliminate glare completely.

The Keyboard.

On the left of the keyboard unit is a section containing the familiar typewriter alphabetic and numeric keys, with the addition of three keys labelled STOP, ALT and EXTRA, whose function will be described in due course.

The SHIFT LOCK key has a light to show when it is engaged. The large key marked RETURN on the right of this section serves the same purpose as Carriage Return on a typewriter.

The keys on the PCW8256 are capable of producing a wide range of symbols, not all of which are shown on the key-tops, and several different programs make use of this ability, though not always in the same way.

LocoScript, for example, provides a range of accents and non-English characters, so that most languages which use a form of the Roman alphabet, as well as Greek, can be accurately represented on both the screen and the printer.

On the right of the keyboard is a group of keys devoted to word-processing and computing. Some of these have a number of different functions, depending on the action you are performing.

We shall examine these in more detail later; for the moment it is sufficient only to point out the four **cursor keys** (with arrows on them) and the four **function keys**, (bearing an f and a number between 1-8).

There are also special key combinations available, which may vary from program to program. In LocoScript, pressing the ALT and ENTER keys together acts as a Caps Lock key; and ALT and RELAY pressed together turns the cluster of keys on the right-hand section of the keyboard into a number-pad. Both of these are cancelled by repeating the same sequence of keys again.

Finally, whatever program you are using, pressing SHIFT, EXTRA and EXIT together will reset the computer completely; anything you have not yet saved onto a disc will be lost for ever, so use this facility with caution.

Starting up.

The various cable connections are shown in Fig. 1.2. Check that the printer ribbon cable is the right way round before pressing it firmly into the multi-pin socket at the back of the monitor, that the printer power plug is in the 24 Volt DC socket and that the DIN plug which attaches the keyboard to the side of the monitor is correctly aligned before pushing it home.

Curiously, the PCW8256 may load the LocoScript disc even if these cable connections are not properly made. For this reason, double-check the keyboard connection in particular if you can get no response when you type anything in.

Unless you are actually printing, there is no need to have the printer connected (although there is no need to unplug it either); knowing this may reduce the number of bits you need to carry with you if you are setting up the machine for a writing session somewhere else.

11

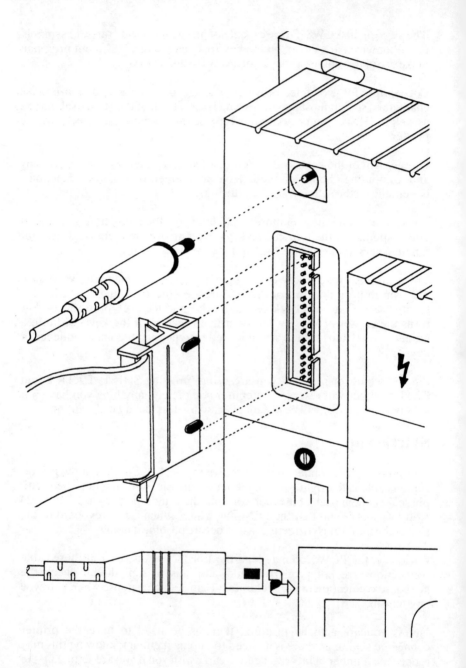

Fig. 1.2

Electrical interference.

The PCW8256 is relatively less affected by fluctuations in mains voltage than many other similar machines, but the office environment can be rather 'noisy' electrically, with other equipment, often drawing relatively heavy loads, being switched on and off; under certain circumstances the power 'spikes' or surges that this causes can affect the machine's operation.

It is most unlikely that these power surges could do any damage, but they can cause word processors and computers to 'lock up', and if this happens it will be necessary to reset the PCW8256 and start again – or even to remove the disc and turn it off and then on again – with the consequent loss of everything you have written and not yet saved on disc.

However, simple voltage regulators are available which will iron out the worst fluctuations, and if you do experience any problems these provide a handy, cheap and complete solution. Perhaps it should be added that the office kettle and coffee-maker are among the worst offenders at creating these annoying high-current spikes!

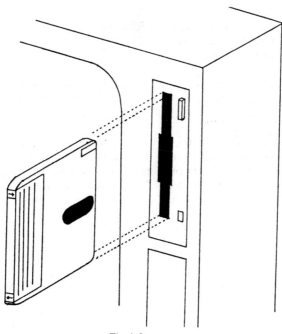

Fig. 1.3

When you are sure that everything has been properly connected up, take out the first disc (the one with LOCOSCRIPT on one side and CP/M PLUS on the other),but *do not insert it into the disc drive yet*. Then turn on the PCW8256 by pressing in the Power button on the front of the monitor at the left.

The screen will gradually 'come up' to a uniform bright green. Insert the disc with Side 1 (LOCOSCRIPT) facing to the left, and press it gently right home, as shown in Fig. 1.2. It should go in without difficulty; if there appears to be any obstruction, make sure that there is nothing blocking it (such as another disc) and that you are holding the disc by the correct end, i.e. the one with the printed label on it.

If after checking these things you still have difficulties, *turn the machine off and consult your dealer* as you will be able to proceed no further now. However, given the reliability of modern disc drives and their associated electronic components, this situation is extremely unlikely to arise.

Starting the PCW8256 in this way is sometimes called 'Loading LocoScript' and sometimes, more graphically, 'booting LocoScript.' This has nothing to do with kicking it out of the door; it's a joking reference to the machine 'lifting itself by its own bootstraps.'

Within a few moments of the disc clicking into place you will hear the drive beginning to operate, and the red 'activity light' to the right of the disc will come up to full brightness.

Next the border of the screen will turn black and a series of horizontal black bars will scroll down the screen. As these reach a point about two-thirds of the way down, the screen will clear again and a message will appear.

This should include the name "LOCOSCRIPT" and a Version Number; if not, you have inserted the wrong disc (or the wrong side of the right disc), and you should remove it by pressing the disc release button. Then reset the machine by pressing the SHIFT, EXTRA and EXIT keys, holding each key down until they have all been pressed, then releasing them all simultaneously; then insert the correct disc.

Assuming that you have inserted the correct disc, the first message (sometimes called a **wake-up message**) will be replaced within a few seconds by the **Disc Manager** screen, which will appear as in Fig. 1.4. We shall look at this in detail in the next chapter; for the moment we shall proceed to set up the printer.

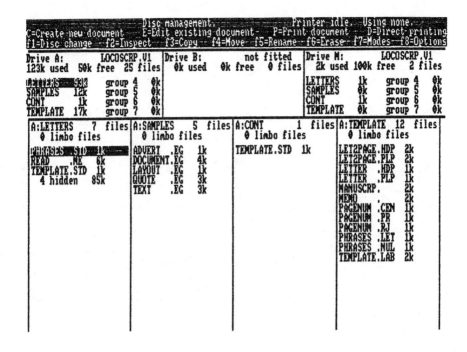

Fig. 1.4 · The Disc Manager Screen

Setting up the Printer.

To insert a single sheet of paper into the printer, lay it on the left-hand side of the paper-rest so that the bottom of the sheet is just caught by the platen. There is no need to wind the paper in by hand; indeed, doing this can inhibit the operation of the printer.

Then pull towards you the paper-feed control located on the knob on the right of the machine, as shown in Fig. 1.5. The bail bar will come forward as you do this, the platen will turn and the paper will be gently drawn into the printer; finally, the print head will move across on its tracks and then return to its rest position on the left-hand side.

You should now check that the paper is straight and that the print-head is not off the edge of the paper; when you are sure that everything is in order, look

15

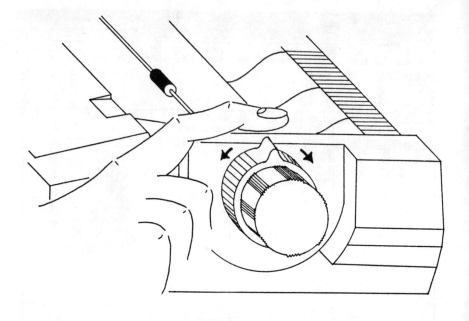

Fig. 1.5

```
            Disc management.                    Printer idle. Using none.
Printer: Online  Top of form              Idle           Draft quality  Single sheet
f1=Options    f2=Paper   f3=Actions    f5=Document/Reprint   f7=Reset   f8=On/Off-Line  EXIT

Drive A:        LOCOSCRP.V1  Drive B:      not fitted  Drive M:        LOCOSCRP.V1
123k used  50k free  25 files  0k used   0k free   0 files  2k used 100k free   2 files

LETTERS   93k    group 4    0k                        LETTERS    1k    group 4    0k
SAMPLES   12k    group 5    0k                        SAMPLES    0k    group 5    0k
CONT       1k    group 6    0k                        CONT       1k    group 6    0k
TEMPLATE  17k    group 7    0k                        TEMPLATE   0k    group 7    0k

A:LETTERS    7  files A:SAMPLES   5  files A:CONT     1  files A:TEMPLATE  12  files
```

Fig. 1.6   The Printer Control Screen

back at the screen and you will see that the topmost section has changed, and now looks like Fig. 1.6.

What has happened is that by operating the printer, you have entered what is

16

called Printer Control Mode. Later you will see that you have to do this whenever you wish to give any instructions to the printer.

The top three lines of the screen are called the **Status Block**; the purpose of this is to keep you informed of the actions which the machine is carrying out. It pays therefore to keep a close eye on the Status Block whenever you are giving instructions of any sort to the word processor.

You will see that on the second line from the top of the screen, the word PRINTER is flashing, as an indication that you are now in Printer Control Mode. We have no further instructions to give the printer at the moment, so get out of this by pressing the EXIT key on the bottom row of the keyboard, and you will see the Status Block change back to what it was before.

Printer Control Mode can be entered in two different ways. The first is to pull forward the printer bail-bar or to operate the paper-loading knob, as we have already done; the second is by pressing the PTR (for PrinTeR) key next to the EXIT key. Either way, the effect is the same.

(The PTR key is actually something of an anomaly in LocoScript; in every other case, the Status Block shows which control keys you can press for any desired result, but the PTR key is never included in this list.)

Now that we are back in Disc Manager Mode and the printer is loaded with paper, we shall experiment with the PCW8256's Direct Printing Option.

There are two reasons for starting in this way: the first is that it provides a particularly straightforward introduction to the simpler word processing commands; the second is that Direct Printing does not rely on saving (i.e. recording) on disc the material which has been written.

If you have at some earlier time tried to follow the instructions in the first section of the LocoScript Manual which came with your machine, and if you have LocoScript Version 1.0, you may well have had difficulty because of this.

The decision by Amstrad to make the Master Discs permanently 'Write protected' so that they cannot be used for recording, was apparently taken after that part of the manual had been written. Because of this, Direct Printing is the easiest way to proceed.

The Direct Printing Option.

The purpose of Direct Printing is to enable the user to treat the PCW8256 rather like an electric typewriter, for filling in forms and the like. The words are not printed as you type, but when you press the RETURN key at the end of the line, the whole line is automatically printed exactly as it was entered.

If you look back at the Status Block, you will see that D stands for the Direct Printing Option; press D now, and you will see one of the most typical features of the PCW8256, a 'pull-down' (or 'pop-up'!) menu which seems to grow down out of the Status Block.

In computer terms, a **menu** is a selection of options open to the user at any particular point, and while using the PCW8256 you will come across a very large number of different menus of varying lengths and complexity.

This particular one is very simple, merely asking you to confirm that you really are intending to use Direct Printing; check-menus of this sort are used frequently in LocoScript to ensure that you don't accidently take any destructive action that could result in your work being lost.

Fig. 1.7   The Direct Printing Screen

Confirm your choice by pressing the ENTER key (in the bottom right-hand corner), and the screen will clear and be replaced by the one shown in Fig. 1.7.

The line at the top of the screen is a 'Rule', to enable you to lay out your typing neatly; the little numbers along the top represent inches, measured from the left-hand edge of your paper (assuming that your paper is located properly in the printer). There is a similar rule on the printer bail-bar itself.

Now type in the following line, errors and all (but don't press the RETURN key); it won't matter if you make a few extra errors of you own as well!

T h i s   i s s   a   s i m p l e o f t h e D i r e c t r P r i n t i n g M o o d .

As you press the keys, the letters appear on the screen exactly like

18

typewritten characters on the page – except that you will be able to electronically correct your errors without any fuss or bother.

If you have previously been used to a manual typewriter, you will need to be particularly careful not to rest your hands on the keys. This is because on the PCW8256, most keys have what is called **repeat action**, which means that they will continue to print characters for as long as you are holding them down.

In fact there is always a short delay before the first repeated character is produced; but after that, the keys repeat at about ten characters per second – it pays to develop a light touch!

The position in which each letter is going to appear is marked by a light-green rectangle, called the **cursor**; this moves along as you type. If you look up at the Rule, you will see that there is a second marker there which also moves along the line in step with your typing.

Fig. 1.8

After you have finished entering the line printed above, you should find that your screen looks something like Fig. 1.8.

With an ordinary typewriter, you would now have to go back over your work with an eraser or correcting fluid to remove the mistakes; you might even decide to retype the whole line afresh.

With the PCW8256, however, you can use the cursor keys (the cluster of four with arrows on them) and the two Delete keys (DEL→ and ←DEL) to correct your work before it is printed.

Move the cursor back to the second word in the line 'iss'; then press the DEL→ key (which is a Forward Delete), and the letter under the cursor will disappear.

Be careful not to hold the DEL→ down for too long, as it has an auto-repeat action and will erase the rest of the line as well if you are too heavy-handed!

Next, place the cursor over the 'i' in 'simple', and type in an 'a' to replace it. As you do so, the line to the right of the cursor will expand to make room, for LocoScript always regards extra characters typed on top of existing ones as Inserts rather than Overwrites. Now use the DEL→ key to get rid of the unwanted 'i'.

To use the ←DEL key, move the cursor to the space between the words **Directr** and **Printing**, and then press it. This key is a Backward Delete, and the incorrect 'r' will be erased; once again, be careful as this key also auto-repeats.

Finally, change **Mood** to **Mode**, using a combination of the cursor keys and Forward and Backward Delete keys to correct the errors.

When you are satisfied that the line is perfect, move the cursor to the end and press RETURN. The PCW8256 will place a Carriage Return Symbol, or **Effector**, on the screen, then your text will disappear from the screen and a moment later the printer will begin to copy it onto paper.

If you watch the printer, you will see that the printer head makes two passes over the line, both of them in the same direction, from left to right; this is the way in which the printer produces 'letter quality' work, and when LocoScript starts, it is taken for granted that this is what you want.

High quality printing takes place at the rate of about twenty cps (characters per second).

There is also a faster printing style of about 90 cps, called 'draft quality', in which the printer passes over each line only once, printing alternate lines in opposite directions, first from left to right, then from right to left.

The Carriage Return Effector is not printed, of course; it was merely placed on the screen to remind you of the point at which the RETURN key was pressed.

At the end of the line, the printer platen turns; this advances the paper so that it is ready for the next line.

Type in a few more lines of your own, and correct them as you go; at the end of each line check your work, and when you are sure that it is right, press RETURN to commit it to paper.

To finish, press the EXIT key, and when the pull-down menu appears asking if you wish to Finish Direct Printing, accept it by pressing ENTER. Then carefully wind your finished sheet out of the printer by hand; later we shall see how to make the PCW8256 do this automatically.

If you are now ready to finish your first session, it is very important that you remember to remove the Master Disc from the disc drive **before** turning the power off, as leaving a disc in the drive when powering up or down could cause it to become corrupted and useless.

Copying Discs.

Because accidental loss of any of the material on the Master Discs would be catastrophic, you will need to make copies of them. You will not be able to proceed any further unless you have at least one empty disc onto which to copy the first Master Disc.

The copying of discs is done using a program on the second side of the same Master Disc that we have already been using – that is, the side labelled CP/M PLUS. If the PCW8256 has been switched off, turn it on again and insert the Master Disc with Side 2 facing left; otherwise, remove it, reset the computer (SHIFT/EXTRA/EXIT)and replace it the other way round.

The machine will go through the now-familiar starting routine, but instead of the LocoScript Disc Manager screen there will be a message telling you that CP/M has been loaded, and ending with the prompt A > .

(If you know nothing about CP/M, all you need to understand at the moment is that it consists of a series of programs which control the operation of the PCW8256 when used as a computer rather than as a word processor, together with several 'utilities' which enable you to copy discs, rename files and perform other useful chores. We shall be looking at CP/M in more detail in Chapters 6, 7 and 8.

The particular utility we need is called DISCKIT. Load this into the PCW8256 by simply typing DISCKIT after the A > prompt; the activity light on the disc drive will come on for a few moments as the program is loaded.

When it is ready, a diagram of part of the keyboard will appear on the screen, showing three of the function keys and the EXIT key. Select the 'Copy' option by pressing key ƒ5/ƒ6.

From this point on,you need only follow the instructions on the screen. The PCW8256 will copy the first 20 tracks of the disc (actually numbered 0 to 19) into its memory, then invite you to replace the Master Disc with the one on which you are going to make the copy.

Next it will automatically duplicate the first 20 tracks onto the new disc before asking you to reinsert the original disc in order to repeat the procedure with the last 20 tracks, numbered 20 to 39.

It is very important for you to note that you *must* copy the whole disc; there *are* ways of copying parts of discs, but if you try to use a disc which contains only the first 20 tracks, you will find that it will not work properly.

Furthermore, if you *have* copied only half the disc and have then tried to do something else with the PCW8256, you will find that you cannot easily copy the second half of the disc. For this reason, **it is extremely important to copy the whole disc in the same session.**

If you have two spare discs available, you can copy all four sides of the two Master Discs. Certainly you will need to do this sooner or later. However, for the moment it will be enough to make copies only of LocoScript and CP/M Plus.

When you have done this, make sure that the new discs are properly labelled and put the originals away in a safe place. In nearly every computer system, the value of the 'software' (the programs and files held on discs) very soon exceeds the value of the 'hardware' such as the computer and printer.

Looking after Discs.

Because discs are vulnerable to physical and magnetic damage, it is important that everyone who uses them should know how to handle them, as well as how to minimise any accidental losses that may occur.

The main rules for disc care are listed below; we suggest that you use the PCW8256 to Direct Print a copy, and display it prominently by the computer.

1. Before turning the PCW8256 on or off, ensure that the disc drive is empty; **powering up with a disc in the drive is the most common cause of disc damage.** In the event of a power failure, remove the disc from the drive immediately.

2. Keep discs away from all sources of magnetism. Telephones, transformers and loudspeakers are all potential sources of damage.

3. Spillages of coffee, etc., will certainly ruin a disc; inserting a wet or sticky disc into the disc drive 'to see if it's all right' may well damage both the disc drive and any other discs which may become contaminated by it.

4. Never pull back the protective metal shutter of a disc, or attempt to touch its magnetic surface.

5. Discs must be kept in moderate temperatures; do not leave them in direct sunlight or near radiators, or in unheated areas.

6. Avoid storing or using discs in dusty or damp environments.

7. Keep a back-up copy of **everything**, and make sure that every disc is accurately labelled.

There is an established procedure for protecting data stored on discs from loss; **when you prepare an updated version of a file, always keep a copy of the most recent update-but-one**. This ensures that at the worst you will lose only one session's work, as the previous version of the file will still be available to you.

LocoScript will carry out this task automatically, putting the previous version of the file into a special category called **Limbo**, from where you can recover it if necessary.

Useful though this is, it is not an absolute guarantee of security, as the disc itself might be lost. It is wise, therefore, to keep a 'backup' file on a separate disc, and to store that disc in a different location.

If you have installed the second disc drive (Drive B), remember that the high-density discs which it uses are not interchangeable with those used in Drive A.

One very annoying problem if you have two disc drives may arise if there is a power failure or power surge when you are copying something from one disc drive to the other.

Under these circumstances, it is not impossible for **both** discs to be corrupted. **If you have a two drive system, play safe and keep a third copy for total security.** Remember, the workings of fate are such that you will **always** lose the one thing of which you don't have a backup copy!

Unintentional erasure of disc-files can be prevented with the **write-protect** device on your discs; the implementation of this differs slightly from one disc manufacturer to another, but the principle is shown in Fig. 1.9.

When the appropriate write-protect hole is blanked off, 'writing' to the disc can take place normally; but if the tab is moved so that the hole is opened, the disc is said to be 'write-protected', and any attempt to record material

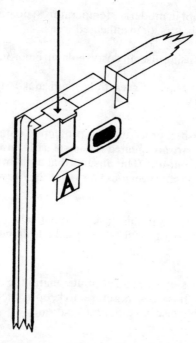

Fig. 1.9

onto the disc, or to erase material from it, will fail, and an error message will be displayed.

The tabs for both sides of the disc are completely independant, and there is nothing to prevent one side of a disc from being write-protected while the other side is not.

The Master Discs provided with the PCW8256 are permanently write-protected. Not all program discs are protected in this way, however. It is generally a good rule never to risk recording anything on any program master disc; always make a copy and use that.

Postscript to Chapter One.

In Chapter One we have already covered a very substantial amount of ground. Indeed, if you started off as a raw beginner, you may find it hard to realise just how much you have learnt.

Before going on, it is particularly important for you to be familiar with all the basics which we have discussed so far; none of the topics is difficult individually, but there are so many different points to bear in mind that it is quite easy to get confused.

Stop now, and go back and try again with anything which doesn't quite make sense. Remember, LocoScript won't break, no matter how many mistakes you make when using it.

CHAPTER TWO

Essentials of LocoScript

Preview

The following topics will be discussed in this chapter:

Using templates
The Disc Manager screen.
The Function keys.
Starting to write.
Choosing a template.
Creating a document.
Writing and correcting.
Making a printed copy.
Re-editing.
Moving text around.
Scissors and paste.
Find and exchange.
Making copies of files.

On the way to real word processing.

There are at least two important differences between Direct Print documents of the sort which we experimented with in the previous chapter and those which are word-processed in the usual sense of the expression.

The most obvious difference is that unlike a text created by Direct Printing, most word-processed documents are stored in the PCW8256 for some period of time – long enough for the whole document to be licked into shape, at least.

After they have been printed out, such documents may be re-edited, printed again in the same or a different form, saved for future use or reference, or deleted.

27

Another important difference is that letters, reports and the like are usually laid out according to certain more-or-less fixed rules or policies. These govern such diverse matters as the size of margins, the location of page numbers and the placing of addresses, dates etc.

This concept is particularly important because in LocoScript, documents of various kinds are classified into groups according to their layout, or template.

Each LocoScript template automatically provides a particular structured framework for the group of documents constructed using it. This framework defines page width and length, type—style and —pitch, line spacing, tab positions, text and page-numbers for headers and footers (where used) and other similar details.

For example, a company might have one standard layout for letters, another for memoranda, a third for reports and a fourth for minutes of meetings. An Estate Agent might add to this list a standard layout for Property details and perhaps another for Auction Sale announcements, and so on.

To get you started, the Master Disc contains a series of standard templates suitable for memos, long reports, letters on headed or unheaded paper and so on. For most purposes, it will be enough to simply adapt one or other of these templates to meet your own requirements.

There is no limit to the number of different templates that can be used; the only restriction is that not more than eight groups can be accommodated on any one disc.

The Disc Manager Screen.

Turn on the PCW8256 and insert a copy (not the original) of the Master Disc. You will see the Disc Manager screen, reproduced here as Fig. 2.1.

The screen is divided into three unequal sections. At the very top, and occupying three lines, there is a Status Bar, which provides the user with either a brief list of the options which are open to him or with instructions.

The bottom two thirds of the screen is taken up by a listing, in columns, of the various document files found on each of the three possible disc drives (A, B and M).

In general terms the files in any particular column were all created according to the same format, or template. (As far as the Master Disc is concerned this

28

is something of an over-simplification, but it is nonetheless an important principle to grasp).

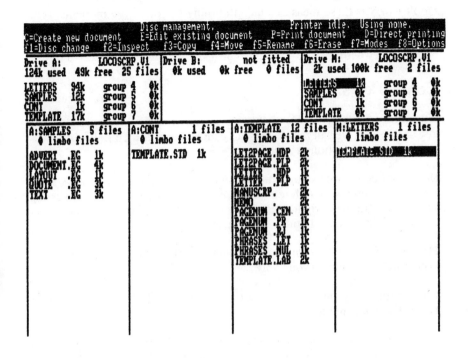

Fig. 2.1   The Disc Manager Screen

Between the Status Bar at the top of the screen and the template columns at the bottom there is a third section containing a listing of the names of the various columns, according to the disc drive on which they are found. If you have not fitted a second disc drive, the middlemost of the three spaces will contain no names.

In each of the two lower sections is a long bar. These bars can be moved around the screen to indicate individual group– and file-names; this is done using the cursor (arrow) keys. In this book, such bars are called **cursor bars**.

Adjacent to each group– and file-name is an indication of how much space each occupies, measured in Kilobytes, abbreviated to K. 1 Kilobyte is the amount of space required to store 1024 characters. There is also an indication of how much disc-space is currently unoccupied ('free'), also measured in Kilobytes.

Don't worry if these measures mean nothing to you at the moment; very soon you will be able to judge whether a particular disc has enough room left on it to hold a new document, and this is the only practical point you need to be concerned with.

Control keys.

All actions involving the Disc Manager screen are initiated by pressing one key or another; we can regard these as **control keys**, as their only purpose is to control the operation of LocoScript.

Because LocoScript is so complex, and because the various keys have different functions at different times in the course of a word processing session, choosing the right control key for any given purpose can be rather confusing until you are familiar with the program.

However, there are two safeguards which greatly reduce the chances of an accidental error ruining your work.

First, before any files are altered or erased, a pull-down menu appears requesting confirmation.

Second, on the top row of keys and located next to the ←DEL key is a key marked CAN. Press this to CANcel the effect of any control key which you may have pressed in error, or which you have changed your mind about.

At the bottom of the Status Block on the Disc Manager screen you will see a list of the options open to you on pressing one or other of the Function keys.

(The even numbered functions are obtained by pressing the appropriate odd-numbered key and SHIFT at the same time; e.g. for f6 you would press SHIFT and f5.)

Five of these keys (f2, f3, f4, f6 and f7) affect the files marked by the long cursor bar in the lowest section of the screen; the other three (f1, f5 and f8) have a more general application.

To select which file will be affected by Function keys f2, f3, f4, f6 and f7, press the cursor keys until the lower cursor bar covers that file-name. To move the upper cursor bar from one **group** to another, press the appropriate cursor key and SHIFT simultaneously.

As you move either of the cursor bars around the screen, the other bar flies automatically to an appropriate position. For example, if you put the lower cursor bar over the file called PAGENUM .CEN in the TEMPLATE group, you will see that the upper cursor bar will move to that group.

There are actually more columns of file-names than can be fitted on the screen. To inspect the other columns, try to move the cursor bar off the screen to the right; the columns will immediately slide across to reveal the extra names, though the Status Block and the section beneath it do not move.

The names given to each Function key are sometimes rather too cryptic to be very helpful until you are used to them, so a brief guide follows.

Remember that this list applies only to the Disc Manager screen; the other screens which appear from time to time, such as the Printer Control Screen and the Direct Printing Screen, both of which we saw in the previous chapter, generally use the various function keys in different ways.

$f1$ – Disc Change. The only occasion on which you should change the disc when using LocoScript is while the Disc Manager screen is displayed, and you *must* then inform the PCW8256 of the change by pressing $f1$. This is called **logging in** the disc.

$f2$ – Inspect. This key enables you to examine the contents of a document without having to edit the whole file. Place the lower cursor bar over the required file-name and press $f2$, and up to three lines of explanatory text will appear. Use ENTER to clear it.

$f3$ – Copy. Use this key to copy any file from one column to another, or from one disc to another. (Instructions for copying files from one disc to another on a single-drive system are given later.) Place the cursor bar over the file you wish to copy, press $f3$ and follow the instructions displayed on the Status Block. The original file is not affected by copying.

$f4$ –Move. Exactly the same as Copy, except that the original file is deleted as the move is carried out. Check-menus appear before either Move or Copy are effected; press ENTER to accept or CAN to cancel.

$f5$ – Rename. With this the user can rename any file, disc or group by placing the cursor bar over the appropriate item and pressing $f5$. A space will be created in which to enter the new details. Erased files (i.e. those in Limbo – see below) can be recovered with this key if you know what their name was; see $f8$ below.

*f*6 – Erase. Used to erase a file; a check-menu is displayed before any action is taken; press ENTER to proceed or CAN to cancel. Erased files are not actually wiped from the disc, but can be recovered with *f*5 *unless the disc is so full that the erasure of Limbo files becomes necessary to create storage space for new files.*

*f*7 – Modes. This key produces a small pull-down menu which duplicates the Create, Edit, Print and Direct Print commands on the middle line of the Status Block. More importantly, it provides space for the future expansion of LocoScript.

*f*8 – Options. With this key, Hidden and Limbo files are revealed in their appropriate columns; when the pull-down menu appears, place the cursor bar over the option you want and press the [+] key, located to the left of the space bar, then ENTER. To conceal such files, press *f*8 and the [-] key, to the right of the space bar.

Starting to write.

The steps to be taken in composing a short document, printing it and finally saving it on disc are briefly outlined below. Read carefully through what follows so that when you try it out you will understand what is happening at every point.

1. Pick (or create) a suitable template. The template you choose will depend on the layout you want your final document to have.

2. Press 'C' to Create a new document. The PCW8256 will suggest a name for it, but you can change this to any name of your choice.

3. The Disc Manager screen will clear and you will be presented with a new Status Block and a Rule showing the tab positions and other features of the template you have chosen. This is where you write and edit your text.

4. When you have finished writing and correcting your work, press EXIT; you will be given a range of options, one of which is to print your work and to simultaneously save it on to disc.

There is no need to print your work immediately, of course; instead you can save it on disc and later print it out directly from the Disc Manager screen, using the P (for Print) command.

Choosing a template.

To get a feel for using the facilities of LocoScript, it is best to start with the very simplest template provided, namely the one called TEMPLATE.STD in the CONT group. There is another TEMPLATE.STD in the LETTERS group, so be sure you choose the right one.

The template for the CONT group is actually designed for use with continuous computer stationery – the kind which has sprocket holes in tear-off strips down each side. However, it can be used for other things as well, as we shall see.

Creating a document.

Move the bottom cursor bar until it is anywhere in the CONT group – it doesn't have to be placed over TEMPLATE.STD; you will see that the upper cursor bar is also resting over the name CONT.

Fig. 2.2   The Create Document Menu

Then press C to Create a document. LocoScript will respond with the pull-down window shown in Fig. 2.2.

You can either accept the document name suggested or amend it. If you choose to change it (and DOCUMENT.000 is hardly the most memorable of names), you can clear the old name from the box with the [-] key by the space bar, and then type in your own choice.

If you do choose to type in your own name, you will see that it doesn't matter whether you use capitals or small letters; LocoScript will always convert them to capitals for file-names.

File names consist of two parts. The first part consists of up to eight letters or numbers. Then type in either a space or a full-stop, and the cursor in the window will jump to the end of the window for you to type in up to a further three letters or numbers, called the file type.

The file name and type can be anything you like, but we suggest that you choose both with care, as otherwise you may have trouble finding the document you want in the future.

When you are happy with your choice of file-name, press ENTER and you will be given the screen shown in Fig. 2.3. Although you are creating a document from scratch, this is called the **Editing screen**.

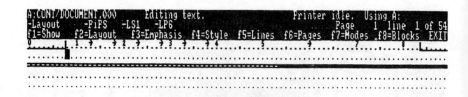

Fig. 2.3   The Editing Screen

The Status Block.

If you look at the Status Block at the top of the screen you will see that it too has changed. Some of the Function key commands available from this screen are extremely complicated, and these are described in subsequent chapters; others are much simpler, and these we shall examine a little later.

Note that on the top line of the Status Block at the left, the document and the disc drive on which the file will be saved are named; on the right are shown the status of the printer and the disc drive.

The second line of the Status Block informs you that the document will have proportional spacing (PiPS), and that the lines will be single-spaced, (LS1) and that the Line Pitch is set at 6 to the inch (LP6).

Finally, at the right of the second line of the Status Block there is kept a running count of your position on the page and the number of the page on which you are working. (Although the page-number is not necessarily displayed, the PCW8256 always maintains the page count as if the numbers were to appear.)

The Rule under the Status Block shows the left and right margins, measurements from the left hand edge of the paper in inches, and tab positions (marked with little arrows,→).

Beginning to type.

You can now start to type in your text. If you are unfamiliar with word processors, you may be surprised to find that there is no bell as you approach the end of a line.

Instead, as your typing reaches the right margin, any half-completed word will be automatically transferred to the start of the next line – a feature called **word-wrap** – so you don't need to worry about watching your place on the line.

You should not press the RETURN key at the end of each line; this is used at the ends of paragraphs only, and leaves behind the same effector that we saw when Direct Printing.

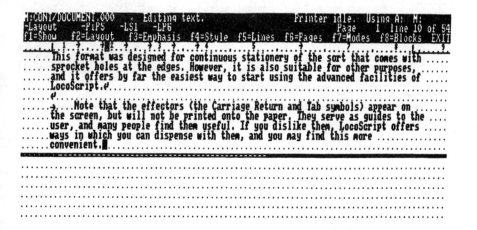

Fig. 2.4   A Simple Document

Attempt to type in the text shown in Fig. 2.4. Any errors that you make can be easily corrected by the use of the cursor keys and the DEL→ and ←DEL keys, as we saw in the previous chapter.

The first line of the second paragraph is to be inset from the margin, so use the TAB key. Note that this, like the ENTER key, leaves a visible effector on the screen (→), but that neither of them will appear on the paper when the document is finally printed.

If a paragraph looks rather ragged after you have finished correcting it, locate the cursor anywhere in that paragraph and then press the RELAY key, located on the bottom row next to $f1$. The whole paragraph will be tidied up as you watch.

Making a printed copy.

When you have the text looking the way you want it, you can make a printed copy of the whole thing; but this time a copy will be automatically saved onto the disc as well. Press the EXIT key and a short menu will appear, as in Fig. 2.5.

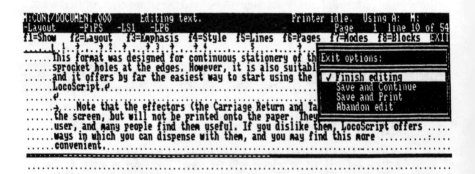

Fig. 2.5

(In Version 1.0 of LocoScript, the Save and Print option appears regardless of whether the printer is connected or not; versions 1.04 and later do not offer Save and Print if no printer is attached, or if the printer is already active and printing some other document.)

36

The various options offered have the following effects: Finish Editing saves your work onto disc but doesn't make a printed copy, Save and Continue saves the work onto disc and then prepares to resume the writing and editing from the point where you left off, Save and Print does just that, and Abandon Edit scraps the work which you have been doing.

The last of these choices is a dangerous one; if you choose this by mistake and you have no other version of your work on disc, then everything will be lost irretrievably.

The option we are going to use now is Save and Print, so make sure that your disc is write-enabled (i.e. that the write-protect hole is blocked). Then with the cursor keys place the cursor bar over the appropriate option, and press ENTER.

Make sure that the printer is loaded with paper, as described in the previous chapter – this can be done now, or it could have been done at any earlier stage. Then wait while the file is saved onto the disc.

When the document has been saved, the printer will begin to work. When everything has been printed, the paper will be automatically fed upwards until it is just held by the bail bar. Pull it out, and the job is done!

By now the PCW8256 will be displaying the Disc Manager screen again, but with one important change: in the column of the CONT group, you will see the name of the document which you have just created, showing that it has indeed been saved onto the disc.

Re-editing.

The procedure we have just followed is quite adequate for a short piece such as a letter, but a longer piece of text, such as a report or a chapter for a book, may have to go through several versions before it is finally finished.

This can be easily done from the Disc Manager screen. Position the lower cursor bar over the name of the file which is to be re-edited and then press E for Edit. The PCW8256 will respond in the usual way with a check-menu, and if you confirm your action with ENTER, the file will be displayed on the Editing text screen.

(Version 1.0 of LocoScript doesn't detect whether a file which you want to re-edit has been loaded off a write-protected disc, but later versions issue a warning, and suggest saving your completed work on Drive M. This is to save you the work of editing a file only to find that you cannot re-save it on the original disc.)

Press E now to edit the new file which we have just created and saved on disc. It will be redisplayed, with the cursor at the top left-hand corner of the screen – the 'home' position.

Moving round the document.

We have already seen how to move around the document using the cursor keys. The PCW8256 also has many other ways of moving the cursor round a file, and once you are familiar with them you will find them very useful.

The keys which govern this facility are grouped around and above the cursor keys; they are LINE/EOL, DOC/PAGE, UNIT/PARA and WORD/CHAR.

If you position the cursor at any point in the first line of the document and then experiment with these keys, the workings of most of them will very quickly become clear.

Their purpose is to move the cursor immediately to the point indicated by the key-name. Thus EOL will take it to the End Of (the current) Line, PAGE to the head of the next page (or the foot of the current page if it is the last one) PARA to the head of the next paragraph and CHAR to the next character.

The other functions are obtained by pressing SHIFT and the appropriate key at the same time; LINE will move to the start of the next line, DOC to the end of the document, and WORD to the first character of the next word.

UNIT is a little more complicated. It allows you to move the cursor forward to a **Unit Marker**, which is a point which you have previously defined in the text; in a long document which is divided into sections, for example, you might wish to place one of these Unit Markers at the start of each section.

The inserting of Unit Markers is dealt with in the following chapter.

The effect of each of the keys can be reversed by pressing ALT (for ALTer) at the same time; ALT/PARA, for example, will move the cursor to the head of the *previous* paragraph, and ALT/EOL will move it to the end of the previous line (not to the beginning of the current line as you might imagine.)

Similarly, SHIFT/ALT/DOC will move the cursor back to the start of the document, SHIFT/ALT/UNIT to the previous Unit Marker, and so on.

Scissors and paste.

Just as the PCW8256 offers fast ways to move the cursor around your document, it also provides extremely sophisticated ways of rearranging the text you have already written.

This process, which is analagous to cutting out a piece of paper with writing on it, and then sticking it down in some other place, is accomplished using the CUT, COPY and PASTE keys on the top row at the right-hand side of the keyboard.

To delete any unwanted portion from your text, simply position the cursor on the first character to be removed and press the CUT key. Then move the cursor to the character *immediately beyond* the last character to be deleted, and press CUT again.

To assist you in this operation, the section that will be affected is highlighted. Once you have established one end of the section to be removed, you can then move the cursor about quite freely until you are certain you have highlighted exactly the right portion; and, of course, you can move the cursor around either with the cursor keys or with the DOC/PAGE, LINE/EOL and other control keys.

There is actually no need to place the cursor at the beginning of the passage to be deleted; if you prefer, you can start at the end and move the cursor up the document instead of down.

Take special care with the location of the cursor when locating the first CUT; if you put this in the wrong place, or if you decide to abandon a CUT half-way through, press the CAN key. The operation will be aborted and the highlighting will disappear.

When you use CUT, the text which you have scissored out is gone for ever. The COPY and PASTE keys, on the other hand, enable you to remove words and phrases, or even substantial portions of your document, from one place and reinsert them somewhere else – or to insert them in more than one place, if you wish.

To do this, proceed exactly as for cutting, but pressing the COPY key at the beginning of the affected section instead of CUT. Then move the cursor to the other end of the appropriate section; it will be highlighted, just as before.

What happens next depends on whether you intend to actually **move** the highlighted text or merely **copy** it.

If the former, press CUT and then any number between 0 and 9. This number will be used to identify the section you have cut out, and until you finish editing that document, or give the same number to another copied section, that number will always refer to that particular fragment of text.

As soon as you have pressed CUT and the identifying number, the highlighted area will slide off the screen, just as if it had been lost for ever. However, if you now move the cursor to the spot where you wish to reinsert the material and press PASTE followed by the same identifying number, the words will reappear, with everything else moving down to make way.

You can insert the same section as often as you want; as long as the appropriate identifying number is pressed each time, there is no limit to the number of times a fragment defined by COPY and CUT can be reinserted into the text.

A variation on this can be achieved by copying the original text without removing it. To do this, follow exactly the same procedure as before, except for pressing COPY (and an identifying number) when you have defined the area, instead of CUT.

Portions of text removed in this way are forgotten once the editing of that particular document has been completed. There is, however, an option which allows *phrases* to be carried in the PCW8256's memory between one document and another.

The procedure for doing this is exactly the same as that described above, except that an identifying letter is used instead of a number. There are a number of such phrases already stored in LocoScript. The majority of them are of the sort that an Estate Agent might find useful – they include "on frequent bus route" and "convenient for the M62", for example.

The only restriction on these saved phrases is that the combined length of all of them is limited to around 550 characters. Later, we shall see how to permanently save phrases of our own onto the disc in the same way as the Estate Agent's phrases listed above.

Spend some time experimenting with these various facilities. Don't be too surprised if you don't always get exactly the results you are expecting, especially if you are a little careless about including carriage returns, spaces and tabs in a section being moved or cut. As far as the PCW8256 is concerned, the end result will always be logical, and a few moments spent tidying it up is all that should be required.

Find and Exchange.

The final way of editing the text you have written is probably the most powerful of all. It is done with the aid of the EXCH/FIND key placed immediately under CUT, and allows you to automatically find, and if you so wish change, any short sequence of characters in your text.

The basic principles of operation of EXCH and FIND are very similar to each other. In both cases a string of characters (the 'search string') is entered by the user.

The document, from the current position of the cursor forward, is then scanned to find a match for the search string. If the length of the document makes it necessary, the text will scroll up the screen as the search takes place.

If you have chosen FIND, the cursor will come to rest at the beginning of the first match found. If you have chosen EXCH, then depending on the precise instructions you have given, the search string can be automatically replaced by an 'exchange string' which you have also specified.

In this way it is possible to go through an entire document, automatically changing every occurence of a given word or phrase, and then RELAYing the text.

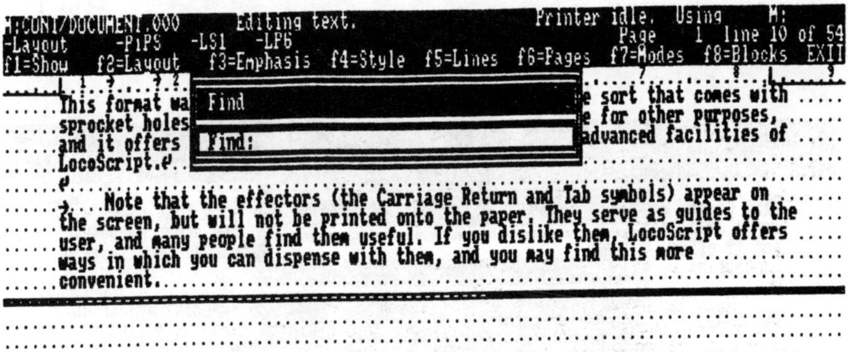

```
:CONT/DOCUMENT.000      Editing text.              Printer idle.  Using    M:
-Layout      -PiPS   -LS1   -LF6                        Page    1  line 10 of 54
f1=Show    f2=Layout    f3=Emphasis  f4=Style  f5=Lines  f6=Pages  f7=Modes  f8=Blocks  EXIT
     .......................
.......This format wa: Find                      e sort that comes with .....
.......sprocket holes                            e for other purposes, .....
.......and it offers  : Find:                     dvanced facilities of .....
.......LocoScript.⊘...................................................
.......⊘
.......2....Note that the effectors (the Carriage Return and Tab symbols) appear on .......
.......the screen, but will not be printed onto the paper. They serve as guides to the ....
.......user, and many people find them useful. If you dislike them, LocoScript offers .....
.......ways in which you can dispense with them, and you may find this more .............
.......convenient..........................................................
```

Fig. 2.6 The FIND Menu

On selecting FIND, you will be offered a special window in which up to 30 characters may be entered (see Fig. 2.6); these will constitute the search string.

41

Type in the word or phrase you want to find, editing it as necessary by using the delete and cursor keys; any spaces will be represented by small triangles. When all is satisfactory, press ENTER.

Only exact matches will be found, so if you are looking for a word written in capitals, for example, the search string will have to be entered in capitals as well.

Another point to be borne in mind is that as all perfect matches are found, if you enter the word 'if' as a search string, FIND will locate it both as a word on its own and inside other words, such as 'tiff'.

It pays, therefore, to be ingenious in choosing your search string; most ambiguities can be avoided by the inclusion of appropriate leading and trailing spaces. If you use the FIND command a second time, the PCW8256 will automatically offer you the same search string again. To clear it, either press the DEL→ key until the window is empty or use the [-] key, which clears all text to the right of the cursor in the window.

To repeat a FIND once the first occurence of the search string has been located, simply press FIND and ENTER, and the search will be resumed automatically. If no matches are found, the cursor will be taken to the very end of the document.

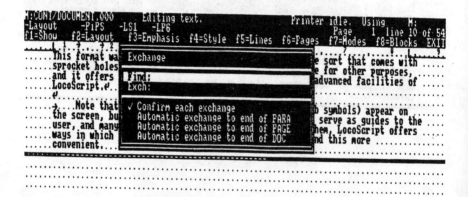

Fig. 2.7   The EXCHANGE Menu

EXCH is only slightly more complicated. The relevant window for entering the search and replacement texts is shown in Fig 2.7, and you will notice that there is a short menu attached to it.

Enter the search string and the replacement string, but *don't* press ENTER after either of them. First you must make a decision about what kind of exchange you require by moving the cursor bar to the appropriate option and pressing [+]. Only when you are certain that you have made the right final choice should you press ENTER.

If you choose one of the three automatic exchange options, the document will be scanned for the search string, and whenever it is located it will be automatically removed, the new text inserted, and the paragraph surrounding the change RELAYed.

Once an automatic exchange has been set in train, it will continue to the end of the section defined; if you realise that you have made a mistake, however, you can abort the search by pressing the STOP key twice. FIND can be abandoned in the same way.

Because of the potential for damage to your document if you have made a mistake, it may be better to limit yourself to the Confirm Each Exchange option until you have gained some experience with the facility.

Confirm Each Exchange will display a cursor at the first character of every match to the search string. To accept the exchange, press [+]; to reject it and carry on searching, press [-].

Ending a re-edit.

As we suggested above, short documents such as letters are unlikely to require much in the way of re-editing, but longer documents such as reports may perforce go through several versions.

Although it is always good policy to keep back-up copies of *everything* which you have on disc, this is obviously even more important with a document which may have taken several hours or even days to prepare.

If you have the second disc drive, Drive B, fitted, there is no problem; from the Disc Manager screen you can simply copy the appropriate file from one disc drive to the other.

If you only have the single drive, the procedure is a little more complicated, though still not difficult.

It would be possible, of course, to make a copy of the whole of the disc on which the relevant document was saved, using the DISCKIT facility described in the previous chapter. However, this is rather time-consuming, and provided you have a **formatted** disc available there are simpler ways to proceed. (See Chapter Six for details of disc formatting).

When you have EXITed from your re-edit, and have saved the appropriate file on disc, use the Copy facility ($f3$) to make a copy of the file onto Drive M, the imaginary internal disc. It doesn't really matter which column bearing the Drive M heading you use to do this, as the file will only be stored there temporarily.

Next, insert the formatted disc onto which the back-up copy is to be made into the drive, and press $f1$ to inform LocoScript of this change. Finally, re-copy the file from Drive M onto Drive A ($f3$ again), and the job is done.

The only point to be careful of is that if there is already an earlier version of the file, with the same name, on the back-up disc, you will have to erase it (with $f6$) before transferring the new version from drive M, as you can't have more than one LocoScript file with the same name sharing a disc.

One last problem which you may experience when working with a long document is that just as you are getting it somewhere near perfection, there is an unexpected power cut, or by some inexplicable blunder you manage to lose everything which you have written.

Fortunately, there is a simple solution: at regular intervals – we suggest about every half-hour – use the Save and Continue option of the EXIT menu. This will update the previous disc file, replacing it with the current version, so that at no time can a power failure or a personal error deprive you of more than half an hour's work at most.

It should be added that this is the sort of good advice which everyone can see the point of, but few people feel troubled to take until they themselves have become the victims of a lost file. Take heed, and don't be caught out yourself!

Postscript.

After reading this chapter and trying out its suggestions for yourself, you should be able to make real use of the facilities of LocoScript.

There is still a lot left to discover, but in the meantime you will be able to write letters and other documents much more easily than would ever have been possible with a typewriter.

You may even feel that you now know enough not to bother reading on any further. We feel that that would be a pity, because many of the most powerful features of LocoScript have still not been mentioned. But before going on, do make sure that you really are familiar with all the material so far.

CHAPTER THREE

Document Layout and Presentation

Preview.

The following topics will be dealt with in the course of this chapter:

Special characters.
The Emphasis and Style menus.
The Lines menu.
The Pages menu.
The Set and Clear menus.
The Show menu.
Controlling the printer.

More sophisticated effects.

Word processing with LocoScript will enable you to obtain without difficulty a wide variety of effects which are not available on ordinary typewriters, and which are often difficult to achieve even with sophisticated word processors.

These include underlines, italics, varying type-styles and –sizes, bold and double-strike characters, accents, foreign language characters and many other special effects.

Some of these are available directly from the alphabetic/numeric section of the keyboard, while others are under the control of the Function keys listed on the Status Block at the top of the Editing screen.

Special characters.

The keyboard of the PCW8256 varies from country to country, in order that every user will have the letters and symbols he most needs easily available.

However, all versions of the PCW8256 can be used to produce the same range of characters; the only different is that some characters are more easily called up on some keyboards than on others.

using ALT --

χ β ↓ μ ç o ÷ ∞ α σ δ ø γ ← ↔ → λ ∴ ⟨ ⟩ θ ε ρ τ

ψ ↑ ⊗ ω π ⅛ ¼ ⅜ ½ ⅝ ¾ ⅞ å æ ø ± ≃

using ALT + SHIFT --

ç • × Σ Δ Γ ⇐ ⇒ ⊙ Ω Π ‰ Å Æ Ø ≡

using EXTRA --

© ß ¦ ¿ \ ª ß † ƒ ↑ « » ® ™ ¥ ↑ º ¶ ¡ ¨ ℞ ¢ ° ´

ˆ ` ↔ 0 ~ ≠

Fig. 3.1   Special Symbols

Special symbols, which are shown on Fig. 3.1, can be broadly divided into two categories. First, there are those which represent accents and other diacritical marks, such as tildes, umlauts, rings etc.

These are reached by pressing EXTRA and the relevant number keys (the top row on the left of the keyboard).

To select, for example, a u-umlaut, the umlaut is printed first (EXTRA/2). However, the cursor does not then move on from the printing position, thus enabling you to enter the 'u' underneath it.

The second type of special symbol does not hold the cursor back for an over-print. Examples of symbols of this sort are mathematical symbols such as Infinity (∞), general symbols such as Paragraph (¶) and a wide range of foreign language symbols, including a Greek character set.

Indents.

We have already observed how the TAB key can be used to indent a single line. Whole paragraphs can be inset in the same way, by use of the Inset TAB command.

This is achieved by holding ALT while TAB is pressed. All following lines in the same paragraph will be inset by the same amount as the first line; however the effect is not carried on beyond the next use of the RETURN key.

Uses of the Indent TAB include setting lists, etc., in from the normal print margin.

Using the Function keys.

In addition to the effects listed above, a very large range of special effects can be achieved with certain of the Function keys.

The relevant keys are $f3$ (Emphasis) and $f4$ (Style); the former is in charge of underlining, bold– and double-strike type and reverse video (high-lighting), and the latter handles type-face, type-size and pitch.

Function Key $f3$ pulls down a short menu which offers four ways of emphasising text: underlining, bold, double strike and reverse video – see Fig. 3.2.

The choices offered are not mutually exclusive – it is possible both to underline and to double strike, for example.

Because of the difficulties of representing such features as bold and double strike on the screen, some lack of consistency occurs between the representation of the Emphasis options on the screen and their printed appearance.

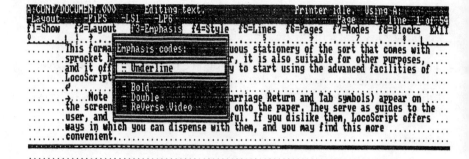

Fig. 3.2　　The Emphasis Menu

Underlining is represented both on screen and on paper, and if this option is chosen (by moving the cursor bar and using the [+] key) a further choice is offered between full underlining and word underlining. Use [+] and ENTER to make your choice.

If full underlining is used for a passage of text which continues beyond the end of a line, it will extend into the space following the last character *on the screen*, but not when printed.

Bold printing is carried out by restriking the affected characters after moving the print head fractionally to the right. **Double Strike** in draft mode is achieved by moving the paper up slightly before restriking; in high quality mode it is indistinguishable from Bold.

Neither bold nor double strike are shown on the screen; they only appear during print out.

Conversely, **reverse video** is shown only on screen, and does not affect the printing. It is used to highlight words which are to be changed during a future re-edit, for example.

If you compose text with one or other of the emphasis options (except underline, which is self-evident) selected, an appropriate message is displayed on the Status Bar.

If you go back to insert underlining into text which has already been composed you will not necessarily see the effect of your action on the screen until that paragraph has been RELAYed, or the cursor has been taken to the bottom of it with PARA, PAGE or a similar command.

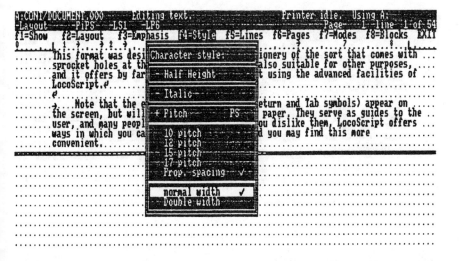

Fig. 3.3   The Style Menu

ƒ4 – Style.
This key and the associated menu enable the user to choose between regular and italic type-faces in a range of pitches. Choose the required effect with the cursor keys and [+]. If you choose the Pitch option, a sub-menu will be shown offering the option of double-width characters, as shown in Fig. 3.3.

Similarly, if you choose half-height characters you will be asked whether they are to appear as subscripts or superscripts; you cannot mix these together except by setting the printer line-spacing to zero, i.e. overprinting a line.

Further effects can be achieved with Function Key ƒ5 (Lines). This is for those occasions within a document when individual lines are to be treated in some special way; accordingly the effect of the Lines menu is limited to the line in which the option is chosen.

To make a choice from this menu, which is depicted in Fig. 3.4, simply move the cursor bar to the appropriate place and press ENTER.

Probably you will most often use the Lines Menu to place an individual line centrally between the left and right margins. To do this, select Centre Line at the beginning of the appropriate line, and remember that most centred lines

51

Fig. 3.4 The Lines Menu

will end with a carriage return.

Individual lines can also be forced against the right margin using the Right Justify Line option of the Lines menu.

Right Justify Line is actually something of a misnomer, as instead of inserting pad spaces evenly through the line in order to create an even right margin, the entire line to the right of the point at which the instruction was given is simply shifted the necessary distance to the right.

True right justification is also available with LocoScript, and will be described in detail in the following chapter.

The Lines menu also has a 'hard' and 'soft' space and hyphen option. These terms may require some explanation: the rule is that a 'soft' space or hyphen does not appear except when, in the course of RELAYing or editing, it occurs at the end of a line; a 'hard' space or hyphen conversely, is always displayed, but is prevented from ever appearing at the end of a line.

The purpose of the first of these changes to the normal word wrap rules is to enable a long word to be broken between adjacent lines; the purpose of the second is to prevent, for example, a person's initials from ever appearing on a different line from his surname.

The final options available from the Lines menu allow the user to vary line spacing and line pitch at any point within the text. These are selected in a slightly different way from the other options: move the cursor bar to the appropriate position, type in the number required and press ENTER.

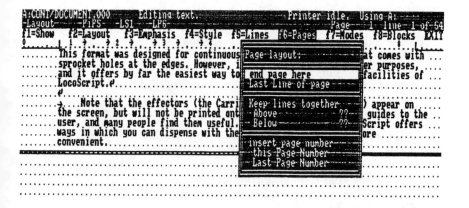

Fig. 3.5   The Pages Menu

Just as the Lines menu obtained from *f*5 can be used to alter the formatting of individual lines, so the Pages menu (Fig. 3.5), reached through *f*6, alters the format of an individual page.

The purpose of the first two options is similar: namely to allow a page-end to be forced at any point. They are selected by moving the cursor bar to the option required and pressing ENTER.

Last Line of Page forces a page break at the end of the current line, causing the next full line to appear at the head of the next page, while End Page Here causes an immediate page break at the very next character, regardless of previous line or page formats.

The Keep Lines Together options allow a given portion of text to be kept as one block by forcing a particular number of lines to be carried together over page breaks.

The precise form of the instruction will vary according to where the text cursor is when the command is given; move the cursor bar in the menu to the required instruction and type a number to show how many lines are to be kept together, then press ENTER.

The final options on the Pages Menu allow either the number of the current page or the number of the final page of the document to be displayed at the point chosen in the body of the text – in this context, 'last' does not mean 'previous!'.

This is particularly valuable with Version 1.0 of LocoScript, as there are undocumented problems in inserting page numbers in headers and footers. These problems have been corrected in Version 1.04.

The purpose of being able to specify the number of the final page is to automate expressions of the "Page 4 of 6" variety. Page numbering is dealt with more fully in the next chapter.

Using the Set and Clear Menus.

So far, all the formatting effects which we have achieved have required the selection of the appropriate function key, the display of the relevant pull-down menu, the making of a choice with the cursor bar and the final confirmation of that choice with the ENTER key.

Once you are familiar with the effects of the various commands, this procedure can be shortened considerably; a further bonus is that you will not need to remember just which Function Key creates which effect.

A:CONT/DOCUMENT.000   Editing text.   Printer idle.   Using A:
Layout   PiPS   LS1   LP6   Page
f1=Show   f2=Layout   f3=Emphasis   f4=Style   f5=Lines   f6=Pages   f7=Mo

........This format was designed for continuous stationery of the sort
........sprocket holes at the edges. However, it is also suitable for
........and it offers by far the easiest way to start using the advanc
........LocoScript.
........Note that the effectors (the Carriage Return and Tab symb
........the screen, but will not be printed onto the paper. They serve
........user, and many people find them useful. If you dislike them, L
........ways in which you can dispense with them, and you may find thi
........convenient.

Bold
Centre
Double
Italic
Keep   ??
Layout   ??
Line-Pitch   ?
Line-Spacing   ??
Last-Line
Last-Page Number
Pitch   ??-?
Page-Number
Reverse
Right-Justify
SubScript
SuperScript
UnderLine
Word-underline
Unit
hard space
hard hyphen

Fig. 3.6

54

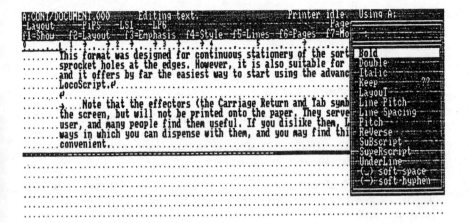

Fig. 3.7   The CLEAR Menu

This is done using two menus which we have not yet seen, the **Set** and **Clear** menus. These are shown in Figs. 3.6 and 3.7. To gain access to them press [+] (for the Set menu) or [-] (for the Clear menu) and wait for a couple of seconds. The chosen menu will be pulled down in the usual way.

To select any item from either menu, move the cursor bar to the appropriate line and press [+]; this is used to confirm the choice for both menus, and not only for the Set menu, as you might imagine.

There are two additional refinements to this procedure. The first allows you to gain access to the Set and Clear menus without even the usual couple of seconds' wait. After pressing [+] or [-], press the key bearing a hatch-pattern and the number '2' which is located in the middle of the cursor-key cluster, and the appropriate menu will be displayed instantly.

To speed matters up even more, pull down either of the new menus and look at it in detail. You will notice that the various options are written in a rather odd mixture of capitals and lower case letters.

Reverse, for example, is written as **ReVerse**, and Unit as as **UniT**. The purpose of this is to enable the user who is familiar with the system to access the editing commands without needing to use any of the menus at all.

By way of illustration, the command **Bold** can be achieved in any one of three ways. First, there is the pull-down menu reached through Function Key *f3*, on which the appropriate choice is made by moving the cursor bar and pressing [+] and ENTER.

Second, there is the Set menu, from which **UnderLine** can be chosen in exactly the same way.

Finally, and dispensing with menus altogether, the same effect can be achieved by pressing [+] *followed by the capitalised letters listed on the various menus*. Thus Bold can be selected with [+] immediately followed by the letter 'b' (either in upper or lower case).

At first, you will almost certainly find it easier to use the various menus which LocoScript provides; however, as you become more familiar with the program, and develop your own writing habits, you will probably find it quicker and simple to use the 'no menus' approach, at least for the commands which you use most frequently.

Making the most of the screen display.

A feature of word processing on the PCW8256 is that you can at any time during the editing of a document rearrange various details of the screen display.

You may remember that the first document which you wrote, using the CONT format, was done against a background of faint dots which marked the spaces which had not actually had anything typed in them yet.

With *f1* (Show), and depending on your personal preferences, you can either show or conceal one or more of a series of editing aids in the text you are working on.

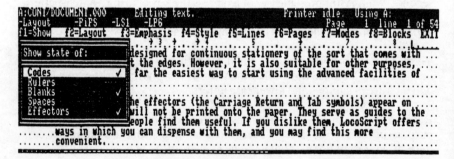

Fig. 3.8   The SHOW Menu

Options from this menus, which is shown in Fig. 3.8, are controlled by moving the cursor bar to the appropriate place and pressing the [+] key to select or the [-] key to deselect, and finally confirming the choice with ENTER.

Working down the menu in order, **codes** are symbols which modify the text on the printer or the screen or both – e.g. by turning on or off such features as underlining or printing text in boldface.

If this option is selected, the codes will show on the screen in the form of letters, words or phrases enclosed in brackets, but the codes do not appear when the document is printed.

Rulers contain variations in tab settings and other template details which have been altered in the course of a document. They are discussed in the next chapter.

Blanks (i.e. unused areas of the screen) and **spaces** are represented by faint dots and little triangles respectively. They provide a useful guide if you need to count the number of spaces between columns in a table, for example.

Effectors are symbols which represent Carriage Returns, Tabs and the like.

Depending on your preferences, you can display any or all (or none) of the editing aids available. The more options you choose, the more cluttered your screen will become; but if you are laying out a particularly complex document, this may well be a price worth paying.

However, the inclusion of codes in particular tends to distort the appearance of your text, and make it harder to visualise it on the printed page.

It does not affect the number of words which can be fitted onto any individual line, however, as when codes are displayed the line will simply be extended into the right-hand screen margin by the appropriate amount; remove the codes with *f*1 and the real length of the line will be made apparent.

We suggest that for most purposes you show only effectors, and possibly codes as well, but that before printing the document you remove all these features in order to see more accurately what the printed text will look like.

A word of caution is necessary at this point. LocoScript with the Amstrad PCW8256 is an extremely powerful and complex word processor, and as such it has many facilities which are lacking on simpler and less sophisticated machines, including many which are very much more expensive.

Inevitably, several of the features which it provides will not be appropriate to all users. If you do not feel that any of the features described will be of use to you, then don't worry about them.

For most normal purposes, the only function keys you are likely to use while actually writing a piece of text are $f1$ and $f3$; and, as you have already seen, it is perfectly possible not even to use those, and yet still produce sophisticated work.

Using the printer.

The printer included with the PCW8256 differs from most others in that it is almost entirely lacking in external controls or switches. This is because it is controlled by the program stored in the computer at any given time.

One result of this is that all the printer's facilities can be manipulated directly from LocoScript, and all the LocoScript commands are compatible with the printer.

If you have never had to 'install' a printer for a particular computer, you may not appreciate what a great advantage this is; underlining, italics, special symbols – in short, everything which can be produced on the screen – are all printed accurately and without fuss.

Printer control is entered through the PTR key, located to the left of the EXIT key on the bottom row of the keyboard. This key, as mentioned in Chapter One, puts LocoScript into Printer Control Mode, and lists the printer control commands on the Status Bar.

Alternatively, the same effect can be obtained by using the paper-feed knob, or pulling the bail bar forward.

Provided that none of the pull-down printer control menus is being displayed, you can return at any time from Printer Control Mode to the Editing Text or the Disc Manager screens by pressing the EXIT key. If you want to abort the use of a menu, use CAN in the usual way.

It must be admitted that the operation of the various function keys in Printer Control Mode is not as clear as it might be; nor are the various key names which appear on the Status Bar terribly helpful.

Because of this it is wise to develop a fixed procedure which can be used for setting up the printer at the beginning of each printing session. Careful adherence to this routine will ensure that your documents always look as you intended them to.

Begin by checking the one control which is actually located on the printer itself, namely the strength of impression lever.

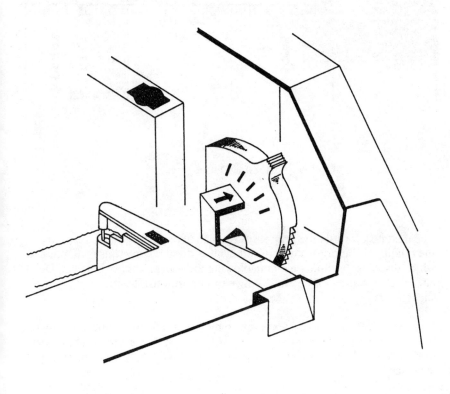

Fig. 3.9   Strength of Impression Lever

This is located inside the printer case on the right – see Fig. 3.9 – and to ensure maximum clarity it should be set to low pressure (pulled back) for single sheets and to high pressure (pushed forward) for multiple copies. Select the lowest pressure consistent with good quality.

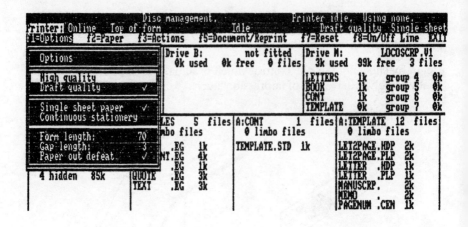

Fig. 3.10   The Print Options Menu

The next task is to set the printer for the size of paper which will be used and the quality of the print-out required. This is done by pressing *f*1 (Options), which displays a pull-down menu allowing the user to choose between Draft and High Quality Mode, and between continuous stationery and single sheets – see Fig. 3.10.

You can select the options you require by the usual combination of moving the cursor bar and pressing [+]. If you change the form of stationery, LocoScript will suggest a suitable length (in lines), which you can amend if necessary.

Line pitch is usually set at six lines to the inch, though eight lines to the inch can be selected – this is described below. Single sheet length is pre-set for A4 paper, and continuous stationery length is pre-set for standard 11" by ½" perforated paper.

When the paper has been loaded using the paper-loading control, as described in Chapter One, it may be necessary to command the printer to carry out certain additional tasks. This is done with *f*3 (Actions).

This menu – see Fig. 3.11 – offers two external printer actions and one internal action.

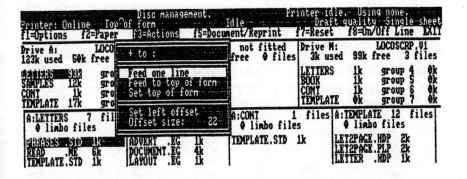

Fig. 3.11   The Print Actions Menu

The first external action forces the printer to advance the paper by either one line or one page. Locate the cursor bar over the appropriate choice and press [+]; several lines can be advanced by pressing [+] repeatedly, but the key does not auto-repeat.

The second external action is to move the print-head away from the left-hand edge of the paper by a certain number of characters. Put the cursor bar over the bottom line of the menu, enter the new value and press [+].

The internal action resets the top-of-form position. This may need to be done when continuous stationery is used and the paper has been manually advanced, in order to inform the printer that the current paper position is at the top of a sheet.

In every case, press ENTER to confirm your choice and leave the menu.

The printer control facilities already described are all that you will normally use; indeed, if you standardise on A4 paper, you will rarely need to change any of the settings from their initial values, except perhaps to alter print quality.

When you are happy with the settings, use EXIT to leave printer control. Subsequent printing of your document when EXITing from an editing session, or with P from the Disc Manager Screen, will done according to the settings you have already given, though you can revise them at any time by re-entering Printer Control Mode with the PTR key.

The remaining keys on the Printer Control Status Line are mostly used to take some action while the printer is working, or to enable you to clear some error which has occurred.

In each case you will have to re-enter Printer Control Mode in order to give the commands; this will cause the printer to stop either at the end of the current line or at the beginning of the following one.

Thus if anything goes wrong while printing is taking place, such as the paper tearing or jamming, the PTR key will stop the printer almost immediately.

Although the printer will stop when you press PTR, it will start again as soon as you press EXIT; to prevent an immediate restart, you can put it off-line, i.e. on stand-by.

This is done with $f8$ (On-line/off-line). When the printer is on-line, it responds to signals from the PCW8256; when it is off-line, it does not. Pressing $f8$ 'toggles' the printer between the two states – i.e. it changes it to the other state, regardless of what state is current.

If you go off-line during printing, you must both restore the on-line state ($f8$) and signal (using EXIT) that you are ready to proceed before the printer will restart.

Occasionally you will need to abandon printing in the middle of a document – perhaps because you realise that there is some error in it which you need to correct.

This cannot be done using the PTR key alone; instead press $f7$ (Reset), which is also used to reset the printer and return the print head to its rest position.

An advanced feature of the PCW8256 is that the printer can be working on a copy of one document at the same time as you are editing another document on the screen. The Document/Reprint menu – Fig. 3.12 – reached by pressing $f5$, gives you details of the document which is being printed, or informs you that the printer is not in use.

A second purpose of this menu is to allow you to reprint either the previous or the current page of the document being printed or the whole text of it, in case the paper has been misaligned or something else has gone wrong with the printing.

The only other occasion on which you may need to return to Printer Control Mode is when the printer stops and the Status Line displays the message

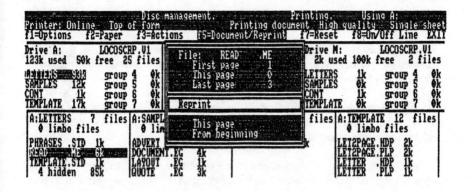

Fig. 3.12   The Document/Reprint Menu

"Waiting for paper," although paper is in fact loaded.

This may happen if you are using continuous stationery but have not set f1 accordingly, or if you have wound the paper in by hand without using the automatic paper-feed. Pressing *f*2 (Paper) and ENTER will enable the printer to continue.

When using single sheets, the printer stops after every page to enable you to insert more paper. Inserting the new sheet automatically returns you to Printer Control Mode, so when the new sheet is ready, press EXIT·to start printing the next page.

Finally, an image of the screen at any time (a **screen dump**) can be obtained on the printer by holding down EXTRA and then pressing PTR. This is always in high-quality print, and the print image is reversed from the screen image: i.e. light green areas on the screen appear as black ink, and vice versa. All the screen images in this book were obtained in this way.

Many printer manufacturers suggest that over-use of so-called 'bit-image printing' of this sort can eventually result in damage to the print head.

We are not aware of any such problems with the PCW8256 printer, but caution is probably wise. Certainly, prolonged printing of any sort can generate considerable heat at the print head, so be sure to keep your fingers well clear of it.

63

Postscript.

Many LocoScript commands can be given in several different ways. In general, it will help you to work faster if you use the methods which require the fewest key-strokes.

At first, however, you will find it easiest to use the Function key menus freely, and only move on to the SET and CLEAR menus, and to give direct commands, when you feel ready.

Other topics described in this chapter have been related to improving the appearance of your printed documents, and to showing how to issue commands to the printer.

CHAPTER FOUR

Using LocoScript Templates

Preview.

The topice to be introduced in this chapter are the following:

> The purpose of templates.
> Using ready-made templates.
> Editing templates.
> Pagination details.
> Page breaks.
> Headers and Footers.
> Extra layouts in a document.

What templates are for.

So far all our word processing has used either Direct Printing or the CONT format. Useful those these are, they make little use of the very advanced formatting facilities available in LocoScript, which we are now going to examine.

By way of illustration, try to edit the file called PHRASES.STD on your copy of the LocoScript Master Disc; the PCW8256 will respond with an error message telling you that you cannot as it is 'Not a LocoScript Document.'

In one sense, of course, this is manifestly absurd; if it is not a LocoScript document, then what else is it?

In a more specialised sense, however, the error message is quite correct: *A LocoScript Document is one which has a LocoScript Header*, and PHRASES.STD does not.

Headers may be defined as portions of documents which do not form a part of the final printed text, but which carry information about margins, tabs, page numbers, type faces, line spacings and other data.

Additionally, headers *may* contain some printed text, which will then form a part of the final document just as if it had been typed in the usual way.

Once a document has been given a header, that header forms an integral part of the document, and can be edited in the same way as any other part of it; we shall shortly see how this can be done.

If you look carefully at the Disc manager Screen, you will notice that the LETTER and CONT columns both have their own TEMPLATE.STD files, and also that there is a separate column made up of new templates.

Using an existing template.

When in Chapter Two we placed the lower cursor bar in the CONT column and pressed C to Create a new document, we were instructing LocoScript to start a new document formatted according to the details of the template for the column in which the cursor bar was placed — i.e. the template suitable for continuous stationery.

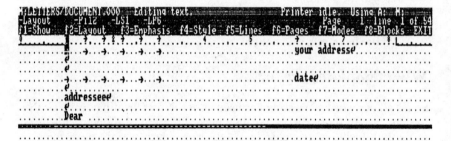

Similarly, if you place the cursor bar in the LETTERS column and Create a document, that document will automatically be given the template applicable to that column. Do this now — Fig. 4.1 shows what you should see on the screen.

Ignoring for the moment the text which appears under the rule at the top of the screen, you will notice that selecting this template has automatically established certain aspects of your letter — left and right margins are fixed, the type-face is pre-set to a pitch of 12 letters to the inch, the line-spacing to 1 and so on.

Assuming for the moment that all these things were satisfactory for your own purposes and practices, this would mean that whenever you wished to write a letter, you would only need to Create a document under this column to have all the incidental details automatically and consistently established.

There are also included in this template, and visible between the rule at the top of the screen and the page-end marker two-thirds of the way down, a number of prompts as to where you might wish to include your address, the date, etc.

Before you can use the template, you would naturally wish to remove these; in any case, your own preferred layout may be completely different.

Choosing another template.

In the TEMPLATE column there are several ready-prepared templates, and no matter what your requirements are, it is very likely that you will find several there which are suitable.

For example, LETTER.HDP is designed for headed notepaper, MEMO for memoranda, MANUSCRP for lengthy reports or books, etc.

You can inspect these by placing the lower cursor bar over each of them in turn and pressing E to Edit. Alternatively, f2 (Inspect) will display a short text to explain what each of the templates is for without taking you out of the Disc Manager screen. We shall now replace the original TEMPLATE.STD for the LETTERS group on our copy of the Master Disc with another template from the selection provided in the TEMPLATE column.

(Normally you should treat your copy of the Master Disc of any program with as much care as the original, and leave all the files on it intact; however, with LocoScript it is often very advantageous to alter the Master Disc copy to make it more suitable for your individual needs.)

First, erase the TEMPLATE.STD file in the LETTERS column — remember, it hasn't necessarily gone for good, but has merely been put into Limbo.

Then put the lower cursor bar over the template from the TEMPLATE column with which you have chosen to replace it — LETTER.HDP, perhaps, though you might choose any one of the various letter templates available — and press f3 (Copy).

Instructions will appear in the Status Block telling you to move the cursor bar to the appropriate destination group, which in our case is LETTERS, and then to press ENTER.

67

When you have done this, the new template will automatically be copied into the new group.

It is now essential to rename this file, as when you create a document, the PCW8256 looks for a file called TEMPLATE.STD in the appropriate column. Do this with *f*5 (Rename), using the Rename Document option to change the name from, in our example, LETTER.HDP to TEMPLATE.STD.

All new documents Created with either the lower or the upper cursor bar in the LETTERS group will now automatically be formatted according to the new template you have chosen.

It is important to realise that any documents which were already in LETTERS before you transferred in the new template will be unaffected by the change; only new texts are Created according to the new template. Note also that each group can only have ONE TEMPLATE.STD attached to it.

Editing templates.

The procedure which we have described so far is quite adequate if you are happy with the various templates offered in the TEMPLATE column. It may well be, however, that although you find that some particular template is generally suitable for your purposes, there are nonetheless certain details of it which you would like to change.

Of all the tasks which you may end up doing with LocoScript, editing templates is by far the most difficult and confusing. This is partly because LocoScript is so powerful that it offers choices which are not available with many other word processors.

The unhelpfulness of the Function Key descriptions on the Status Block is another potential source of confusion, though this is in part a consequence of the large number of menus and sub-menus which are offered to the user.

The structured approach to template editing which follows will enable you to get the precise results you need with the minimum of difficulty. As you become more used to the procedures, you will be able to develop your own short cuts.

As with very many computer operations, a little time spent in planning before sitting down in front of the PCW8256 will save you a great deal of trouble and effort later. Specific choices which you will need to make include the following:

(i) What size of paper will you be using?

(ii) How many lines of printing do you want to have to a page?

(iii) Are any features of the layout governed by physical limitations, such as the location of windows on envelopes?

(iv) How large should the margins (on all four sides of the printing) be?

(v) What type-size and –style do you want?

(vi) What text or page-numbers will be displayed in Headers or Footers? Will all pages be alike or will the first page (for example) be different?

If the template which you are designing is a particularly difficult or important one, you may find it helpful to take a sheet of paper of the size which you are going to use, and lay out various trial designs on it with a ruler.

Remember that a standard template may will serve for several hundred letters, for example, so time spent developing its design will certainly not be wasted.

When the planning work is complete, set up the Disc Manager screen, place the lower cursor bar over the particular TEMPLATE.STD which you wish to change and copy it (with ƒ3 (Copy)) to any column under Drive M. In the examples which follow, we have used the LETTER.HDP Template.

(It would be quite possible to leave the template which we are editing on Drive A; however, for reasons which are explained in the following chapter, it is often advantageous to move files which are being edited onto Drive M).

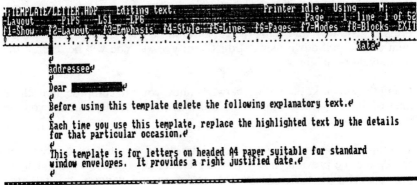

Fig. 4.2   The LETTER.HDP Template ready for editing

With the lower cursor bar on the template file-name in Drive M, press E to Edit it. The screen will clear and you will be offered the display shown in Fig. 4.2.

Before beginning to edit the template, it is comforting to know that whatever may go wrong, you can dump all your emendations and go back to the original template at any time; in this respect, editing the template is exactly like editing all other documents with LocoScript.

Identifying your work.

If a filing cabinet is allowed to become untidy because of pressure of work or carelessness, at least it is possible to tidy it up with relatively little trouble – just looking at the contents will serve to identify most of them.

When documents are stored on discs, identification becomes very much more time consuming. With LocoScript, however, you can create an identifying text for your work (to be later read from the Disc Manager screen with *f2* (Inspect)),and this is best done right at the beginning, before you forget.

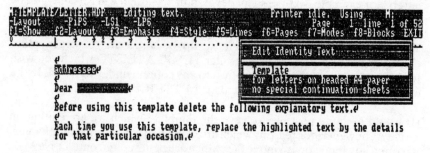

Fig. 4.3   Identifying text with the Edit Identity Text Window

Press *f7* (Modes), and using the cursor bar and ENTER select the second item on the pull-down menu, Edit Identify Text. You will be offered the window shown in Fig. 4.3.

Using the cursor keys to move between lines, you can compose up to three lines of thirty characters apiece of information about the template you are working on.

This information will replace the previous identifying text; if you wish, you can delete the previous text with the DELete keys or use [-] to delete all previous text to the right of the cursor in the window, as with the EXCH/FIND windows.

Apart from this, the editing of text in the windows is rather basic, and words will not 'wrap' from one line to the next as you type, as they do in ordinary LocoScript text files.

When you are happy with the Identify Text, press ENTER to confirm it and to remove the window in which it was written.

General principles of template editing.

Editing a template is not unlike peeling an onion: there are several different layers one inside the other.

The innermost layer controls the physical appearance of the document – matters such as tab settings, type-style, margins and the like.

Outside this is a 'pagination' edit, which affects the text, page-numbering etc., which is to appear on the Headers and Footers of the final document.

Furthest out is a 'text' edit, which allows you to specify any text which will become part of any document written with the template, such as your address at the head of a letter.

Pagination. Paradoxically, the easiest way to edit LocoScript templates is to plunge in to the deepest layer and then to work outwards.

Press ƒ7 (Modes), select the first option (Edit Header) by pressing ENTER, then choose ƒ7 again from the new choices which have appeared on the Status Bar. This time the name given to ƒ7 is Options; again, one wishes that the terms chosen were a little clearer.

Fig. 4.4   The Editing Header Screen

Looking at the Status Bar now – the screen that you should have is shown in Fig. 4.4 – you will see that you are editing the **header**.

This term too is rather apt to confuse, as 'header' in this context means not the text that would appear at the head of a page (as a Footer appears at the bottom of a page) but rather the form of the rule which will govern the shape of your document, and on which tabs, etc. are set.

71

In an attempt to avoid confusion, this book refers to printed text at the head of a page as a **Header** and the LocoScript template feature as a **header**, without the initial capital.

Fig. 4.5   Editing the Base Layout

Press *f*1 (Layout) and the Status Bar will become an editing window marked **Editing Base Layout**, as shown in Fig. 4.5.

Letter pitch. There are *two* editing cursors in this screen, though you may be unaware of this initially. The first is a bar located on the extreme left of the second line of the Status Bar, where the word **Pitch** appears.

To alter the number of characters per inch in each line, type in the appropriate number – 10, 12, 15 or 17 to the inch, or PS for proportional spacing.

Proportional spacing means that instead of each letter occupying the same amount of space on the paper, the thin ones like 'i' are allocated less room than the wide ones, like 'w'.

On average, over a line of printing, proportional spacing works out about the same size as 12 Pitch. However, numerals in proportional spacing are all of the same width, to avoid untidiness in tables.

Because proportionally-spaced characters are of different widths, text which employs proportional-spacing may seem either too wide or too narrow for the rule on top of the screen. When printed, however, the effect will be correct.

Apart from this, your choice of pitch has no effect on the way printing is displayed on the screen.

Confirm your choice of letter pitch with ENTER, then move the cursor bar to the right with the cursor key.

Line pitch. Line pitch refers to the number of lines per inch. The usual is six lines per inch, but eight is also possible. If you wish to change the setting, enter the new number and ENTER, otherwise move the cursor bar on to the third choice.

Line spacing. A line spacing of 1 selects single line spacing, which means that there are no blank lines between lines of printing; a line spacing of 2 means that you have double line spacing, and so on.

You can also choose a line spacing of 1, ½ or 2½, for example, or even a line spacing of zero; this will cause the second line to be printed directly on top of the first. This is usually only necessary for texts that require both superscripts and subscripts, such as some mathematical material.

Whichever line spacing you choose will have no effect on the way your document is displayed on the screen; that always has a line spacing of 1.

Once again, if you wish to change the line spacing provided, type in the new value and press ENTER.

Italic printing. The fourth choice on the Status Bar doesn't require a number to be input. Instead, if there is a tick by the word **Italic**, then text will be printed in italic type, though appearance on the screen will not be affected.

Remove a tick by pressing [-], or insert one by pressing [+]. In either case, all you are establishing is the norm for your document; you can additionally select or deselect italics at any point in the document from within the Emphasis menu.

Justification. The final choice offered on the Status Bar is whether you want your text to be right-justified, i.e. with the spaces padded out so that both right and left margins are straight. Where a fixed pitch is chosen, the effect can be a little untidy to some eyes; with proportional spacing, however, an extremely neat effect is obtainable – though some people object to it on the grounds that it makes it obvious that the text has been word-processed! This option is chosen in the same way as Italic printing, with [+] or [-].

Margins. The second cursor which we mentioned above can now be brought into play. Reveal it by pressing the ↓ cursor key; you will see a little cursor rectangle, similar to the one which you use when writing a document, appear at the left of the rule at the top of the screen.

This marks the only occasion in LocoScript when two cursors are visible simultaneously but do not move together. (Usually the appearance of a menu with a cursor bar on it implies that the usual text cursor has been hidden).

As long as this small cursor is visible, only it will respond to the commands of the cursor keys; to move the long cursor bar, remove the smaller one with the ↑ key.

Place the small cursor on the rule at the point where you wish the left margin of your document to appear, then press $f1$; next, move it across to the site for the right margin and press $f2$. The rule will immediately indicate where the new margins are to be.

LocoScript does not restrict your documents to the width of the screen. If you try to move the cursor square off the screen to the right, you will find that all the rest of the screen (except for the Status Bar, which remains stationary) will slide over to the left; the only practical factor limiting the width of a document is thus likely to be physical length of the printer-platen.

Tabs. The small cursor is also used to fix or remove tabs. Removal is straightforward, requiring only the placing of the cursor over the symbol marking the unwanted tab, followed by the [-] key. Insertion of tabs is more complicated, however, as the PCW8256 has no fewer than four tab types.

Ordinary tabs. The small right-pointing arrow represents the most common type of tab, and the only sort available on most typewriters. If the TAB key is pressed while a document is being written or edited, and the next tab-symbol is of this type, then all text which follows on the same line will be aligned to start at the tab.

Right tabs are represented by a small arrow pointing to the left. Their effect is directly the reverse of ordinary tabs. If the TAB key is pressed and the next tab symbol is of this sort, following text will be aligned so that its right end is aligned under this tab.

Centre tabs are represented by an arrow with a head at each end $\longleftrightarrow$; text tabbed to this symbol will be laid out so that it is centered underneath the symbol. Experiment with centre tabs before committing yourself to their use, as with very short lines of text the effect may not be what you intended.

The final type of tab is the **decimal tab**, represented by a dot. These are invaluable when setting out tables of numerical information, as any decimal point in text tabbed to them is forced to appear underneath the tab symbol, regardless of the number of places before or after that decimal.

When you are happy with the layout details, press EXIT and you will be returned to the 'Editing Header' screen; however, if you have any second thoughts at any time, you can easily go back to $f1$ (Layout) to make any necessary further modifications.

The next three editing possibilities will probably not be used very frequently; but the fact that they are present does give some indication of the power and scope of LocoScript, and there may be occasions when you will find them invaluable.

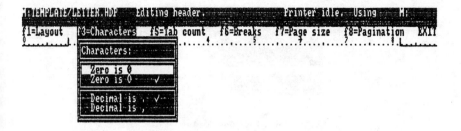

Fig. 4.6   The Characters Menu

Changing characters. Pressing Function Key *f*3 will reveal the pull-down menu shown in Fig. 4.6.

The purpose of this is to enable you to alter the form of the zero character, and to specify whether a comma or a full-stop is used as a decimal point.

The convention has arisen in computer programming of showing Zero as Ø, with a bar through the middle, rather than as O; this is in order to make a clear distinction between it and the letter O.

LocoScript offers you the choice of which symbol you prefer to use; move the cursor bar to the appropriate position and press [+].

The second option on this menu is to choose the form for the decimal, either as a point (for British, North American or Australasian use) or as a comma (for many other countries).

This option does not change the form of the symbol – you must still choose a stop or a comma as you wish – but it selects which of the characters will be aligned automatically with the decimal tab described earlier. Make your choice with the cursor bar and [+].

When both options are set to your specifications, press ENTER and the menu will disappear.

Tab count. A feature of LocoScript which we shall examine later is that although each document is written according to one base template, it can have a number of other templates which can be called up in the course of the document.

A possible use of this might be, for example, to set up a consistent pattern for long quoted inserts in scholarly works, setting them in from both margins and using a different type-size and line-spacing.

75

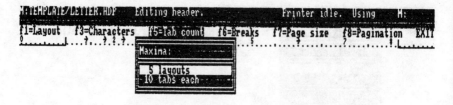

Fig. 4.7   The Tab Count Menu

LocoScript allows a maximum of 99 different templates per document, with a maximum of 99 tab settings for each one, and these are chosen with the Tab Count menu, controlled by the Function Key *f*5 – see Fig. 4.7. However, the larger the number you select, the more space your documents will require on disc.

To give some indication of the increase in storage space demanded by a larger number of templates and tabs, increasing both to the maximum permitted of 99 will result in a template needing 11K of disc space, instead of the 1K which is usually sufficient.

A maximum of five layouts with ten tabs each should deal with all but the most demanding requirements, and less will suit many purposes. Use the cursor bar and the number keys to change the preset values if necessary, pressing ENTER to confirm each value; then press ENTER again to remove the menu.

Fig. 4.8   The Page Breaks Menu

Page breaks. The options offered on the Breaks menu shown in Fig. 4.8, which is revealed with Function Key *f*6, determine the way in which individual lines and paragraphs are treated towards the end of pages.

Widows and orphans are single lines left at the bottom of one page or at the top of another. These generally look unattractive, and certainly add nothing to the readability of a document, so if you wish to avoid them, place the cursor bar over 'prevented' and press [+].

An alternative, especially where work is to be printed, and where complete clarity is therefore essential, is to avoid all paragraph breaks completely. If this option (Broken paragraphs Prevented) is chosen, any paragraph which would over-run a page boundary is automatically forced to the top of a new page.

A useful feature of LocoScript is that the user can tell at a glance exactly where he is in writing a page – indeed, there are two quite different indications.

First, in the Status Bar at the top of the screen, there is an explicit statement of which line on the page is currently occupied by the cursor, and what the maximum number of lines per page is.

Second, as you type in your text, vacant spaces in the page-boundary marker immediately underneath your current line are gradually filled up; you may well not have noticed this taking place, but if you watch the page-boundary marker closely you will observe it change slightly as you reach the end of each line.

With these guides available to you, there is a danger that you might try to force a particular section of your text onto a new page by typing in a number of 'empty' carriage returns; indeed, with some other word processors, this is the only way to achieve page control.

However, this technique will not work with LocoScript, as blank lines at the top and bottom of pages are ignored when printing.

The Breaks menu is thus invaluable for establishing rules for the behaviour of individual lines and paragraphs at page breaks.

As with the Characters menu, choices are made with the [+] key and the cursor bar, and are confirmed with ENTER.

If any further changes are necessary in the actual course of composing the text of a document, the Pages menu (*f*6) on the Editing text screen should be used, as described earlier.

Page size. Function Key *f*7 calls up the Page size menu, which is shown in Fig. 4.9.

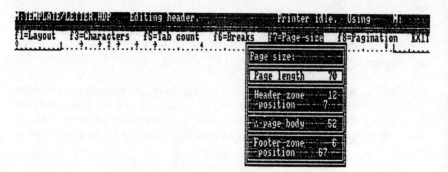

Fig. 4.9   The Page Size Menu

The purpose of this menu is not merely to establish the paper size for any particular document, but also to fix the amount of space to be set aside for Headers and Footers, and to specify where within that space the Headers and Footers are to appear.

The numbers which appear in the menu refer to numbers of lines. In the example given in Fig. 4.9, the page is 70 lines long (standard A4 when using a line pitch of 6) and the top 9 lines and the bottom 7 are set aside for Headers and Footers.

Within the blank space at the top of the page, the Header starts seven lines down, and thus two lines from the start of the main text. Similarly the Footer starts 66 lines down from the top of the page – after 9 lines of Header, 54 lines of text and 3 blank lines.

One figure on this menu is not entered by the user; the 'page body' size. This is worked out by LocoScript, which detects whether the value is a sensible one, and will issue an error message (i n c o n s i s t e n t) if it is not.

Pagination. The last template feature which can be edited from the Edit Header screen is pagination, using a menu called up with Function key *f*8. This menu controls two separate features, the first of which is page numbering.

Even if page numbers are not displayed, LocoScript keeps track of them, and during writing or editing the number of the current page is always displayed on the Status Bar.

Enter the number of the first page by positioning the cursor bar in the appropriate place and typing in the number, then ENTER. The highest number possible for any page is 9999.

The second feature which is under the control of the Pagination menu is the allocation of Headers and Footers to different pages.

There are certain circumstances under which some pages may need Headers or Footers while others do not. For example, every page of an article may require to have "more follows" or "mf" at the bottom except for the last, which would probably have "ends".

Similarly, the second and subsequent pages of a letter might carry a page number, but the first page generally would not.

The Pagination menu makes it possible to determine what variations you wish to have in the allocation of Headers and Footers. It is even possible to have odd and even numbered pages handled differently, so that when they are mounted in a binder their page numbers will always be on, say, the outside corner.

Choices in this section of the menu are made with the cursor bar and [+]; when you have the layout you want, confirm it with ENTER.

Leaving the Header editing screen. When you are certain that you have all the details of the template header just as you want, press EXIT to return to the next-outer layer of the onion, so to speak.

At this point, you will be asked to confirm that you really do wish to use the new details which you have entered. Press ENTER and the screen will clear, leaving you ready to edit the actual text and page numbers that will go into your template's Headers and Footers.

There is nothing to stop you from returning to the Editing Header screen again at any time; however, in the interests of following a fixed and organised routine in creating a document, it is better to try to get it right the first time, if possible.

Headers and Footers.

Creating text for insertion into Headers and Footers is no different from entering any other text, except that the amount of space available is more limited, and you are more likely to use such features as right justification and page numbering.

Consequently, the various Function Keys displayed on the Status Bar are the same as those used during normal writing, and can be used to call up the Show, Emphasis and other menus which we have already seen.

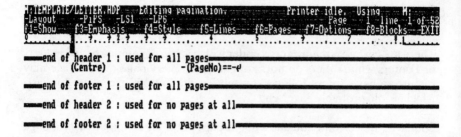

Fig. 4.10   Editing pagination–inserting Headers and Footers

Figure 4.10 illustrates the appearance of the screen at this point, with the Show option enabled to reveal Effectors and Codes. The most prominent feature is the series of bars across the screen, each one of which marks the end of a Header or Footer, as appropriate.

Each bar is identified with a brief text which also specifies where each particular Header or Footer will be used. This is derived from the Pagination option (ƒ8) on the previous screen, which is why we have worked back to this point after establishing the pagination choices.

Page numbers in LocoScript Version 1.0.

In LocoScript Version 1.0, due to an apparent 'bug' in the program, page numbers cannot be inserted into Headers or Footers using the commands intended for that purpose, and the routine described in the User Manual does not work.

Consequently, the only straightforward way to have page numbers in the Headers or Footers of a document is to use a ready-prepared template which already has the Page Number code in more or less the right places – reveal the code with the Show Codes option on the Show menu.

You will find that the Page Number code can be moved from one part of a Header or Footer to another part of the same Header or Footer, and that it can be deleted, but it cannot be moved from one Header or Footer to another, nor can it be reinstated once it has been removed.

The only practical way around this problem, if you insist on having page numbers at the top of a page, for instance, and you are using a template which does not provide them ready-placed there, is to insert them into the ordinary text at the desired location.

To do this, put the cursor on the appropriate line and use the Pages menu (ƒ6), choosing the **Insert Page Number– This Page Number** option, using the cursor bar and the [+] key.

In addition, you will then need to insert the appropriate symbol or symbols to show how the numbers are to be located, and to allocate space for them; this is described below.

Page numbering.

The problem described above has been corrected in LocoScript Versions 1.04 and onwards.

To insert page numbers, it is necessary to make three choices. The first of these is the general location of the numbers in the Header or Footer, which is probably best done using the Centre or Right Justify commands from the Lines menu (f5).

Next, you must decide how many spaces you are going to allocate to the numbers, and whether you want the numbers to sit on the right, the left or the centre of the space chosen.

Both these choices are handled by the form and number of the symbols which you must type in immediately following the PageNo command – which is a good reason for using the Show menu to reveal exactly where the code for PageNo is placed.

The PageNo command itself can be inserted in various ways; use the Pages menu (f6) or the SET menu, or call it directly by entering [+]**pn**.

The symbol ‹ locates the page numbers to the left of the space provided; › places them to the right of the space; and = centres them. The number of times the symbol is repeated defines how much space the numbers will be allowed to occupy.

Thus the combination ‹‹‹ leaves space for up to three numbers, and locates them as far to the left as possible – useful if you need the numbers to appear immediately after the words "Page Number" or something similar.

Similarly, the instruction -(**PageNo**)====– allows space for up to four numbers, and prints them centrally between the two hypens.

Another option for page numbering allows the number of the last page to be entered – 'last' in this case meaning 'final'. This permits such expressions as 'Page 4 of 6' to be achieved without any need for counting on your part.

Leaving the screen. When you are satisfied that you have achieved the results you want – or alternatively, if you feel that you have made a total mess of the job and you want to start all over again – press the EXIT key, and the menu shown in Fig. 4.11 will be shown.

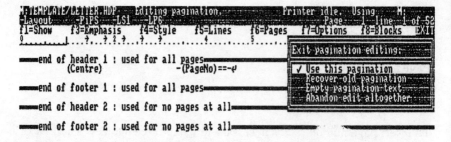

M:TEMPLATE/LETTER.HDP   Editing pagination.   Printer idle, Using   M:
Layout   PiPS   LS1   LP6   Page   1 line 1 of 52
f1=Show   f3=Emphasis   f4=Style   f5=Lines   f6=Pages   f7=Options   f8=Blocks   EXIT
0............?..?..2..?..?..?...........4...........5.

Exit pagination editing:

✓ Use this pagination
  Recover old pagination
  Empty pagination text
  Abandon edit altogether:

━━end of header 1 : used for all pages━━
      (Centre)   -(PageNo)==-↵

━━end of footer 1 : used for all pages━━

━━end of header 2 : used for no pages at all━━

━━end of footer 2 : used for no pages at all━━

Fig. 4.11   Exiting from editing Headers and Footers

The first choice – **Use this pagination** – confirms that you have completed this portion of the editing and are ready to move on to the next section.

Recover old pagination, the second option on the menu, allows you to abandon all the changes you have made and revert to the previous format.

The third line – **Empty pagination text** – is a kind of bulk delete, clearing everything from both Headers and Footers and leaving you still in the same screen. It is best considered not as an EXIT option at all, but as a fast way of clearing Header and Footer space before entering new text.

Finally, **Abandon edit altogether** returns you to the Disc Manager screen, but with all your work lost for good; this allows you to escape from an editing session which has somehow 'gone wrong' without messing up the original template.

Template text

The outermost level of the template editing procedure takes you back to the regular text-creation screen, on which you can enter in the usual way whatever information or messages you want.

These will then form an integral part of the template whenever you use it to create a document; the facility is most useful for such features as addresses at the top of letters, but other uses will probably come to your mind.

If the text which you enter here is not intended to form part of a final printed document, you may find it worthwhile drawing attention to it by using the Reverse Video option from the Emphasis menu (*f*3).

Other layouts.

At this point, you might think that the editing of the template was completed; and in the sense that the main template is now ready for use, you would be quite right.

However, one of the most useful features of LocoScript is that it allows you to have various subsidiary templates in addition to the **Base Template** – the one which is automatically selected when you begin an edit.

Earlier, on the Editing Header screen, we established how many different layouts we might need, using *f*5 (Tab Count). There is no need to define all of them now – indeed, it is perfectly possible that you might not wish to define any of them at the moment – but the advantages of having a couple of subsidiary formats ready for use are so great that we will assume that you will proceed with this now.

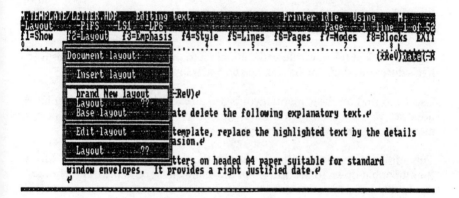

Fig. 4.12   The Layouts Menu

Press *f*2 (Layout), and the long menu shown in Fig. 4.12 will appear. Some of the terms on this are a little complicated, and will repay closer examination.

The menu offers two main choices. The first, (**Insert layout**), allows the user to pick one of the numbered layouts which has already been prepared, or to return to the Base layout (i.e. the main template which we have spent so long creating already) or to choose a Brand New Layout.

The second choice (**Edit layout**) makes it possible to choose one or other of the numbered layouts and to amend it.

So that you can see exactly what is happening, it is best to use the appropriate option from *f*1 (Show) to reveal Rulers. This is not a choice we have used so far, but if you are composing a complicated document, it may be very helpful.

Many of the ready-made templates supplied with LocoScript already have some subsidiary layouts attached to them. To see whether this is true of the one you are using, press *f*2 (Layout), move the cursor bar down to **layout ??** and type in the number 1, followed by ENTER.

The menu will disappear, and provided you have set the Show option to reveal rulers, you will see the new ruler flash into view immediately under the line on which the cursor is resting.

There are two checks you must make before you can be certain whether you have actually called up a layout which previously existed or not.

First, check the Status Bar. A different layout may well have different line spacing, type-style or pitch.

Second, look at the new rule and compare it to the rule under the Status Bar; if it is different, then you have called up a new layout.

Use *f*2 to find out how many layouts are already defined. When you have done so, you can then, if you wish, set out to edit any of them to conform more closely with your requirements.

This editing is also done with *f*2, but with the second half of the menu. Move the cursor bar down to the bottom of the menu and type in the number of the layout that you wish to edit.

The layout details will appear at the top of the screen exactly as they did when you were working with the Editing Header screen earlier.

The only difference now is that, when you have made your choice and pressed EXIT, you will not be offered the same progression back through the Editing Pagination screen (since pagination remains consistent throughout the whole document), but will be taken immediately back to the text editing screen.

In order to help you to remember the details of each subsidiary layout, you may find it helpful to call them all up onto the screen, immediately under one another, with the Rules revealed.

Then load paper into the printer and make a screen dump for your records by pressing EXTRA and PTR together.

Brand new layouts.

If you have allowed yourself five different layouts, as suggested, it will probably be quite sufficient for most purposes to set one or two of them ready for those changes that you can anticipate wanting to make in the internal layout of documents, and to leave the rest undefined.

These 'spares' will then be ready to define and use whenever you find in the course of creating or editing a document that it would make your work easier to have a new layout.

When this need arises, select ƒ2 (Layout), choose the Brand New Layout option and press ENTER.

You will immediately be offered the Editing Header display in place of the Status Bar. Although you have asked for a brand new layout, the layout offered will actually be identical to the one you are already using, as LocoScript always offers this as a starting point.

When you have made the necessary changes, press EXIT and the new layout will immediately be given the next available free number, and the rule will appear across the screen (provided you have chosen to show it).

Changing the layout of an existing document.

It is perfectly possible to change the layout of a document which has already been written. To do this, simply position the cursor at the point in the text from which you wish the change to take effect and use ƒ2 to call up the appropriate layout number.

If you then move the cursor down through the following section with UNIT, PARA, etc., or use RELAY, you will see your text being reconfigured to match the changed layout.

To return to the original layout at any time, use ƒ2 and select the option marked **Base Layout**.

Finally, if all this work has been done on Drive M, remember that you will have to retransfer your new TEMPLATE.STD back to a suitable group on Drive A before switching off, or everything that you have done will be lost.

Postscript.

Templates provide both one of the most powerful features of LocoScript, and one of the most difficult to understand and come to grips with.

However, once you have mastered them, they enable you to produce documents which are clear and consistent with a minimum of time spent working out a suitable layout for them.

Because of the complexities of templates, it may be well worth your while spending a considerable amount of time getting them right, at least if you are interested in understanding and using the great flexibility they provide.

Despite this, it is perfectly possible to produce high-quality documents with LocoScript without ever editing a single template; if you find the whole subject uninteresting, or think that it will not repay the effort of learning about it, then you will still find that you can carry out useful word processing without it.

CHAPTER FIVE

More About Files and Discs

Preview

This chapter is devoted to the following topics:

> Special files.
> The READ.ME file.
> The PHRASES.STD file.
> Disc types and the Start of Day disc.
> Working discs.
> Un-named groups.
> Moving text between documents.
> Disc managing from the Edit screen.
> Handling long documents.

Special files.

We have already seen that LocoScript enables up to eight different 'groups' or formats of files to be kept on any one disc, and that each group consists, in general, of documents which have been composed using the particular TEMPLATE.STD for that particular group.

As a result, there should normally be an individual TEMPLATE.STD for each column, with each template containing formatting details for up to 99 different layouts.

Deviations from this rule are possible, however. For example, there are two columns on the Master Disc which contain no TEMPLATE.STD. One of these is the special column of ready-made templates, and the other is the SAMPLES column.

The READ.ME file.

If you load your copy of the Master Disc and look at the Disc Manager screen, you will find that there are two other important cases where document files do not really belong to the group in which they are located. These files are those named READ.ME and PHRASES.STD, both of which are to be found in the left-most column of the screen. The READ.ME file was devised as a way of passing on to the user any new information on the operation of LocoScript which had not been included in either the User Manual or in any additional printed material.

In order to read this file, it is only necessary to Edit it in the usual way; alternatively, a print-out of it may be made, which can then be kept with the other user documentation.

There is, however, another use for this file. When Locoscript is first loaded, the file-names *in the first column only* are searched, and if there is a file there entitled READ.ME, a suitable message is displayed to draw the user's attention to it. If the READ.ME file has been erased (or placed in Limbo) the message will not appear.

This is useful because a new READ.ME file can be created to pass on any sort of information to anyone using LocoScript.

The only restrictions on such a file are that it must be saved in the first column of the LocoScript program disc, and that it must have the right name.

Of course, there is nothing to stop you from creating the file to some completely different format, if you wish, and then transferring it across to the first column.

The PHRASES.STD file.

Another file which must be located in the first column of the LocoScript program disc is the PHRASES.STD file.

This is an unusual file in many ways. In the first place, it has no header, and therefore is 'Not a LocoScript document.' Because of this, it cannot be edited or amended in any of the usual ways.

Second, unlike ordinary documents it is automatically loaded into the memory of the PCW8256 when LocoScript is started, provided it is found in the appropriate place.

We have already seen how to create 'new' phrases which we can then PASTE into any document, but so far these have been lost when power was turned off at the end of the session. We shall now see how to make these new phrases immediately available whenever LocoScript is started.

First of all, using your copy of the Master Disc, use Function key *f*4 from the Disc Manager screen to Move (not Copy) the PHRASES.STD file from column 1 to any column under Drive M. Then, in that column on Drive M, create a new document and display in it all the original LocoScript phrases.

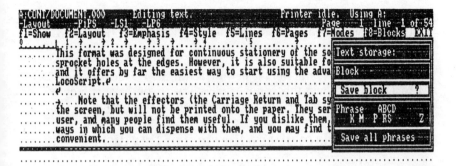

Fig. 5.1   The Blocks Menu

If you don't know which letters are already occupied by phrases, you will find them listed on the pull-down Blocks menu, which is reached via Function key *f*8 – see Fig. 5.1. Unless you are an estate agent, you will probably find that few of these ready-made phrases will be of very much use to you!

By now you will probably have found several phrases of your own that you would like to keep permanently. Obvious examples might be your Company's name, address and telephone number, the name of your product and standard greetings and closes for letters.

As there are only about 550 characters available for phrase storage, start off by deleting all the ready-made phrases which you don't want. A good place to begin is with Phrase Z, which takes up over a hundred precious characters.

You can delete it by pressing COPY, followed immediately by CUT Z; this has the effect of saving a 'null phrase' in Z, with a consequent saving of space. Alternatively, type in a new phrase and then save it as Phrase Z.

If you have a large number of phrases it can be difficult to remember which phrase is represented by which letter; either print a list and pin it up near the PCW8256, or save the phrases according to some logical rule – A for your address, S for 'Yours sincerely' and so on.

When you have stored all the phrases you want, call up the Blocks menu again with *f*8. Make sure that all the phrases you want to save are really there – check that their identifying letters are listed under the word **Phrase** – and move the cursor bar down to the bottom option, **Save all phrases**. Then press [+].

You should now leave the Edit by pressing EXIT and choosing the Finish editing option. All your phrases will now be saved in PHRASES.STD on Drive M.

All that remains is to transfer the new PHRASES.STD file back from Drive M to Drive A. When this is done, the phrases you have chosen will be automatically available to you in every word processing session.

Different kinds of discs – the start of Day disc.

The original Master Disc which came with your PCW8256, and the copy which you made of it and have probably now amended, contain both the LocoScript program and a series of document files.

Because LocoScript takes up a large proportion of the space on these discs, there is relatively little room left on them for the many documents you will wish to create.

One way round this problem would be to delete all the document files already on the Master Disc copy. Even then the amount of room is still very limited, and you would soon find yourself running out of disc space to store your document files.

Because of this it is a common procedure to have two different types of disc. In this way, you can start a word processing session by loading the LocoScript program from a disc which contains it, and then remove that disc and replace it with another which has only document files on it.

A disc which has the LocoScript program on it is sometimes called a **Start of Day disc**; one which has only document files on it is called a **Working Disc**. In order to make the best use of LocoScript, it is as well to spend some time getting these properly organised.

We have seen that the LocoScript program disc has three functions: it carries the LocoScript program; it checks for a document entitled READ.ME in the first column, and if it is there it draws attention to it on the first screen; and it checks the first column for a file named PHRASES.STD, the contents of which it places in memory.

In addition to these, there is one other task which is carried out by LocoScript when the program is first loaded. This is to automatically allocate certain group-names to Drive M, and to Copy certain files from the program disc on Drive A to Drive M.

This is done by scanning the names of each group on Drive A and setting up matching groups on Drive M.

Setting up the matching groups is carried out regardless of whether there is a TEMPLATE.STD associated with a group or not. However, if a TEMPLATE.STD *is* provided for a group on Drive A, then additionally a column is set aside for that group on Drive M, and the TEMPLATE.STD is automatically copied across into it.

Bearing all of this in mind, we can now reorganise our copy of the Master Disc to provide a useful Start of Day disc that will make subsequent document creation and grouping as easy as possible.

The first and most obvious requirement of the Start of Day disc is that it must have the LocoScript program on it. The easiest way to do this is to copy your whole Master Disc, and later to erase all unwanted files.

Before carrying out these erasures, however, you will recall that up to eight different columns – i.e. eight different document formats – can be stored on a single disc.

Begin by working out which eight of the templates that you have devised you are most likely to use (if there are even that many), and transfer them onto the LocoScript program disc, renaming the various groups as appropriate.

If you have more than four TEMPLATE.STDs, then you will need to use one or more of the un-named groups on the disc. If you are uncertain how to do this, read the following section on un-named groups first.

If you have more than eight TEMPLATE.STDs, keep those you will use least often in a TEMPLATE column of their own, as they were on the Master Disc, or put them onto a second Start of Day disc with another copy of LocoScript.

Next, you can if you wish use Function key *f*6 (Erase) to remove any unwanted files from the disc. This is not strictly necessary, or course, but you may find that it helps to avoid confusion among less experienced users.

Finally, copy to the first column on the disc the PHRASES.STD file which you have prepared, and any READ.ME file which you wish to include.

When this is done, write-protect your disc (with the write-protect tabs) to guard the files against accidental erasure, then make a back-up copy of it.

Working discs.

With your Start of Day disc ready, it is time to prepare one or more Working discs.

How many of these you will have depends largely on whether or not you intend to continue to keep printed 'hard copies' of all your documents, or whether you intend to keep 'soft' copies on disc only.

If the latter, you will find that your disc-space will fill up quite rapidly – especially as everything should be duplicated on a back-up disc – and therefore it will be wise to set aside one working disc for each type of document.

An alternative is to continue to keep actual printed copies of all documents – either photo-copies or printed using Draft Mode, for speed – in which case only the most recent documents might also need to be kept on disc (in case you found you needed another high-quality copy).

If you favour this approach, one Working disc would serve for documents of several different kinds.

Un-named groups.

On the original Master Disc, only four of the possible eight groups were actually named and used – LETTERS, SAMPLES, CONT and TEMPLATE. The remaining four groups contained no files, and instead of real names, they were identified by numbers – Groups 4, 5, 6 and 7.

In preparing your Start of Day disc, you will almost certainly need to use one or more of these un-named groups; and although there are no real problems in dealing with them, there are a couple of points which should be borne in mind.

First, to rename any group – whether initially unassigned or not – place the upper cursor bar over it, using SHIFT and the cursor keys, and press Function key ƒ5 (Rename), selecting the Rename Group option.

Merely renaming the group will not assign a column to that group in the lower section of the screen. To do this, it is necessary to actually transfer one or more files into the group, using either Function key ƒ3 (Copy) or ƒ4 (Move).

It is good practice to begin by moving over an appropriate TEMPLATE.STD file, or a different Template which you are intending to adapt for the group.

However, because the group does not yet have a column of its own, you cannot do this in the usual way, by moving the lower cursor bar into the appropriate column.

Instead, when you have identified the file you wish to Copy by pressing Function key ƒ3, you will have to place the *upper* cursor bar over the appropriate group name.

When you do this, the lower cursor bar will not have a corresponding column to go to, so it will lie flat along the dividing wall between two other columns. However, as soon as the first file has been transferred into the new group, the lower cursor bar will be placed over it in the usual way.

Moving text between documents.

So far we have regarded document files as self-contained portions of text. However, LocoScript offers certain facilities for transferring text from one file to another.

There are various reasons for doing this. The most obvious is to insert one rather lengthy piece of text – too long to be fitted into the 550 or so characters allowed for phrases – into a number of different documents, or to remove a section from one file and place it in another one.

Alternatively, it may be necessary to print only a portion of some document; LocoScript doesn't offer a 'Print part text' option, so the only way to proceed is to transfer the relevant section of the document into a file on its own, and then to print that.

The process can be broken down into two steps: the removal of a text fragment from one document, and its insertion into another document.

The first of these is carried out by the normal process of COPY and CUT (or COPY and COPY, if you wish to keep the text in the original document as well).

Normally, the text which has been removed would be abandoned when the Edit was finished. To keep it, press Function key ƒ8 (Blocks) before EXITing. The Blocks Menu will appear once more; it is shown again in Fig. 5.2

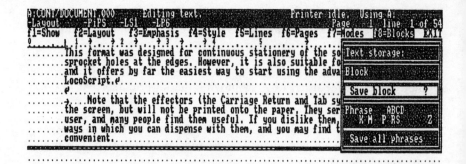

Fig. 5.2   The Blocks Menu

On this menu will be listed all the numbers which you have allocated to blocks of text removed with COPY. Choose the number of the block which you wish to transfer to another document, and with the cursor bar in the Save Block part of the menu, enter that number and press ENTER.

Because all LocoScript documents are identified by a name and a group, you will immediately be shown the Disc Manager screen, and invited to place the cursor bar in the group in which the text fragment is to be placed, and then to press ENTER.

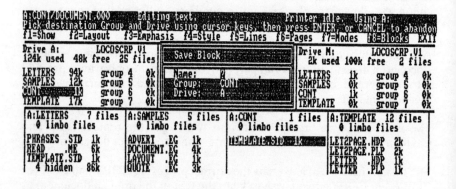

Fig. 5.3   The Save Block Menu

When you have done this, you will be offered the window shown in Fig. 5.3, and asked for a document name for the text. As soon as you have typed this in and pressed ENTER to confirm it, you will be taken back to the document on which you were originally working.

The fragment of text which you have now named and saved is rather a curious document, inasmuch as it has no header, and is therefore 'Not a LocoScript document.' It cannot therefore be either directly Edited or Printed, although it can be transferred from one column to another, or copied from one Drive to another.

In order to Print or Edit the text fragment, it is necessary either to Insert it in another document, or at least to assign it a header.

The procedure is broadly the same in both cases: Edit the document into which the fragment is to be Inserted, or Create a new file with the appropriate header, and then press Function key f7 (Modes).

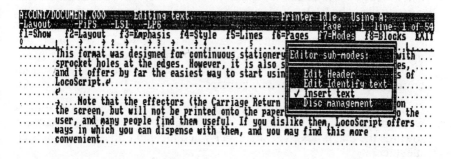

Fig. 5.4   Inserting Text with the Modes Menu

As you will see from Fig. 5.4, the third choice offered on the Modes menu is Insert text. Move the cursor bar down to this, and press ENTER.

Once again you will be taken back to the Disc Manager screen, in order to identify the document which is to be inserted. When you have done this, you will be returned to your document, and will see the text fragment being fed in in the appropriate place.

Disc management from the Edit screen.

You will observe that one of the choices on the Modes menu reached with f7 is Disc Management. If you select this option, the text Edit or Create on which you are working will be temporarily stopped, and the Disc Management screen will be shown.

The most important reason for choosing this option would be to allow you to move or delete files in order to give more space for the document on which you are currently working. As far as possible, avoid any disc manager activity that could affect the file on which you are actually working.

When you are ready to return to the Edit screen with the original document, press EXIT.

Working with long documents.

Although LocoScript is a very advanced word processing program with many very useful features, it is generally at its best when dealing with relatively short documents, such as letters or reports.

One reason for this is the way in which LocoScript documents are RELAYed after editing. The general rule is that all text in any given paragraph *above* the cursor is automatically RELAYed when you insert new text or take the cursor below the bottom of the paragraph, but text *below* the cursor will not be RELAYed without a specific command.

As all LocoScript documents are saved in a fully RELAYed form, this means that whenever you EXIT from the Editing text screen (unless you are abandoning the document), the whole text will scroll up the screen so that any necessary RELAYing can take place.

On long documents, this procedure is painfully slow, and about as exciting as watching paint dry. To minimise it, always edit from the start of a document towards the end if possible, and EXIT when the end of the document is on the screen.

Another point to be aware of is that when you edit an existing document with LocoScript, you are not working with the actual document at all – that is always waiting 'in the wings' as it were, in case you decide to abandon the edit.

This means that there are always two copies of every current document – the original, which is untouched until you save the new version (at which time it is erased and becomes a Limbo file) and the new version.

Long documents are not loaded into the PCW8256 in one go; instead, as you move through the text, new portions are taken off the disc.

One result of this is that working through long texts can be rather slow, with frequent pauses for the disc drive to operate. We have also found under certain circumstances that portions of lengthy documents have become corrupted with extraneous symbols, though this has not proved to be a serious problem.

Edited text is stored on Drive M until you are ready to save it, though this is generally not apparent. No document can therefore be longer than the total amount of space available on Drive M.

If you are working with a very long document, and especially if you already have several other files on Drive M, it is possible to run out of room on Drive M for the text on which you are working.

None of these problems is serious, especially for the typical user, whose documents will rarely exceed several hundred words. If they do arise, however, there are various techniques which should prove helpful.

First, limit the length of individual documents to a maximum of about 15K; longer documents can be made by piecing together a number of short files.

Second, Create and Edit long documents on Drive M, rather than Drive A; this will eliminate delays caused by the disc being accessed in the middle of a document.

If you do this, it is particularly important to backup the Drive M file onto Drive A at frequent intervals, to reduce any loss as a result of power failure. Your guideline here should be, *How much work am I prepared to retype?* – if retyping half a dozen pages doesn't bother you, then backup your work every six pages; if you don't want to risk losing more than two pages, then make a backup copy at the end of every second page.

Finally, as far as possible limit Drive M to the document on which you are working and the usual TEMPLATE.STDs. There is no advantage in having a large number of files on Drive M in any case.

Postscript.

Within the last few chapters we have investigated most of the important features of LocoScript, and you should by now have a good grasp of how it works.

Over the next few months, it is likely that there will be several additions to LocoScript, in the form of 'extensions'. One probable extension which will be particularly useful if you ever need to send out a series of individually addressed form-letters should be a **mail-merge** facility, which will take details such as names, addresses and the like from a second file and 'merge' them into individualised letters.

A limitation which you should be aware of is that, because of the way in which LocoScript documents are stored, it is inherently difficult to arrange spelling-checkers and similar utilities to work with it.

For similar reasons, there are problems in merging non-LocoScript documents – the output of a spread-sheet, for example – into LocoScript texts.

It appears that new versions of LocoScript currently under development may offer a facility to store text files in a different way, so that these problems will cease to apply.

In any case, for the vast majority of users, the failings mentioned are not serious. Remember that all word processors – indeed, all serious computer programs – are the result of hard choices between ease of use on the one hand and sophistication on the other.

There are other word processing packages available for the PCW8256, and some of these are more sophisticated than LocoScript. It is our view that choosing a word processor is a very personal business, and the only real guide to the value of a program is whether you as a user find it useful.

CHAPTER SIX

Starting with CP/M

Preview.

In this chapter, we shall cover the following topics:

> About operating systems.
> What is CP/M?
> Loading CP/M.
> CP/M Utilities.
> Programming languages.
> Applications programs.
> What CP/M expects.
> Using DIR.
> Copying and formatting with Disckit.
> Resident and transient commands.
> Examining text files on the screen.
> Using the printer with CP/M.
> Erasing files from discs.
> Renaming files.
> Copying individual files with PIP.
> The Show utility.

A little about operating systems.

So far, most of our work with the PCW8256 has used one particular program, the LocoScript program provided on one side of the Master Discs supplied with the machine.

However, the PCW8256 is a fully-fledged computer as well as a word processor, and the other three sides of the Master Discs contain a variety of other useful programs.

We have already remarked that when you turn on the PCW8256, unlike many personal computers, there is 'nothing in it'. Only when the LocoScript program has been loaded does it begin to operate.

If you pause for a moment to think of what LocoScript is actually doing inside the machine, you may realise that it is responsible for far more than merely transferring characters from your key-presses onto the screen.

For example, LocoScript kept an index of the contents of the disc, so that when you saved a new document it wasn't recorded on top of something which was already there.

A second task which LocoScript handled was regulating the flow of information inside the PCW8256, sending the appropriate stream of data to the printer, the screen and the disc drive.

Finally, LocoScript knew exactly where in the memory of the PCW8256 all your information was stored, so that whenever you needed to look at something which had already been typed in, you could find it again without any trouble.

These tasks of organising the disc drives, directing information around the various parts of your computer system and keeping track of what is in the memory are usually carried out not by a particular program, like LocoScript, but by something called the **operating system**.

There are many different operating systems used on personal computers; some of them are used only by one or two manufacturers' models, while others are widely used on a variety of different computers.

The advantage of an operating system which has been used by many different manufacturers is that programs which will run on one computer with that operating system will generally also run on other computers from different makers with the same operating system.

What is CP/M?

On the Amstrad PCW8256, the operating system supplied is known as CP/M (standing for Control Program for Microcomputers). This is probably the most popular operating system ever devised for small computers, and there is an enormous library of programs designed to use it – to 'run under CP/M' as the jargon goes.

As with LocoScript, you don't actually need to know much about *how* CP/M works; the two most important facts which you should bear in mind are that CP/M wasn't designed specifically for the PCW8256, and that most of the time, you won't really be aware that you are using it at all.

When we first looked at LocoScript, we compared learning to use it to learning to drive a car; you don't need to know *how* the various mechanical bits all work together, you only need to know what the consequences are of pressing this pedal or of turning that switch.

To continue that analogy here, using an operating system is a little bit like driving a car with automatic transmission. Most of the time, you don't need to know which gear you are in, or when it is time to change up or down, because the car's 'operating system', in the form of the automatic gearbox, takes care of that for you.

Similarly, most of the programs that you will be using on the PCW8256 use CP/M like an automatic gearbox; you won't know what is going on at any given moment, but that doesn't matter.

But just as there are occasions when you will need to select the car's gears manually – to park, for example, or reverse – so there are some tasks for which you will need to use CP/M directly.

The last point which we should make here is that LocoScript is *not* a CP/M program, and so it can't be run on any other type of computer. Indeed, LocoScript has many features which clash with the way in which CP/M works.

Usually you will be completely unaware of this, but there is one point which does need some care: **don't store LocoScript files on discs which you will use for CP/M as well**, as they are not compatible and you might find, for example, that you had unintentionally erased a file.

Loading CP/M.

Loading CP/M is done in exactly the same way as loading LocoScript: turn on the PCW8256 and insert the Master Disc which has **CP/M+** (or better, your copy of it) into the disc drive.

After the usual series of scrolling lines, you will find a brief copyright message and the usual CP/M prompt, **A>**. This is because CP/M always prompts with the name of the current disc drive, and we have started off on Drive A.

At this point, there are a variety of different things which we might do. We could, for example, load a word processing program (not LocoScript) or a spreadsheet into the PCW8256, or load a computer language, like BASIC which is a popular 'programming language' often taught in schools and widely used all over the world. Alternatively, we could use some of the various **utilities** which are available under CP/M.

A first look at utilities

As their name suggests, **utilities** are programs which are useful for something – not just anything, but specifically for what we might think of as computer housekeeping.

We have already seen one example of this sort of thing when we made back-up copies of our Master Discs, using Disckit; Disckit is a utility for, among other things, copying the contents of one disc onto another one.

Other utilities will enable you to make a list of what files you have on any particular disc, to rename files, to erase them, to alter which character will appear on the screen when any particular key is pressed and so on and so on. There is even a utility to help you when you get confused!

Not all possible utilities are actually included on the Master Discs, of course. As you become more familiar with your PCW8256, you may find that there are other, specialised utilities which you would find useful and which you will buy.

Thinking of languages.

These are not languages like French or German, but computer languages – special ways of presenting things to computers so that they can understand your instructions.

We have already mentioned BASIC, and there is in fact an excellent, and very advanced, version of the BASIC language included on the Master Disc which we have just used to load CP/M+.

On the other disc, there is the bonus of a second computer language, called LOGO. This is best known for so-called **turtle graphics**, by means of which various shapes can be drawn on the screen (although you can do very many other things with LOGO as well).

LOGO is primarily a language for teaching computing to children, but don't let that put you off trying it; what makes it particularly good for learning with is that you can see the results of your instructions almost immediately. If nothing else, it may increase your respect for computer programmers!

Applications programs.

The last sort of program which you will find on CP/M is the sort of program which is actually intended to **do** something – to organise a spreadsheet, for instance, or work out a company's payroll and accounts.

No CP/M applications programs are actually included with your PCW8256. However, whatever your needs, you will certainly have no difficulty finding applications programs running under CP/M which will do everything you need.

There are thousands of such programs, ranging in price from several hundred pounds right the way down to nothing at all – so-called 'free-ware' – though in reality most people end up using programs drawn from a relatively small list.

Part of the reason for this is that a reputable 'software house', or manufacturer of programs, will 'maintain' its programs, advising the registered users of any problems which may have developed, and what to do about them.

Also from time to time they will bring out 'up-grades' – newer versions of programs with enhanced capabilities – and these are frequently offered at a discount to registered users of the earlier versions. The most popular programs are generally those which have the best track-record of accuracy, maintenance and up-grading.

What CP/M expects.

We have already seen that CP/M works on a very large number of different computers. However, it does expect that certain things will be more or less the same on all of them, and this can cause some confusion.

First of all, CP/M only works with computers which have at least one disc drive (though it can handle up to 16!).

Second, it expects certain keys to be present on the keyboard; if they are not there, then other keys must take on their job. Because of this, the keyboard of the PCW8256 produces slightly different results when used with CP/M than with LocoScript.

The most important differences are that the small ENTER key in the bottom right-hand corner no longer has a special purpose but is treated just like the large RETURN key; that the EXIT key becomes an **Escape** key, (usually abbreviated to ESC); and the ALT key becomes a **Control** key, usually abbreviated to CTRL or CTL.

When the ALT key (or CTRL, as it now becomes) is pressed in conjunction with any other key, it produces what are called **control characters**. (These are used in very many CP/M utilities and applications programs to give instructions to the computer.)

In this book a convention has been followed which you will also find in many other books and instruction manuals. According to this convention, control characters are marked by a special symbol called a 'caret,' which looks like a circumflex accent: ^. Thus ^C (Control + C) is merely another way of saying 'Hold down the ALT key while pressing the letter C'.

A slightly different convention which is occasionally followed marks control characters with an upward-pointing arrow. Under this convention, Control + C would appear as ↑ **C**.

Returning to the requirements of CP/M, the last important one is the way in which files are named.

By now you are probably already used to the requirements of LocoScript for file-names. Those of CP/M are exactly the same.

To recap briefly, CP/M file-names consist of two parts. The first part, consisting of not more than eight letters or numbers, is usually called the **file-name** and the second part, consisting of up to three letters or numbers, is called the **file-type**. The two parts are separated by a dot.

Some file-types can be important if you begin to develop a serious interest in CP/M, because CP/M treats some names in special ways, but if you are only using data-files of one sort or another with various applications programs, you can simply make up a file-type that makes sense to you – TXT for Text, perhaps, or DAT for Data. Or, if you prefer, you can simply leave the file-type blank, and use only the file-name part.

Useful utilities.

We have already seen that on sides 2, 3 and 4 of the Master Discs there are a large number of CP/M utilities programs.

The most useful of these have been grouped together on Side 2 of the Master Discs – the side marked CP/M+. Many of them will prove invaluable, especially at carrying out the various housekeeping tasks which will be needed to keep your discs in order.

Looking at the Directory.

When you use LocoScript, the names of all the document files were automatically displayed on the Disc Manager screen for you to see.

Some CP/M applications programs do this as well, but there are may occasions when you may want to know what programs are on a disc without wanting to run a particular program.

There is a useful inbuilt command in CP/M which enables you to find out exactly what is on any disc. Simply insert the disc into the disc drive and type D I R (which is short for DIRectory).

```
CP/M Plus  Amstrad Consumer Electronics plc

v 1.1, 61K TPA, 1 disc drive, 112K drive M:

A>DIR
A: J11CPM3 EMS : BASIC    COM : DIR      COM : DISCKIT COM : ED       COM
A: ERASE    COM : KEYS     WP  : LANGUAGE COM : PALETTE COM : PAPER    COM
A: PIP      COM : PROFILE  ENG : RENAME   COM : SET      COM : SET24X80 COM
A: SETDEF   COM : SETKEYS  COM : SETLST   COM : SETSIO   COM : SHOW     COM
A: SUBMIT   COM : TYPE     COM : RPED     BAS : RPED     SUB
A>█
```

Drive is A:

Fig 6.1 The effect of a **D I R** command on the CP/M+ Master Disc

The activity light on the front of the disc drive will immediately come on, and within a few moments you will see a complete listing of the names and types of every file on the disc. Fig. 6.1 shows what you will find if you carry out a D I R on the CP/M+ disc.

The letter A, followed by a colon, appears in the left-hand columns, to show that the computer is working with Disc Drive A, and after this the various file-names and –types are listed in five double columns down the screen.

The majority of the files are of file-type COM, which is a very important type for CP/M. It stands for COMmand, and the various programs listed with COM as their file-type can be run by simply typing their names, sometimes together with other information. All the utilities we shall be looking at are of this type.

If we wished, we could also use the DIR command to find out what is on some other drive, such as the internal Drive M. To do this, we would type

```
DIR  M:
```

There are a couple of points to note here. First, CP/M doesn't care whether you enter commands in capitals or lower case letters, or any combination of them; it will always convert your instructions to upper case.

Second, CP/M always assumes that one particular disc drive is the **default drive**, that is, the one which it will use unless it has been told differently. When CP/M is first started, Drive A is the default drive, and this is why the CP/M prompt reads **A >**.

After CP/M has checked to see what files are stored on Drive M (you will get a 'NO FILE' message, unless you have been using Drive M for something else) it will return to the A› prompt.

If you wish to change the default drive to Drive M, simply type

    M:

at the **A >** prompt, and CP/M will prompt you with the new drive letter, **M>**.

You can also use DIR to find out whether any specific file, or files, are on a disc, by giving the name of the file after the DIR command; for example, to find out whether ERASE.COM was on the disc, you would type **DIR ERASE.COM**.

If the file is present, then its name will be listed in the same way as with the usual DIR command; if not CP/M will respond with **No File**.

Wild cards.

There are many occasions when it is inconvenient to have to type in a complete file-name and file-type; for example, you might have a series of spreadsheet data files called SPREAD1.DAT, SPREAD2.DAT and so on, up to perhaps SPREAD9.DAT.

CP/M allows you to specify *all* of these files by using special ambiguous characters called **wild cards**. There are two of these: * represents any one or more characters, and ? represents a single character.

Taking the example given above, you could discover whether the spreadsheet files were on the disc by entering

    DIR SPREAD?.DAT.

The question mark in the seventh place in the file-name means that the DIR command would find SPREAD1.DAT, SPREAD2.DAT, and any others which are present, and list them all in the usual way.

Similarly, typing

    DIR *.DAT

would produce a directory listing of all files with the file-type DAT, regardless of what the file-name was. And

    DIR *.*

would produce a listing of every file on the disc, regardless of file-name or file-type.

Experiment with the DIR command and the wild cards until you feel that you understand how they work; this is particularly useful because the wild cards are used in many other areas of CP/M, including a lot of applications programs.

Finding out the size of a file.

Another use of the DIR command is to discover the size of any file or group of files.

```
CP/M Plus  Amstrad Consumer Electronics plc
v 1.1, 61K TPA, 1 disc drive, 112K drive M:
A>DIR *.* [SIZE]
Scanning Directory...
Sorting  Directory...
Directory For Drive A:  User  0
A: BASIC    COM   28k : DIR       COM   15k : DISCKIT  COM    8k
A: ED       COM   10k : ERASE     COM    4k : J11CPM3  EMS   40k
A: KEYS     WP     1k : LANGUAGE  COM    1k : PALETTE  COM    1k
A: PAPER    COM    2k : PIP       COM    9k : PROFILE  ENG    1k
A: RENAME   COM    3k : RPED      BAS    7k : RPED     SUB    1k
A: SET      COM   11k : SET24X80  COM    1k : SETDEF   COM    4k
A: SETKEYS  COM    2k : SETLST    COM    2k : SETSIO   COM    2k
A: SHOW     COM    9k : SUBMIT    COM    6k : TYPE     COM    3k

Total Bytes    =    171k  Total Records =     1313  Files Found =    24
Total 1k Blocks =    171   Used/Max Dir Entries For Drive A:   27/ 64
A>
                                                      Drive is A:
```

Fig. 6.2   Using the SIZE option of the DIR command

107

The format of this command is

DIR *filename.filetype* [SIZE]

where instead of *filename.filetype* you insert the actual name and type of the files you are checking, using wild cards if required. Thus

DIR*.* [SIZE]

will produce the listing shown in Fig. 6.2 of the sizes of all the files on the CP/M+ Master Disc

Similarly,

DIR*.COM [SIZE]

would produce a listing, with sizes, of all the files of file-type COM on the disc.

Disckit.

You have probably already used the Disckit utility when you made a copy of the Master Discs for LocoScript. There are in fact three options within the Disckit program, and we shall now examine these.

Remember that before you can do any of these things, you will need to load the Disckit program from the CP/M+ Master Disc by inserting that disc into Drive A, and typing DISCKIT.

(When using CP/M+ Command files – that is, those with the file-type COM – you must not enter either the COM or the dot which precedes it. Just typing in the file-name is all that is necessary.)

When you have loaded Disckit, the screen display will resemble Fig. 6.3. This is in effect a representation on the screen of part of the keyboard.

Formatting discs.

A newly-bought blank floppy disc is not unlike a new car park. Before you can park cars on it in an orderly and sensible way, there need to be white lines to outline the individual parking spots.

Similarly, a floppy disc needs to have the equivalent of electronic lines placed on it so that your data can be stored properly. Indeed, **an unformatted disc is completely useless**.

One drive found

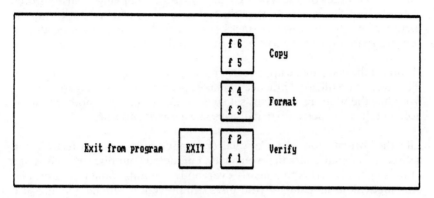

Fig.6.3 The DISKIT Menu

If you copy a disc with the Disckit COPY facility, you don't need to format it first, as the formatting is done at the same time as the copying. This one exception apart, all discs must be formatted before they are used, and it is obviously worth-while formatting both sides of a disc one after the other – or even all your blank discs in one session.

Generally, only new, blank discs will be formatted. However, there is nothing to prvent you from reformatting old discs. If you do this, everything that was previously recorded on the discs will be completely erased. Indeed, reformatting a disc is a standard way of obliterating old information in such a way that it can never be recovered.

As with the other Disckit options, all that you need to do is to follow the instructions which appear on the screen, making sure that the disc which you wish to format is inserted before answering **Y** to the word **VERIFY**.

Check too that the write-protect holes on the new disc are in the 'write–enabled' position, i.e. with the holes blanked off.

Copying discs.

You have probably already made copies of your Master Discs with the Disckit Copy option. As with the Format command, using Copy is mostly a matter of following the on-screen instructions after you have selected Copy (with *f*5), inserted the disc you are going to copy *from*, and pressed 'Y' in response to the prompt **Copy**.

109

The only important point to note is that you *must* copy the entire side of a disc, and that this involves two separate copying operations.

First, the contents of tracks 0-19 of the disc you are copying from are stored in the PCW8256's memory, then that material is transferred back from the memory onto the first twenty tracks of the new disc; next, the procedure is repeated with the last twenty tracks, numbered 20-39.

If you get the discs mixed up, an error message will be displayed to warn you. However, it is still good practice to make sure that the disc you are copying *from* has the write-protect tabs set so as to make sure that nothing can be accidentally recorded onto that disc if some error does occur.

Like the Format command, Copy will erase anything previously recorded on a disc, so first make sure that you haven't muddled your discs up; this is one of those ghastly errors that nearly everybody commits sooner or later, and only meticulous labelling of your discs will prevent it, though making sure that you have proper back-ups will help to avoid the worst consequences of a mistake.

Unfortunately, the Disckit Copy utility doesn't work with all types of disc. If you get an error message warning you that the disc from which you want to copy is 'old style data format,' then you will have to use the PIP utility instead; this is described further on in this chapter.

Verifying discs.

The final option on Disckit is Verify. This is used to ensure that a disc formatting has been correctly completed; it can be carried out safely on old or new discs without damaging their contents. But set the write-protect tabs just in case you make a mistake!

Transient commands and resident commands.

If you think back to your use of the two commands which we have already studied, you may realise that there is a strange difference between them.

To use Disckit, you first had to load it off your copy of the Master Disc on which it was supplied. If the Disckit program had not been on the disc, then CP/M would simply have responded with **DISCKIT?** to show that it couldn't find any program with that name.

DIR, on the other hand, doesn't have to be loaded off a disc before you can use it; it is always available, and you can summon it up merely by typing its name, no matter what disc is in the drive.

This is because CP/M has two kinds of utilities: there are those which are always ready for use, like DIR, and which are called **resident commands**, and those which have to be loaded from the appropriate disc before use, called **transient commands**.

Occasionally, a CP/M program hovers a little uncertainly between the two classificiations. The DIR command, for example is resident – that is, you can do a DIR of any disc, without having to call up the DIR program off the disc first. However, if you want to find out the *size* of a program with DIR, then you will need to use the DIR.COM utility provided on Side 2 of the Master Disc.

Typing out a text file.

There are many occasions when you may need to use CP/M to find out the contents of a particular file, especially if you can't remember exactly what the file-name stands for!

There is an extremely useful resident command to do this. Simply enter

        TYPE filename.filetype

and the contents of the file will be displayed on the screen (assuming that the file is present on the disc, of course).

This useful command only works properly with text files, that is files which contain documents of some sort, rather than programs.

Another name which you will come across for such files is **ASCII** files. ASCII (pronounced Askey) stands for the American Standard Code for Information Interchange. This code assigns a number to every letter, number and symbol used in computing, and the words 'ASCII file' are therefore generally used to mean 'any file containing the text of a document'.

Unfortunately, LocoScript is an exception to this rule, as LocoScript text files are *not* stored according to strict ASCII rules. For this and other reasons, it is a very good idea to follow the example of the Master Discs themselves and keep CP/M files and LocoScript files well away from one another, on separate discs.

As mentioned in Chapter 5, versions of LocoScript may be produced in the future which will provide the option of storing text in ASCII format, for use with spelling-checkers and similar utilities. We would expect that the CP/M TYPE command could be used on such files in the normal way.

Using the printer in CP/M. Just as in LocoScript, the printer is controlled by pressing the PTR key on the keyboard or using the paper-feed mechanism on the printer itself.

```
CP/M Plus  Amstrad Consumer Electronics plc
v 1.1, 61K TPA, 1 disc drive, 112K drive M:
A>█
```

Printer:On line | Top of Form | LF | FF | Draft quality | PO defeat:On | Hex:Off | RESET

Fig. 6.4 The CP/M Printer 'Buttons'

However, instead of the LocoScript pull-down menus, you will be shown a set of options along the bottom of the screen, and a cursor bar which can be moved along by using the ← and → keys.

These options are called 'buttons' because they take the place of the actual push-buttons found on most other printers. Fig. 6.4 shows what these 'buttons' look like.

The number of choices offered by the buttons varies according to what the printer is actually doing. Most are reasonably self-explanatory, but the following notes may help.

LF and **FF** stand for Line Feed and Form Feed respectively; to advance the paper by a single line, or to move to the end of the sheet, place the cursor bar over the appropriate button and press [+].

PO defeat, (standing for Paper Out) should be set On for single sheets and Off for continuous stationery.

Hex:Off is not used for document printing, but for programming purposes.

Finally, **Reset** stops printing, causes any text which has not yet been printed to be abandoned, and sets all the printer options back to their original values.

To 'press' any of the buttons, place the cursor bar over them and press [+] or [-]. Press EXIT when you have the printer set up as you want it.

Applications programs that use the printer will generally take care of all these details without any help from you, but if you want to keep a record of your disc housekeeping, or anything else you are doing with CP/M, you can make a printed copy of everything which appears on the screen by pressing ^P (i.e. the ALT key and 'P' simultaneously).

This is sometimes called 'turning the printer on,' although this is obviouly not meant literally. To 'turn the printer off', press ^P again.

By using the printer in conjunction with the resident TYPE command, you can produce a hard copy of the contents of any text file, if you wish.

Erasing files.

To erase files from a disc, merely type

```
ERASE filename.filetype
```

and the named file will be deleted from the disc. ERASE in this form is a resident command, and so is always available when you are using CP/M.

Unlike LocoScript, CP/M has no straightforward way of resurrecting a file which has been erased, so be very careful not to delete any file which you may need again.

ERASE can also be used with wild cards to delete a whole series of files. For example,

```
ERASE *.COM
```

would delete every file with the file-type COM, and

```
ERASE FR*.*
```

would delete every file with FR as the first two letters of its file-name. Most powerfully of all,

```
ERASE *.*
```

will delete everything on the disc.

Because wild card erasures can be potentially very destructive, CP/M always checks them by repeating the command you have typed in and asking for confirmation with Y or N. *Be extremely careful with wild card erasures.* For safety's sake, always do a DIR first, or you will assuredly find that you have unintentionally wiped out some important file.

An additional safeguard is provided by the **Confirmation option** of the ERASE command, by typing

```
ERASE filename.filetype [C].
```

If you use this option, CP/M will present every individual file to you for confirmation before carrying out any deletions. However, ERASE with this option is a transient, not a resident, command, so you will need to have ERASE.COM available on either Drive A or Drive M before you can use it. (There is a way around this restriction, as we shall see later.)

To erase files from a disc other than the 'default' disc drive, type the name of the drive, followed by a colon, after the ERASE command. For instance,

```
ERASE M:*.*
```

would erase all files from drive M.

The ERASE command is frequently shortened to ERA – it makes no difference which form you choose.

Renaming files.

You can give a new name to any file on a disc by typing

```
RENAME nfilename.nfiletype=ofilename.ofiletype
```

where *nfilename* represents the new name and *ofilename* represents the old name.

Remember that with CP/M the **new** name always comes in front of the equals sign, and the **old** name always comes after it.

For example,

```
RENAME NEWCASH.DAT=CASH.DAT
```

would rename the file CASH.DAT to NEWCASH.DAT.

RENAME can be abbreviated to REN

Another way to move files – using PIP.

We have already seen that there are certain cases in which it is not possible to use the Disckit Copy option to make copies of files.

For example, the disc from which you want to make the copy may be of a type which Disckit cannot use, or you may only want to copy one or two files instead of the whole disc. In these cases, it is necessary to make use of a transient program called PIP.COM, which is on Side 2 of the Master Discs.

In the following chapter, we shall be examining PIP in more detail. For the moment, we shall see only how it can be used to transfer a file from a disc in Disc Drive A to the internal Drive M.

First, with your copy of the Master Disc in Disc Drive A, load PIP.COM into the PCW8256 by typing

```
PIP
```

(note once again that you do *not* type in the C OM part).

As always when you load a transient program, the activity light on the front of the disc drive will come on as the PIP program is loaded into the computer.

The computer will signal when PIP is ready to use by displaying

```
CP/M3 PIP VERSION 3.0
```

and will then place an asterisk on the screen.

The asterisk is CP/M's way of telling you that PIP is ready for use. To copy any file from the disc in Drive A to the internal Drive M, you only need type the following immediately after the asterisk:

```
M:=A:filename.filetype
```

followed by RETURN

If you think back to the RENAME command, you will see that there is a similarity between the way the PIP and the RENAME commands are entered. In both cases the *new* name or drive comes first, followed by an equals sign and finally the *old* name or drive.

For example, to transfer Disckit from Drive A to Drive M, you would enter

```
M:=A:DISCKIT.COM.
```

or a shorter form of the same command:

```
M:=DISCKIT.COM
```

Of course, PIP only *copies* files from one disc to another. The contents of the original disc are not affected in any way by copying with PIP.

You can also use wild cards with PIP. For instance

```
M:=A:*.COM
```

would copy all files of file-type COM from Drive A to Drive M.

You have probably realised by now that you can use P I P to copy files onto a completely new disc. All you need to do is to copy them first onto Drive M, then replace the copy of the Master Disc in Drive A with the formatted disc onto which you want the files to be copied. Finally copy the files onto Drive A from Drive M.

In this case, you would probably want to copy the entire contents of M onto the new disc in one go. To do this, you would only need to type

```
A:=M:*.*
```

and all the files would be transferred automatically.

When you have transferred all the files you want, leave PIP by pressing RETURN one more time when you see the asterisk prompt, and CP/M will respond with the usual A >.

Of course, if you actually have the second real disc drive fitted – Disc Drive B – then you could copy files directly between the two real drives without using the internal Drive M at all, by typing

```
B:=A:filename.filetype
```

By now you may be wondering what PIP stands for. The answer is that the name is made up of initials which are short for Peripheral Interchange Program. **Peripherals** are things like the disc drives, the printer and the keyboard – everything except the processor, in fact.

Actually, PIP is not restricted to copying files between discs – you can also use it to move information from the keyboard to the printer, for example, or indeed from any one part of your system to any other.

These and other more advanced uses of PIP are outside the scope of this chapter however. Some reference to them will be made in Chapter Eight, but for fuller details you should consult a specialist book on CP/M.

The only problem you are likely to meet with PIP, provided you type in the various commands *exactly* as they are given here, is that PIP will fail if it cannot find enough room on the new disc to store the file it is copying.

The solution to this problem is to be sure that the disc onto which the files will be copied has ample room to hold them, preferably by using the Show command discussed below.

The space problem is likely to be most severe when copying files onto Drive M, because Drive M has much less capacity than a real disc in Drive A. You may even find that some individual files are so large that they cannot be fitted on Drive M, even if Drive M is otherwise empty.

We shall be dealing with this special case and a few other related difficulties in the following chapter. For the moment, you will probably find that PIP, in the form given here, will do everything that you want it to.

How much room is there left?

The last CP/M command which we shall meet in this chapter is SHOW, which is used to find out how much room is left on any disc (including Drive M).

SHOW is a transient command which you will find on Side 2 of the Master Discs. To use it, just type

```
SHOW
```

and the PCW8256 will at once respond with information about how much free space is available on the discs.

The only point to watch with the SHOW command is that it will only give you details of the drives you have actually been using during the current CP/M session. For example, if you have not used Drive M at all, it will not tell you anything about how much space is available on it.

You might assume that the fact that SHOW is a transient program would limit its usefulness. After all, you might reason, to find out how much room is available on some particular disc, you would first need to transfer SHOW from the Master Disc copy to Drive M, using PIP, and then replace the copy of the Master Disc in Drive A with the disc you wanted to SHOW the details of.

There is however a rather curious way around this problem. The solution is one which people unused to computers tend to regard with suspicion, but it does work perfectly well, and in fact is often indispensible for carrying out certain tasks, as we shall see in the following chapters.

Put Side 2 of your copy of the Master Disc in Drive A and then enter

    SHOW B:

(Don't forget the semi-colon after the name of the drive in this command.)

The activity light will come on as usual as the PCW8256 loads the SHOW program off the Master Disc copy; then the following message will appear at the bottom of the screen:

Please put the disc for B: into the drive then press any key

In other words, although you actually only have Drive A (and Drive M) fitted to your computer, under certain circumstances CP/M will treat Drive A as though it were actually Drive B!

Insert the disc on which you want to use SHOW into the disc drive, then press a key. (This instruction to press 'Any key' is one you will find in many programs, but it never really means what it says – any alphabetic or numeric key will do, but SHIFT, ALT and a few others won't work. The RETURN key is a good one to standardise on.)

Within a few moments, you will be told how much space is available on the disc which is now in the drive.

Some people find what has happened a little tricky to understand. The best way to visualise it is to think that you can sometimes fool the computer into thinking of Drive A as Drive B.

This is almost as good as getting a second disc drive for nothing. Only 'almost as good', of course, because if you really did have a genuine Drive B you would be able to leave one disc in A and the other in B all the time, whereas with only one drive you will need to keep swapping the two discs around in the one drive.

If the above doesn't make sense, read it again carefully and then try it out a couple of times to see how it works. You will find that by using this technique you can carry out a DIR, an ERASE and many other commands by specifying Drive B and then swapping discs. Usually there's not much point in doing this with resident commands, but with transient commands it can simplify some tasks considerably.

Postscript.

CP/M was originally designed for people who understood computers pretty well. Over the years, certain of its features have been changed to make it easier for non-experts to use, and the majority of commands, particularly those used for elementary disc housekeeping, shouldn't cause you any problems.

One feature which hasn't changed much, however, is the need to enter most commands *exactly* as they are specified. Even a misplaced space is quite enough to cause a CP/M command to fail.

If any commands don't work as they should, go back very carefully over what you have typed, and make sure that no errors have crept in.

In particular, make sure that you have entered as much of the file-name and file-type as is appropriate for the particular command you are using. For example, loading a COM program only requires you to type in the file-name and *not* the file-type; but TYPE and PIP, for instance, require both the file-name and the file-type to be specified, or at least filled in with wild cards.

This can be extremely confusing even for people who are fairly familiar with computers, so don't be surprised if it causes you problems from time to time. If you are stuck, look up the command in the manual and then try it again. Once you have entered the command correctly, and assuming the appropriate disc is in the right drive, everything will work properly; CP/M is extremely reliable!

In this chapter we have only scratched the surface of what CP/M has to offer, and even the commands we have discussed often have other forms which have not been mentioned.

If you ever start programming yourself, you may develop an interest in CP/M beyond what would be necessary merely to use your PCW8256 as an effective business tool. If not, no matter; simply become as familiar as you can with the various housekeeping tools which CP/M provides.

CHAPTER SEVEN

Using CP/M Programs

Preview. The topics covered in this chapter are as follows:

What is installation?
Choosing suitable programs.
Making a copy of the Master Disc.
First steps in installation.
Using PIP. (This CP/M program is dealt with in more detail in Chapter Eight.)
Installation without INSTALL.COM.
Changing the screen.
Changing the printer.
Changing the keyboard.
Putting all the instructions together.
The CP/M SUBMIT command.

What does 'installation' mean?

In the previous chapter we saw that CP/M was designed to work with many makes and designs of computer, regardless of differences between their various keyboards, printers and screens.

This has many very important advantages; the most obvious is that there are thousands of CP/M programs already available for your use, covering every aspect of office work. In addition, computer languages, statistical packages and games of many different kinds can be obtained.

As nearly always in this life, there is a price to be paid for these benefits: **not every CP/M program will necessarily work on every CP/M computer**, and even those that do work may require some changes to be made.

In this chapter, we shall first be looking at ways to find out whether a particular program will actually work on the Amstrad PCW8256, and then seeing what changes may be necessary to get the best out of various programs on the machine.

The process of making these alterations to a program is called **installation**. To explain briefly why installation may be necessary, we shall consider one particular detail which may need changing: the screen format.

The screen on the PCW8256 can accommodate a display 90 characters across by 31 lines high. Such a large display is uncommon – the most usual screen size is 24 or 25 lines high and only 80 characters across – but the benefits which this non-standard size offers, especially when word processing with LocoScript, make it very worth-while.

However, a program which gives a clear and useful diplay on a computer using one size of screen may not look so good on one with a screen of a different size.

Installation will enable you to modify programs in such a way as to make them work most effectively with your own system. You can think of installation as a process of individualising programs to meet the requirements of your PCW8256. (Actually, it is not usually the programs themselves that have to be altered, but certain details of the way in which your PCW8256 handles them.)

Programs that can't be used.

The first requirement in getting a CP/M program to work on the PCW8256 is that it must be supplied on discs of the appropriate type.

The disks that the PCW8256 uses are double-sided, measure 3" across, and are enclosed in a rigid plastic case. **No other sort will work**, at least with the machine as it is supplied.

As time passes, other kinds of disc drive will certainly become available for the PCW8256; when this happens, and if you buy and fit an appropriate additional disc drive, you will be able to use programs supplied on these other types of disc, but this does not directly concern us now.

Programs which are supplied on 3" discs of the correct type can be divided into three groups: they may be specifically designed (or modified) for the PCW8256 alone; they may be adaptable for the PCW8256 and other machines; or they may be designed for other machines altogether.

The first of these types should pose no problems at all, although it is possible that in some cases there may still be a little simple installation left for you to do yourself.

Programs in the second group are harder to make generalisations about; they may present no problems at all, or they may require you to carry out quite a lot of work. However, they should all work in the end, though in some cases the installation procedure may be a little time-consuming.

Programs in the final category *may* work perfectly without any difficulty. Some of them, on the other hand, will not work at all, unless they are substantially rebuilt by an experienced programmer.

The only safe course, if the documentation for a program mentions other specific machines but not the PCW8256, is for you to ask to see it working on the PCW8256 before you buy it. Assurances that a particular program can easily be made to work are sometimes helpful and honestly given, but on occasion they can be wildly over-optimistic.

Making a copy of a program disc.

Before trying to carry out any kind of program installation, it is vital that you make a copy of the disc(s) on which your new programs have been supplied.

Almost all software suppliers now recognise that purchasers have a legitimate right to make backup copies of their programs for their own use. Sometimes, the number of copies that can be taken is specified in the program documentation, and sometimes it is left to the user's discretion.

Because making copies is generally so easy, there is sometimes a temptation to 'make an extra copy' for a friend. **This is a clear breach of copyright.**

Many programs are identified with registration codes of various kinds, so that all copies can be traced back to the original purchaser – the CP/M+ Masters are protected in this way.

Another point worthy of consideration is that software producers rely on the sale of programs for their livelihood; if they are forced out of business by the easy availability of pirated copies, then one day the supply of good software may dry up altogether. Alternatively, manufacturers may protect their programs against copying in such a way that even the routine making of legitimate backups may become impossible.

Returning to legitimate copying, the easiest way is to use the Disckit utility on side 2 of the CP/M Master Disc supplied with the PCW8256. This has the additional advantage that there will be no need to format the disc onto which the original will be copied, as Disckit can format and copy simultaneously.

Disckit will not work, however, if the disc on which the program was supplied was of the incorrect format. This is most likely to arise if the program was intended for a range of machines, perhaps including the Amstrad 6128, 464 and 664 personal computers.

If this happens, first take a look at the printed documentation which accompanies the program to see if there is any specific advice about making copies on the PCW8256. This may well be in the form of a loose Addendum sheet which can be easily overlooked.

Failing this, check exactly what files are available on the new program disc (using DIR). If there is a file called READ.ME, or some similar name, it may contain helpful information about copying the disc.

To read such a file, use the CP/M resident TYPE command – i.e., enter:

> **TYPE READ . ME** (or whatever the file is called)

at the keyboard.

When the screen is full, you may be invited to press the RETURN key to see more. Scan what appears on the screen to check whether there are indeed any useful guides to copying.

Assuming you find such hints, either make a note of them with pen and paper or, for a more complete record, put paper in the printer and then 'turn it on' (i.e. enter ^P – that is ALT+P – as outlined in the previous chapter), and then repeat the **TYPE READ . ME** command.

This time, everything that appears on the screen will be copied onto the printer as well – **echoed** is the computer jargon. When this is finished, 'turn the printer off' with another ^P.

If you can indeed find directions for the copying of the program disc, then provided you follow them carefully, your problems should be over.

However, since the production of programs is often carried out by different people from those who write the instructions (!) you may still find it worth your while to read the following suggestions.

If Disckit fails, there are at least two other ways of copying the Master Disc. It is worth following both of these in some detail, because of the insight you may gain into the ways in which program files can be stored and copied; this may be of use to you if you ever meet a really awkward copying job.

Incidentally, it is frequently the case, especially with long and complicated programs, that there are several program files on the same disc.

The safe assumption to make, unless you know positively that the reverse is true, is that every one of these files is necessary to the proper operation of the program. In the notes that follow, it is assumed that copying the program from one disc to another will involve copying a number of different files.

It is also assumed that the disc onto which the files are going to be copied will have been formatted (using Disckit) before you start to do anything else.

The easiest route to understand is to make a list of all the files on the program disc (using DIR), and then use the CP/M PIP program to copy them one by one onto the internal Drive M. Finally, copy them back from Drive M onto the new disc. Such a sequence would look like this:

1. Make sure that the write-protect tabs of the program disc are in the 'protect' position (i.e. with the holes open). Then insert that disc into Drive A, type DIR, and make a note of all the file-names and –types present on the disc.

2. Remove the program disc. Insert Side Two of the CP/M+ Master Disc into the drive, and type PIP. When that program is ready, it will signal the fact with an asterisk.

3. Reinsert the program disc, and move individual files from Drive A to Drive M by typing

M:=filename.filetype

Where several files are of the same type, you can copy them in one go with

M:=*.filetype

4.When all the files have been moved onto Drive M, remove the program disc from the drive, insert the blank disc, and copy the files onto it with

A:=M:*.*

5.Finally, leave PIP by typing an extra RETURN, then *try out the new disc*. If all is well, repeat the steps outlined for the second side of the Master Disc (if there are files on it), then label the new disc appropriately and put the original Master away safe.

The problem that is most likely to arise with this technique is that, because Drive M has a smaller capacity than a real disc, it may not hold all the files from one side of the Master Disc in one go. If this happens, you must either use the technique described below or copy the files a few at a time, making sure that Drive M never becomes too full.

Another potential difficulty is that you may find you have not actually copied all the files, although you had checked them with a DIR command.

This may happen because software manufacturers use a variety of techniques for hiding certain files from prying eyes. These dodges are unlikely to deter computer users of even fairly modest experience, but they can make copying individual files hard for the total non-expert.

In either case, the easiest way to proceed is to use the PCW8256's ability to treat its single disc drive as if it were actually two drives, A and B. Proceed exactly as for the individual file copying shown above as far as the end of Step 2, then continue as follows:

> **3.** Put the program disc in the drive and type
>
> `B:=A*.*`
>
> then follow the various instructions which appear on the screen. As they appear, these instructions will be signalled by a short 'beep' from the loudspeaker. You will be told to insert the new disc and the program disc alternately, until all the files have been copied.

When all the files have been copied, leave PIP by pressing RETURN again, and then test the new disc. If all is in order, label it and put the original disc away safely. In theory, the above arrangements should work perfectly every time. In practice, there are occasions when they do not, for a variety of reasons.

One error message which you may find if the original disc was particularly full is **ERROR DISK WRITE NO DATA BLOCK**. This may be because the PCW8256 believes, perhaps wrongly, that the new disc is too full to accept any more files.

If this happens to you, the easiest solution is to check whether there are not some files on the original disc which you can do without on your copy, and to ERASE them from your copy disc (not the original program disc!) to leave room for the others.

If the disc has indeed been prepared for more than one type of computer, you may very well find such files, often with some indication of the name of the machine for which the files are intended embedded in their name.

PIP even has a special option, allowing you to specify exactly which files you want to transfer, even though you have used the wild card command. If you type

```
M:=A:*.*[C]
```

when P I P prompts you with its usual asterisk, you will be given the name of each file in turn and asked to confirm whether you do actually want to copy it.

If you just can't get a program disc to copy properly, get straight back in touch with your dealer; if he is unable to help, contact the distributors or manufacturers of the program, who will certainly not want you to have problems with their product.

Either way, do resist the temptation to say, *bother it!* and settle for using the original program disc without a backup, or you will lose everything when the only disc you have gets worn out or lost.

Of course, most of the preceding problems will disappear completely if you have the second disc drive – Drive B – fitted to your PCW8256. If you do have this, then you will be able to transfer files from a program disc in Drive A to a backup in Drive B by using the same PIP sequence outlined above, but without the need to swap discs around in the single drive.

First steps to installation.

If the program you are using has not been bought in a format specially prepared for the PCW8256 *and nothing else*, then you will almost certainly have some installation work to do before it works properly.

Assuming that you don't have a specific PCW8256 version, and that there is nothing helpful in either the printed documentation or in a READ.ME file, follow the instructions printed below.

Place your copy of the program disc in Drive A and do a DIR, ιο check the various filenames present. If you are lucky, you may find one with a name something like INSTALL.COM, which you can run by typing the filename (but not the .COM part).

To take a specific example, Fig. 7.1 shows the results of a DIR command on a copy of the Accounts program produced by Sagesoft (of Regent Centre, Gosforth, Newcastle-upon-Tyne).

```
CP/M Plus  Amstrad Consumer Electronics plc

v 1.1, 61K TPA, 1 disc drive, 112K drive M:

A>DIR
A: ACCOUNTS COM : BRUN     COM : UTILITY  COM : POST     COM : ALLOCATE COM
A: REPORTS  COM : NOMINAL  COM : COMPANY  DTA : CODELIST DTA : STATMENT COM
A: CONTROL  DTA : INSTALL  COM : POSTINGS DTA : ACNTLIST DTA
A>
```
                                                                    Drive is A:

Fig. 7.1 DIRectory of Sagesoft Accounts Program, showing the INSTALL.COM program

You will observe that, as is the case with many programs, there are actually several program files on the disc, and that one of these is indeed called INSTALL.COM.

```
CP/M Plus  Amstrad Consumer Electronics plc

v 1.1, 61K TPA, 1 disc drive, 112K drive M:

A>INSTALL

1)  6128
2)  8256
WHICH MODEL ARE YOU USING ? :
```

Fig. 7.2 The Installation Routine for Sagesoft Accounts

When you run this, you will be presented with a simple question as to which computer you are using – the Amstrad PCW8256 or the Amstrad 6128 – see Fig. 7.2. The question is answered with a single key-press, after which the activity light on the disc drive comes on briefly as the necessary modifications to the program are made.

Many installations are of this simple sort, taking no more than a minute or two. Moreover, the procedure is usually a 'once for all' affair, and does not need to be repeated unless you decide in the future to run the program on a different type of machine.

At the other end of the spectrum, you may find that some installation routines require a whole host of changes in any – or all – of three different areas. In terms of the relative ease of making adjustments, these are their use of the screen, the printer and the keyboard.

None of this is difficult, but it can be tricky to follow the first time through, so take things easy and don't let yourself become flustered if things seem to go wrong.

Make notes as you work, and where possible test the effects of everything at every stage. This way, whenever you find something that seems not to work, you will know exactly at what point things have gone wrong.

If on the other hand you try to set everything up at once and make a mistake, you may never find out exactly where the problem lies. This is yet another one of those cases where computers reward you for taking things easy and thinking out your course of action first!

A complex installation routine on the program disc may ask you a long series of questions about the equipment on which it is to work. In particular it may ask you about the type of printer and the kind of VDU or Monitor (i.e. the screen) which you have.

One great advantage of installation routines of this sort is that they enable you to change the equipment which you have without having to completely change your programs to match. For example, if one day you choose to replace the Amstrad printer with a different kind, you would only need to let the installation routine know what the change had been, and everything else would be taken care of automatically.

Options to watch out for in the routine are a Zenith Z19/Z29 screen and an Epson FX– type printer, especially the FX-80. If these exact types are not listed, don't worry as for most purposes you can select other types with almost as good results.

More important than matching the printer type exactly is making sure that you specify one with the same *general* characteristics. For example, some printers produce underlines by back-spacing and printing a second character; others are not capable of back-spacing, but underline by overprinting two characters in the same place.

A particular problem is the Pound sign (£). This arises because ASCII is, as its name suggest, an American standard, and so there is no universally agreed code for this British sign. You may find that some programs (or printers) will need you to press the # key to produce a Pound sign on paper.

Installation without a routine.

In some cases you may find that there is nothing like INSTALL.COM on the disc, and that you will have to manage on your own. This is not usually as bad as it sounds; the reason some programs don't have an installation routine is because they don't really need one.

On Side 2 of the CP/M+ Master Disc there are a series of Utility Programs which can be very helpful in making programs of this sort work well. Put that disc into Drive A and try out some of the effects to see what happens.

Changing the screen.

First, with certain sorts of program you may prefer to change the colours of the screen – that is, to have black on green rather than green on black. The utility that does this is called PALETTE.COM.

The reverse effect from the usual is reached by entering:

```
PALETTE 1 0
```

Returning to the normal screen is done by entering:

```
PALETTE 0 1
```

Experiment with these effects to see which you prefer; in most programs, there is nothing to stop you from using the display combination which you find most restful. If you do use the reversed screen, however, you may notice a slight movement on it at times, due to interference from the disc drive. This is always present, but is much less obtrusive with the normal screen colours.

A more necessary change with many programs is an alteration to the 'screen size'. (This doesn't mean the physical size of the screen, of course, but rather the proportion of the screen which is used to display text.)

To change the screen size to the more common 24 lines in height by 80 characters in width, use the program SET24X80.COM on side two of the Master Disc.

To reduce the screen to the smaller size, type either of the following commands:

```
SET 24X82 or
SET 24X80 ON
```

To return the screen to its usual dimensions, type:

```
SET 24X80 OFF
```

Changing the printer.

So far all our use of the printer has assumed that we are using single-sheet A4 paper. However, there may be many occasions when we need to use some other paper-type, such as labels (usually mounted on special backing paper with sprocket holes), cheque forms and the like.

Many applications programs will make the necessary changes automatically; others will require you to make these changes yourself at installation time. This is done with the PAPER.COM program found, like the others, on Side 2 of the Master Disc.

PAPER.COM is a little different from the other programs we have looked at so far, inasmuch as it requires a list of instructions after the command-word PAPER. The effect of the program is rather similar to setting the paper-type in LocoScript.

The commands are as follows:

A4
sets the printer to expect A4 single-sheet paper, 70 lines per page and 6 lines per inch.

A5
sets the printer for A5 single-sheet paper, 50 lines per page and 6 lines per inch.

C
prepares the printer for continuous stationery, the length of which may be set later.

Fn or FORM LENGTHn
sets the length of the page in lines to the value of n up to a maximum of 99.

Gn or GAP LENGTHn
tells the printer to leave a gap of n lines at the bottom of a page, up to a maximum of 99.

L8 or LINE PITCH 8
sets the line pitch to 8 to the inch, L6 resets it to the normal pitch of 6 lines to the inch.

S or SINGLE SHEET
if A4 or A5 have not been set, this prepares the printer for single sheet stationery.

n
informs the printer that continuous stationery will be used, with a page length of n inches (*not lines*), up to a maximum of 17 inches.

Any number of these options may be set together on the same line as the **PRINTER** command, and separated by commas; if contradictory values are set on the same line, the last one given will be observed.

For example,

PAPER S,F64

will set the printer for single sheet printing, with each page 64 lines in length. As the Line Pitch has not been set, it is assumed to be 6.

Similarly,

PAPER C,10,G3

informs the printer that continuous stationery will be used, with each page 10 inches in length; the last three lines on each page are treated as a gap and left blank.

```
CP/M Plus  Amstrad Consumer Electronics plc

v 1.1, 61K TPA, 1 disc drive, 112K drive M:

A>PAPER S,F64
Single Sheet
Paper Out Defeat On
Line Pitch   6 (lines per inch)
Form Length 64 (lines)
Gap Length   0 (lines)

A>PAPER C,10,G3
Continuous Stationery
Paper Out Defeat Off
Line Pitch   6 (lines per inch)
Form Length 10 (inches)
Gap Length   3 (lines)

A>█
```

Drive is A:

Fig. 7.3 CP/M's response to two PAPER commands

After you have given these or similar instructions, the PCW8256 will always respond by confirming what you have done, and setting out the full details of the new page form. Fig. 7.3 illustrates its response after each of the commands given above.

Pressing the RESET 'button' on the bottom line of the CP/M screen will cause all these values to be lost, and the printer will return to the state it is set to when CP/M is first turned on. To avoid this, enter the option at the end of every PAPER line, and the new settings will be maintained even after a RESET.

Changing the keyboard.

People who are used to manual typewriters, on which there is a direct mechanical link between the individual keys and the letters which strike the paper, often find it hard to understand that there is no such direct connection between the keyboard of a computer and the characters which appear on the screen.

To prove this to yourself, make sure that you have Side 2 of the CP/M Master Disc in Drive A and type

LANGUAGE 7

This loads and runs the utility program LANGUAGE.COM, which sets different symbols for certain keys, depending on the language which is chosen. LANGUAGE 7 calls up the Spanish set. Now press EXTRA and the full-stop key. You should see a lower case n-tilde (ñ).

Return to the default setting (the one which is automatically chosen when CP/M is first loaded) by typing

LANGUAGE 0

and try the same key combination again. This time you should get a vertical bar ⌶.

There are eight different variations build in to CP/M, as follows:

    LANGUAGE 0 – USA
    LANGUAGE 1 – French
    LANGUAGE 2 – German
    LANGUAGE 3 – English
    LANGUAGE 4 – Danish
    LANGUAGE 5 – Swedish
    LANGUAGE 6 – Italian
    LANGUAGE 7 – Spanish

It may help to explain briefly how these changes are carried out. Every key when pressed sends an individual signal to the processor. The processor in effect looks up each of these signals in a table to see what symbol it represents, and then displays that symbol on the screen. LANGUAGE.COM merely changes the contents of the table.

In addition to the pre-arranged changes which can be reached through LANGUAGE.COM, it is possible in CP/M to make further alterations to the keyboard. (The key settings in LocoScript cannot be altered, however, as they are fixed by the LocoScript program itself).

If you think about the keyboard of the PCW8256, you will realise that it offers a number of keys, such as PASTE and CAN, which have no equivalents on most other keyboards, either on typewriters or computers.

Despite this, it is still possible when word processing on other computer keyboards to get broadly similar effects. In general, the word processing programs which are designed for use on such keyboards do this by using the Control key (ALT on the PCW8256) in conjunction with various other keys.

It would be possible to continue to do this when using these programs on the PCW8256. For example, the famous CP/M word processing program called Word Star will run perfectly well on keyboards lacking even cursor keys, by substituting various combinations of the Control and alphabetic keys, and it can be used in the same way on the PCW8256.

Although this is possible, however, it would obviously be rather a shame to have the cursor (and other) keys available on the keyboard and not use them.

To get around this, there are provided on the CP/M Master Discs two complete key definition files, one for word processing programs and one for use with the LOGO computer language. The first of these is on Side 2 of the Master Discs, and is called KEYS.WP; the second is on Side 4, and is called KEYS.DRL.

We shall assume here that we are going to be using a word processing program of some sort (other than LocoScript) and that KEYS.WP will give us the key-changes we need.

KEYS.WP doesn't actually contain any instructions, as such, but rather a list of key definitions. If it interests you, you can see what it looks like by entering

    TYPE KEYS.WP

when Side 2 of the Master Disc is in the drive. Fig. 7.4 will give you some idea of what to expect, though the actual file is quite lengthy.

```
14  N  S    "^E"         ^E
14  A  SA   "^'£9E'"     ^QE
 6  N  S    "^D"         ^D
79  N  S    "^X"         ^X
79  A  SA   "^'£98'"     ^QX
15  N  S    "^S"         ^S
 5  N       "^D"         ^D
 5  A       "^S"         ^S
 5     S    "^F"         ^F
 5     SA   "^A"         ^A
13  N       "^'£9C'"     ^QD
13     S    "^'£9C'"     ^QD
13     SA   "^'£9D'"     ^QS
12  N       "^C"         ^C
12  A       "^R"         ^R
12     S    "^'£90'"     ^QC
12     SA   "^'£91'"     ^QR
20  N       "^'£92'"     ^QF
```

Fig. 7.4 Part of the KEYS.WP File

The instructions to CP.M to change the key definitions are contained in another program on Side 2 of the Master Disc, called SETKEYS.COM. To use this for our purposes, type

SETKEYS KEYS.WP

and the effects of the various keys will be amended accordingly.

(Similarly SETKEYS KEYS.DRL will set the keyboard for LOGO; however, as SETKEYS.COM is on Side 2 of the Master Disc, and KEYS.DRL is on Side 4, you will have to PIP both files onto Drive M before using them. Check the instructions for PIP given above if you're not sure how to proceed.)

It is possible to use the SETKEYS facility to create your own key definitions, though you will probably never need to do this unless you become interested in programming. For this reason, this facility is not mentioned any further in this book, except to note that one of the minor hazards of redefining the keyboard is that it is all too easy to do it in such a way that it becomes totally unusable. When this happens, you can usually only get out of the mess by resetting the computer!

Putting the instructions together.

The appropriate time to make all these alterations would be before actually running the applications program itself.

Thus if you wanted to run a particular word processing program that requires a 24 by 80 screen, with the screen set to reverse video, the printer set for A4 paper and the keyboard changed to the KEYS.WP standard, you would insert Side 2 of the Master Disc and type the following:

```
SET24X80
PALETTE 1 0
PAPER A4,DEFAULTS
SETKEYS KEYS.WP
```

before finally starting your word processing program by inserting the disc which contains that program and typing the program name to start it off .

None of this is actually difficult, but it can be a bit of a nuisance, especially as you will need to type in the same sequence of commands every time you use that program. Certainly it is not nearly as straightforward as starting off with LocoScript!

However, it is possible to overcome all these difficulties, and to arrange to make the PCW8256 actually carry out all these installation chores for itself, by giving it detailed instructions on exactly what you want it to do. In other words, you will still have to carry out an installation procedure once, but when you are satisfied with it, you can make everything happen automatically from then on.

The CP/M SUBMIT command.

We have already seen that although there is nothing to stop you from using any series of up to three letters or numbers as possible file-types, certain file-types have a special significance in CP/M. The most obvious example of this is file-type COM, standing for COMmand files, that is programs which can be started by simply typing in their file-name.

One of the reasons for carrying out a DIR on a new applications program disc is to see whether there is an INSTALL.COM or similar file on it. Another reason is to discover whether there is any file with the file-type SUB, which is short for SUBmit.

```
CP/M Plus  Amstrad Consumer Electronics plc

v 1.1, 61K TPA, 1 disc drive, 112K drive M:

A>DIR
A: NW        OVR : NWPRINT  OVR : NWINSTAL COM : SETKEYS  COM : KEYS128  WP
A: NW128     COM : KEYS256  WP  : NW256     COM : SUBMIT   COM : SETKY256 COM
A: GO256     SUB : NWMSGS   OVR : GO128     SUB : GO256    BAK : NWREAD   ME
A>
```

Fig. 7.5 SUB files on the pre-release NewWord Disc

A SUB file is one which is pre-arranged to carry out all sorts of resetting of the screen, printer and keyboard *without you having to enter the individual items yourself.*

For example, Fig. 7.5 shows a DIRectory of a pre-release edition of a word processing program called NewWord. You will see that there is a file listed under the name of GO256.SUB (and another called GO128 for the Amstrad 6128 computer).

All files of file-type SUB can be run by typing the command SUBMIT followed by the file-name (but not the file-type, which must always be SUB). In the particular case under consideration, you would therefore type:

SUBMIT GO256

and the PCW8256 would respond by carrying out all the keyboard changes necessary, finally running the actual NewWord program itself (NW256) without any further intervention by you.

The SUBMIT command is not limited to carrying out installation procedures, of course; it can be used for any situation in which there is a need to run several COM programs one after the other.

The effect is exactly the same as if you had entered each of the COMmands separately; the advantage is that once you have typed the SUBMIT *filename* command, everything else is taken care of.

With NewWord, there was a suitable file with file-type SUB already on the disc. You will often find that this is the case, and then all you will need to do to use the program is to type in the SUBMIT command as outlined.

However, there may be occasions when you would like to be able to achieve the effect of a SUBMIT without there actually being a suitable SUB-type file on the disc. You can do this by actually creating such a file for yourself, and in the following chapter we shall be looking at ways in which this can be done.

Creating an appropriate SUB file almost belongs in the category of programming; if it does not interest you, or if you are confused by it, then it is far better that you should give it a miss and move on to Chapter Nine.

It is included in this book for the sake of completeness, and because many people find it easier to handle a SUB file which they have created themselves than to have to remember to type in a series of different commands before using a particular applications program. If you don't think that category includes you, then feel free to skip!

Postscript.

Programs which run 'under CP/M' are designed to work with a variety of different computers; because of this, they may need a certain amount of adjustment before they will work properly on the PCW8256. This adjustment is called **installation**.

To ease this process, there may be a program with a name like INSTALL.COM on the disc. Run this (by typing its file-name) and be prepared to answer certain questions about the machine you are using.

If there is no INSTALL.COM, there may be a file with the file-type SUB. To use this, type the word SUBMIT, followed by the file-name of the SUB file, and a series of different procedures will be carried out automatically.

Failing this, you may have to enter separate command lines to set the printer, the keyboard and the screen.

We have already suggested that what follows in the next chapter falls into the category of 'nice to know' rather than 'read, mark and digest'. Most of the material in *this* chapter does not fall into the same class. However, instead of trying to learn the commands cold, it makes much more sense to use it as a reference book when you need it.

CHAPTER EIGHT

Automating CP/M

Preview. This chapter deals with the following topics:

> Putting information into a file.
> Using PIP.
> Using the ED Editor.
> ED commands.
> Turnkey discs.
> Options with PIP.
> User Numbers.

Putting information into a file.

Creating a file with file-type SUB (for the purposes described in the previous chapter) is not basically a difficult operation. There are many different ways to go about it, and we shall discuss some of them here in order of increasing difficulty.

As you will see, the method you choose will depend in part upon the other programs you have available to you; but it is perfectly possible to get by with nothing but the programs included on the CP/M Master Discs.

What all the methods have in common is that they make it possible for you to type in a series of instructions from the keyboard which will then be stored on a disc-file with the file-type SUB.

Before you start, you will need to be sure that have sufficient room on the Program Disc to include the extra file; have that disc ready to insert into the drive.

The other requirement is that there has to be a copy of the CP/M SUBMIT.COM program on the program disc; whichever way you intend to create the SUB file, you can copy the SUBMIT.COM file from Side 2 of the Master Disc with the PIP utility discussed earlier.

Creating a disc file with PIP.

PIP can be used for many purposes beside copying files from one disc to another as we have just done: it can be used to transfer a file from a disc drive to the screen or the printer, for example, or – as we shall do now – to transfer information from the keyboard to a file which will be stored on a disc.

Start by using PIP to transfer the PIP.COM program itself from your copy of Side 2 of the CP/M Master Disc to Drive M. This is done by typing:

```
PIP M:=PIP.COM
```

CP/M will confirm your command and the disc drive activity light will come on. When the copying is complete, check that PIP.COM is really on Drive M by typing:

```
DIR M:
```

Insert the disc onto which the new file will be saved into Disc Drive A ; this disc will normally be a copy which you have made of the purchased program disc, because you should never take the chance of recording onto the Master disc.

We now have to return to PIP, and at the same time give a command that will enable the disc to store what we shall type in at the keyboard. Do this by typing:

```
M:PIP A:PROG.SUB=CON:
```

As is usual with CP/M commands, it is important that you type in this command *exactly* as it is given here. The colons are particularly important.

What the command does is tell PIP to take input from the CONsole (i.e. the keyboard) and to store it on Drive A in a file to be called PROG.SUB. You can actually choose any file-name you like, as long as the file-type is SUB.

You may be surprised to see that there is now no prompt of any sort on the screen. Don't worry – this is just as it should be! From now on, everything you type in will be stored on Disc Drive A in the SUB file which you are creating. However, the disc drive activity light will not come on until you leave the PIP program.

Now just type in the various lines which will form the SUB file, being careful to make no mistakes. The only point to watch (and it is a very important one) is that at the end of every line you *must* type in RETURN *and* ^J (ALT/J).

Your first two lines might be something like:

```
PAPER A4 (RETURN^J)
PALETTE 1 0 (RETURN^J)
```

That will probably be enough for a first try; if you were creating a real SUB file, the last line in it would of course consist of the file-name of the COM program that you were setting up the system for, but for now we shall merely take that for granted.

When all is complete, leave PIP by typing ^Z (ALT/Z), and the disc activity light will come on as the file you have created is copied onto the disc.

Check that it is there with DIR. If all is well, test that it works by typing **SUBMIT** and the name of the file, but not the SUB file-type. The Drive should work, the two commands you have entered will appear on the screen, and will take effect as they appear. And that's all there is to it.

Although it is so easy to create a file by using PIP in this way, there is one important limitation: PIP places *everything* typed in at the keyboard onto the disc. This should be no problem if you are an accurate typist, but if you make a mistake while typing in one of the command lines for the SUB file, you will discover that you can't use the cursor keys or erase the error with the DEL keys in the usual way.

Instead, you will have to use ^H to move the cursor back to the error, and then type in the correction on top of the mistake. Corrections that you need to make in previous lines are more awkward still, and it may even be worth while abandoning a file and starting again if there is such an error. Still, none of these problems are insuperable, and as most SUB files are very short, you are unlikely to have real difficulties.

Using a word processor.

A second way to create a SUB file is to use an ordinary commercial word processing package, *provided it stores files in ASCII code.* As we have already observed, early versions of LocoScript do not offer this option, and so unfortunately they cannot be used, but other word processing programs are available. A word processing program which offers this facility is discussed in Chapter 12.

Since most word processing programs offer a full range of editing facilities, you should not experience the same problems with them as you would with PIP. On the other hand, it would obviously not be worthwhile investing in a new word processor for this purpose alone!

The ED text editor.

The final way of creating a SUB file is provided by another of the programs on Side 2 of the CP/M Master Disc. This is a text editor called ED.COM. Files created with it are stored in straightforward ASCII code, making it very useful for creating SUB files. However, ED is very much a 'programmer's program', rather than a simple word processor.

The biggest difference between ED and a program such as LocoScript is that ED is 'line-based'; in other words, although it is quite straightforward to alter individual lines with ED, it is not practical to use it for moving text from one line to the other, as you would normally want a word processor to do.

Even so, many people *have* used ED as a word-processor when nothing else was available; and for creating simple text-files of the sort we need for a SUBMIT operation, it is really perfectly satisfactory. If you ever get involved in programming in BASIC on the PCW8256, you may find that ED provides the best way to input and edit lines.

The best way to get used to ED is to try it out, so use PIP to copy ED.COM onto Drive M, then place the program disc onto which the SUB file is to be put into Drive A.

ED Commands.

From this point on, we shall show what happens on the screen on the left of the page, and comment on it on the right. Everything in **bold type** represents the responses of the PCW8256; this type-face represents what you should type in; and {E} means 'press ENTER or RETURN."

M:ED PROG.SUB{E}	Your instruction to create a new file called PROG.SUB.
NEW FILE	CP/M confirms that the file is a new one, and reserves space for it on the disc.
:*I{E}	ED prompts with an asterisk to show that it is in Command Mode. You respond with I for Insert Mode.
1: PALETTE 1 0{E}	ED prompts each new line of the SUB file with a number. You type in the line in the usual way.
2: SET 24X80{E}	

142

3:^Z	ALT/Z takes you out of Insert Mode and back into Command Mode.
*	ED responds with the Command Mode Asterisk prompt.

And that's about all there is to it! However, before we learn how to make corrections to what we have written, there are a couple of points worth knowing.

The first is that if you find you have made a total pig's ear of a line, you can get out of it by pressing ^U. This has the effect of cancelling that whole line, and ED will respond by prompting for the same line again.

The second point is that, in common with many other text editors, ED works with a **Character Pointer**, or CP, which is located at some particular point in the text you have created.

However, this does not take the form of a visible cursor. Instead, ED prompts you by telling you which line it is on, and then you can move it by giving it specific commands.

However, this does not take the form of a visible cursor. Instead, ED prompts by telling you which line it is on, and then you can move it by giving it specific commands; for example, before you can make any corrections to what you have written, your first task is to get the CP back to the beginning, which we do as follows:

B{E}	Stands for 'beginning'. If you had typed a minus sign in front of it, it would have sent the CP to the *end*. Logical!
1:*#T{E}	ED types the number of the line you are on, and prompts with the Command Mode asterisk. You respond by typing # (which means *everything* and T (for Type), and ED displays on the screen everything that you have input so far ....
1: PALETTE 1 0 (etc)	... and when it has finished typing all the lines, it returns to Line 1, where the CP is, and prompts you again.
1:*1L{E}	You may have already realised that many Command Mode instructions take the form *n*C, where *n* represents a number (or # for 'every-

	thing') and C represents a Command. The Commands are listed in detail in Table 8.1. Briefly, 1L means that the CP moves 1 Line down, so ED prompts to show that it is now on Line 2;
2: * 1 K { E }	Your input Kills (erases) the next line, so you move the CP back to the start again and relist what you now have.
: * B { E }	
:PALETTE 1 0	
1: * E { E }	Finally you leave ED by typing E (Exit). ED saves your SUB file and returns you to the usual CP/M A› prompt.

Using ED to edit a file which already exists is just as easy: after you have typed ED and the file-name and file-type, type # A (for Append Everything) and the entire contents of the file will be placed in a special area called the **buffer**, from which you can display them with the #T command.

You can then Kill, Insert, or whatever else you want, saving your work at the end with the E command.

By now you have very probably become quite used to many of the LocoScript commands, even though there were perhaps times at first when you couldn't seem to see how they worked. ED is a little similar; the commands take a bit of getting used to, but once you are familiar with them, the creation of text files becomes very simple indeed.

However, as we have already noted, ED is something of a programmer's program, and not everybody finds that they can get on with it. If that includes you, use a standard word processing package or concentrate on honing up your typing skills and use PIP to create those SUB files.

If you do use ED, there is one special thing to be careful of: be sure that you have plenty of space on the disc to store the SUB file you are creating – otherwise, ED will report a disc error and dump you unceremoniously back at the CP/M A› prompt, with all your work lost – a real disaster as there is no way to get it back!

What we have had so far has merely been a brief look at some of the ED facilities. If you want to try them further, test out the commands listed in Table 8.1 and see how they work.

Table 8.1

*n*A	Append *n* lines – i.e. read and move them from an existing file into the Text Buffer. #A reads and moves everything. Use this before trying to Edit an existing file.
B	Move CP to the Beginning of the text; –B moves CP to the end.
*n*C	Moves CP forward *n* characters – ENTER counts as two characters. A negative number moves CP towards the start of the file.
*n*D	Deletes *n* characters forward – backwards if *n* is negative.
←DEL	In Insert Mode the ←DEL Key repeats the character which it has deleted – this can be rather irritating for those not used to it! In Command Mode the ←DEL Key functions normally.
E	End ED, save the file on disc and return to CP/M.
H	Save a copy of the file on which you are working and then return to ED; this is a backup routine to help avoid accidental loss of a file during long ED sessions.
I	Insert text and move existing lines down as required.
*n*K	Kills (deletes) *n* lines forwards – backwards if *n* is negative.
*n*L	Move CP forwards (backwards if negative) by *n* Lines, leaving it at the start of the appropriate line. If *n*=0, place CP at the beginning of the current line.
O	(For Original). Scrap the version of the file on which you are working and return to the previous version of the file. Follow by A to append the Original file.

*n*P	Move CP forward *n* lines and type the intervening lines – move backward if *n* is negative.
Q	Quit – ED will ask you to confirm this. If you do, it will abandon the ED session without updating your files.
*n*S*os*^Z*ns*	Replace (Substitute)*n* occurrences of *os* by *ns*, and leave CP immediately after the last occurrence.
*n*T	Type *n* lines forward from CP, or up to CP if *n* is negative. The CP is not moved by this command
n	Move forwards *n* lines and type that line – backwards if negative.
n:	Move to the line numbered *n*, and type that line.

End of Table 8.1

Turnkey discs.

All of the above assumes that you have become pretty familiar with your PCW8256 system, and the way in which it uses CP/M. Indeed, an interesting feature of computing is that many people who at first assumed that everything to do with computers would be uninteresting and far too complicated for them to become involved with, find that they are interested in trying out new ideas to see how they work.

Perhaps the fact that you can't actually break anything by trying things out acts as an incentive; in any case, it is certainly true that the more you play around with your PCW8256, the more benefit you will derive from it.

Even so, there will be many occasions when you wish to give simple instructions to someone else about how to use some particular program; and the more straightforward those instructions are, the less chance there is that that person will become confused or worried.

Probably the simplest instruction which it would be possible to give would be something like *Turn the computer on and put the right disc into the disc drive; everything else is automatic*. The ability to do this is indeed available in CP/M; discs which behave in this way are called **Turnkey Discs**, because they are as simple to use as turning a key in a door.

If you want to see how this sort of thing works, there is an example on Side 2 of the CP/M Master Disc. If you do a DIR on that disc, you will find a file there called PROFILE.END. Rename it to PROFILE.SUB, using the RENAME command introduced in Chapter Six, then reset your PCW8256 (SHIFT/EXTRA/EXIT).

As CP/M restarts, you will see that instead of giving you the immediate, and by now familiar, A› prompt, a whole series of commands appears on the screen first, and at the same time the most useful transient utilities are copied across from Drive A to Drive M.

If you think that having the Master Disc do this will be useful to you, then simply leave things as they are; if not, change the name of the file back from PROFILE.SUB to PROFILE.END, and when you load CP/M in future you will be left at the A› prompt without any of the copying taking place first.

You will have realised that the file named PROFILE.SUB controls what has happened. Quite simply, any file with that name is automatically executed when CP/M is started, because the program which starts CP/M working always checks to see if there is a PROFILE.SUB file to work through before showing you the prompt A›.

Creating a turnkey disc of your own from scratch involves three separate steps: first, make sure that the disc is suitable for turnkey operation; second, copy the CP/M start-up program onto it; and finally, make up a suitable PROFILE.SUB file to carry out whatever instructions you wish.

Choosing suitable discs.

A disc which will be used for turnkey operation must have enough room on it for the various programs which make turnkey operation possible.

The amount of space this will take varies, as you will see, but as a general rule you can assume that turnkey operation can swallow 50K or more of disc space; if you don't have that much room spare on the program disc, turnkey operation will not be practical.

Second, although you can use a PROFILE.SUB to carry out most sorts of operation, it is most useful when the disc has on it one particular program which you want to load and run automatically, rather than a suite of programs which might be related but which you would actually want to run separately.

For example, the NewWord word processing program (published by Newstar Software of California) is available in the 3" disc format used by the PCW8256. On one side of the disc is the NewWord program itself, and on the other side are a variety of extremely useful 'extensions' to it, including a spelling checker, an anagram solver, a word-finder (all of these are invaluable for cheating at crosswords!) together with various other useful word-processing-related programs.

NewWord itself would obviously be suited to turnkey operation; all you would then need to do would be to turn on the PCW8256, insert the disc and start to use it. On the other hand, there would be far less point in extending the same turnkey facility to the programs on the other side of the same disc, unless you routinely wanted to start off with the same one each time.

Putting the necessary programs on the disc.

On Side 2 of the CP/M Master Disc you will find a program with a name something like J11CPM3.EMS (though the number after the initial J may vary according to the version of CP/M+ with which you have been supplied).

It is this program which automatically starts CP/M when you turn on the PCW8256 and insert the Master Disc; any disc which has this program on it becomes a **Start of Day Disc** which you can use to initiate a CP/M session, in the same way that a disc with the LocoScript program could be used as a LocoScript Start of Day Disc.

Using PIP, copy this file from the Master Disc to the program disc which you are adapting for turnkey operation. Next, copy the SUBMIT.COM program on to the new disc in the same way. (Without SUBMIT.COM, the PROFILE.SUB file will not have any effect, so you must have this program available).

The last stage is to create a suitable file with all the instructions which you want CP/M to execute when the new program disc is inserted, and then to save this under the name of PROFILE.SUB.

You have the same choice of ways of doing this as you did earlier in creating an ordinary SUB file, using a word processor which creates text in ASCII, or ED or PIP.

When the PROFILE.SUB file has been saved, there will probably be some other files to be put on the disc as well.

For example, it is obvious that the final line of the PROFILE.SUB instructions should consist of the name of the applications program which is going to be automatically loaded and run, and that therefore that program must be on the disc; but it is much easier to forget that if you are changing the keyboard, or the paper size, or the screen, then you will need to have all the appropriate CP/M utility programs, plus any files *they* use, on the disc as well.

By now you will see that the space requirements for the program disc are a little tighter than you had probably imagined, as in addition to the CP/M Loading program J11CPM3.EMS, SUBMIT.COM and PROFILE.COM, you may need SETKEYS.COM,KEYS.WP,SET24X80 and perhaps others too. All this in addition to the applications program itself!

Second, if your purpose in using turnkey operations is to make life easier for users who are unfamiliar with computers – which we think is one of the most pressing reasons for using them – then you will have to put yourself into the shoes of a totally naive operator, and this is something which is easier said than done.

For example, you may have told an operator that if the PCW8256 was turned off, then it should be turned on and the appropriate turnkey disc inserted, but that if it was already turned on and using CP/M, it would only be necessary to insert whatever program disc was required and to type SUBMIT PROFILE.

(You could also have told your operator to place the new disc in the drive after first resetting the machine, but restarting CP/M unnecessarily takes several seconds, so let's assume that you didn't.)

You may have set the PROFILE.SUB on one of the programs to change the paper-size or the keyboard settings to something rather unusual; the other program didn't need to have these settings changed from the normal switch-on values, so *its* PROFILE.SUB contains no corresponding SETKEYS or PAPER instructions.

Everything will work properly as long as the program which sets new values for the printer or the keyboard is always run second; but if it is ever run first, then when the user tries to run the program which relies on the keyboard or printer being set to their normal values, they will find that those values have been changed to suit the other program and not changed back!

The moral is, either tell the user to reset the machine every time they insert a new turnkey disc, or make certain that you have taken into account the possibility that you may need to explicitly restore the keyboard, the screen and the printer to their switch-on values.

Despite all this, there are many real advantages to turnkey operation, and we strongly recommend that you use it when you can, as it greatly decreases the chance of human error fouling up the operation of a program.

Final points about SUBMIT files.

If you get into the habit of using SUBMIT files regularly, either in the PROFILE.SUB form for turnkey operation or in connection with a SUBMIT command for changes in your system to accommodate particular programs, there are two other things you need to know. One of these is about a limitation of SUBMIT files, and the other is about a useful extra facility which they offer.

First, the limitation. *Not all utilities will work in SUBMIT files*, though most will. Specifically, all the resident commands will work (that is, DIR, ERASE, RENAME, SAVE, TYPE and USER), as well as *most* of the transient commands.

However, you may find that some utilities which need to ask a lot of questions will not work properly, and some applications programs may refuse to work properly as well.

The useful extra facility is that you can arrange a SUB file (but not a PROFILE.SUB) to make use of certain additional information which you will type in with the SUBMIT command.

For example, suppose that you regularly wanted to copy certain types of file to Drive M, but that the type of file involved was not always the same – you might want to do it with all the COM files on one occasion and all the TXT files on another, for instance.

To move all the COM files, you would simply include in the SUB file (we shall call it COPY.SUB for convenience) the line PIP M:=*.COM, but obviously this same command could not be used to move any other sort of file.

It can be done, however, by means of what are called **parameters**. That means that in the SUB file, instead of actually including the file-details after the command PIP, you would include only those parts which did not change, and replace the rest of them with a dollar sign ($) and a number – $1, $2 and so on. Thus the PIP command we have shown above would change to PIP M:=*.$1.

Then when we typed the S U B M I T command, instead of entering it as

    S U B M I T C O P Y

as we had done before, we would enter

    S U B M I T C O P Y C O M

to move all the C O M files, or

SUBMIT COPY TXT

to move all files of file-type TXT.

CP/M would then substitute the COM or TXT part of the command for the $1 in the COPY.SUB file.

Options with PIP.

Although we have not needed to use them so far, PIP offers certain options which can prove useful under some circumstances, especially when you are copying files using the wildcard characters ? and *.

PIP options are selected by placing appropriate letters, each representing one option, inside square brackets immediately after the rest of the command; there must be no spaces between the first section of the command and the opening bracket.

The most useful options are C (which asks for confirmation before making a copy), O (which makes doubly certain that the whole file has been copied as required, and that the end-of-file has not been found too soon) and V (which Verifies the copy by comparing it to the original to ensure that no errors have occurred).

If more than one option is required, the various letters inside the square brackets must be separated by single spaces. They can appear in any order. Thus, for example,

PIP M:=A:*.*[C V]

would copy all files from Drive A to Drive M, checking first that each one was to be copied, and would verify that each one had been correctly copied.

User Numbers.

There may be occasions when it is useful to be able to 'hide' certain disc files. There are various ways in which this can be done, but the most practical way is by means of the CP/M User Numbers.

These were originally devised to simplify searching for individual files on systems which had a high-capacity fixed disc instead of removable 'floppies'. Because such a disc might hold hundreds of different files, searching for any of them with a DIR command was difficult; the individual names would scroll up the screen before they could be spotted.

User Numbers permit all files to be labelled with a number between 0 and 15. When CP/M is turned on, the User Number 0 is automatically chosen, and all files created will be of that number.

If you change the number by entering:

USER *x;*

where *x* represents a number between 1 and 15, all new files will belong to this new number. They will therefore not be accessible to any other User Number, even on a DIR command.

Whatever User Number you enter, you will still be able to use the various system files which were originally labelled USER 0.

Like various other of the CP/M facilities, it is not a good idea to make use of User Numbers on discs containing LocoScript files, as these are divided into template groups by virtue of LocoScript 'borrowing' the CP/M User Number facility.

Postscript.

The facilities described in this chapter can be used to make CP/M programs on the PCW8256 easier to use, at the expense of some extra work in setting them up, and some loss of disc space for applications programs because of the need to store additional files needed for turnkey or SUBMIT operations.

The SUBMIT facility allows several operations necessary either for installation (such as resetting the keyboard or printer) or for convenience (such as copying files onto Disc M) to be carried out automatically with only one command.

With PROFILE.SUB, certain operations can be carried out automatically when CP/M is first loaded so that, for example, an applications program can be set up and then run without any command being entered. This is particularly useful in circumstances where a program will be used by people who are unfamiliar with computers.

152

CHAPTER NINE

A brief introduction to applications programs

Preview.

The following topics will be discussed in this chapter:

> What are applications programs?
> Buying a system.
> One job or two?
> Types of system.
> Security.

What are applications programs?

In the days of computing's stone age, back in the 1950's, using a computer meant, almost inevitably, writing your own programs for it.

If you couldn't do that, then you either had to pay someone rather a lot of money to write a special program just for you, or you learned to program for yourself. And if you had neither the money to pay nor the patience to learn, you forgot about the computer and made do with pen and paper instead.

Custom-designed programs are still being created, though as programmers now are paid rather more than they were thirty years ago — even allowing for inflation — buying one will set you back quite a lot of money.

All the same, for certain highly specialised purposes like landing a rocket on the moon or handling an airline's world-wide ticket reservation system, research institutes and big companies have no choice but to pay the price.

For most normal commercial and domestic tasks, however, there are now available an enormous number of ready-made programs for different types of computer. Those which are designed to *do* something for the user – rather than help him write programs or organise his disc-files – are called **Applications Programs** and it is with these that the rest of this book is concerned.

Before looking at individual programs, however, it is worth while taking a general look at such programs in order to see what features are most useful, and what should be avoided.

First, it has been estimated that there are something over 8,000 commercial programs available for CP/M computers. It is fair to point out that most of them — like the majority of books, paintings and whatever else you care to name — are not very good.

Often this is either because they were written a long time ago and have not been properly updated, so that they fail to make full use of the power of modern computers, or because they were designed for a totally different market from the one in which they are now being offered.

For example, accounting programs from the USA may ask you questions about 'State taxes' and 'Federal taxes' which have no relevance in the UK. Even if they avoid this sort of trap, they may make it impossible to print money amounts with a Pound sign (£) in front of them. Since most computer software comes from the United States, this sort of problem is more common that you might expect.

Another area that needs care is that of **user friendliness**, as ease of use is called.

The theory is straightforward enough; a user friendly program is one which you can use without needing to remember a string of different commands (perhaps it uses menus, like LocoScript), and which tries to stop you making destructive errors by double-checking that you really mean to do what you have said.

These goals are admirable in themselves, and programs which take no account of them are often awkward to use; the lack of friendliness of some of the older CP/M utilities is a frequent source of complaint.

At the same time, some programs are so friendly that they positively get in the way of your work by presenting you with menu after menu, even after you have become quite familiar enough with the program to be able to get along without that help.

In these terms, LocoScript offers the sort of compromise which you may find satisfactory: help is available for when you need it, but you can usually avoid it when you don't. Most *good* software follows the same principles.

Buying a system.

Good applications programs almost always involve you in buying a special system for doing whatever task they set out to perform. Because they were designed for general use, and not for your own specific purposes, you will need to adapt your present practice to fit the new system.

Many small businesses, particularly sole proprietorships, struggle along without any particular system for the various chores which crop up.

In such organisations, doing the payroll may involve nothing more complicated than sitting down with the appropriate tax tables and record cards; and keeping accounts sometimes degenerates into a squalid system of putting receipts and cheque-stubs into a drawer for the accountant to puzzle over sometime in the future.

More organised concerns will have provided themselves with one or the other of the various excellent manual payroll and accounts systems. It is with these that an accounts or payroll program should be compared. You must therefore be sure that the system which you buy is one that meets your own particular needs, or is easily adaptable to them.

The keynote here is flexibility. An accounts system which insists on a full set of books being kept may well be very rigorous and accurate, but it may be more than you need. Perfectly good accounts for typical small business purposes can be maintained with a simple spreadsheet program, and we shall show how to do this shortly.

The other problem is the converse of this; it is common for users to start off with a program which is too limiting for their long-term needs, and to find out too late that converting to what they should have had all along would be a slow and expensive business.

The only advice which will always apply is to look very carefully at a program before you buy it; if this is not possible, you may have to rely on reviews in the various business and computing magazines.

At all events it is a sad fact that not all the people who sell programs will be of much help to you. Partly this is because they will be largely unaware of your particular problems, and partly because most companies are geared up to the selling of hardware rather than software. The proverbial pinch of salt can be a great help in choosing applications programs.

One job or two?

Until quite recently, applications programs assumed that when you wanted to do accounts, you would load an accounts program into your computer;

when you wanted to write a letter, you would use a word processing program, and so on.

Gradually this concept has begun to change, so that it is now possible to buy applications programs which will do more than one task.

Imagine writing a quotation for work which you are going to undertake, for example. The majority of the task would count as simple word processing, but in addition you might need to carry out some simple calculations — adding up the cost of several individual operations, perhaps.

Instead of having to stop word processing, load a program to carry out calculations, write down the answers on a piece of paper, reload the word processor and copy the figures off the paper and into the document, some programs now permit you either to carry out word processing in the middle of, for example, a spreadsheet, or to do simple arithmetic in the middle of a word processing job.

The ultimate in this sort of mixed operation is sometimes referred to as **messy desk**computing, because it allows you to handle several different sorts of operations simultaneously, just as you can have papers relating to several different jobs on your desk at the same time.

In general, software for this kind of operation tends to be expensive, is sometimes not very user-friendly, and no doubt many users fail to make full use of its facilities.

However, there is no denying that an ability to do more than one thing in a particular applications program, or at least to import the results of a calculation directly into a word processor without writing things down on a scratch-pad, can be a great time-saver.

The spreadsheet and database programs discussed in the next two chapters have the ability to output text as well as the normal results of their calculations, and this can be a most worthwhile facility.

Adapting to a computerised system.

When changing over from a manual to a computerised system, there will inevitably be occasions when things don't work as they should. There are some real horror stories about big companies which computerised their payroll accounting and only then found faults with their new system which meant that no-one could be paid on time!

The golden rule, particularly where money is concerned, is:*never abandon a manual system in favour of a computerised one without a period of running both at the same time.*

This may seem wasteful, but the advantages are two-fold: if something goes wrong with the new system (and because is is new and unfamiliar, no-one will know what to do if that happens), then the old system is still there to fall back on; and if you get different results from the two systems, you will know that there is something seriously wrong with either the one or the other.

There is a distressing human tendency to believe what the computer tells us, even if closer scrutiny would show it to be manifestly absurd; to chain your accounts payroll to a system which may be making errors, without any way of double checking the result, is extremely dangerous.

Trying to explain to an employee that he has been underpaid this week because of a computer error (which is usually shorthand for operator error) is bad enough; but an error of just a few percent on a budget forecast, caused perhaps by carelessness in entering formulae on a spreadsheet, could mean the difference between success and receivership. Be warned!

Incidentally, it is all too possible when you are converting from a manual to a computerised system that you will be too easily satisfied with what you have and thus make no further progress.

This has happened in so many businesses that the bizarre combination of high-tech equipment and old fashioned methods has become a modern commonplace.

The classic army equivalent is the true story of how men were detailed to hold the horses in artillery companies which had been mechanised for decades, because nobody understood the consequence of the rule that changes in technology should mean changes in techniques as well. 'Nuff said!

Program maintenance.

Buying a program is a little like buying a car; usually it works perfectly well at first, but sooner or later you may have problems with it.

The reasons for this are pretty much the same for both cars and programs, and have to do with the fact that both are highly complex products used, in the main, by non-specialists. Of course, a program should never actually 'wear out' in the same way as the parts of a car, but otherwise the analogy is a fair one.

Unexplained errors in the operation of a program are called **bugs,**and it is safe to assume that nearly every program has them, just as nearly every book has misprints in it. Generally speaking these bugs are pretty harmless, and in most commercial programs they are unlikely to cause you any real inconvenience; but you will assuredly meet them from time to time.

Several of the better producers of commercial software offer schemes for 'maintaining' their programs, perhaps in conjunction with telephone advice — often rather dramatically called a *hotline service.*

In some cases these services are provided free for all registered purchasers of the program, thus helping to freeze out users of illegitimate copies; sometimes there is a small annual charge to pay.

Either way, the provision of proper after-sales service, or **software support,** is something which you should investigate when choosing programs — particularly those, like payroll, which may cause embarrassment if there is a substantial delay in running them.

File Security.

A final problem of computerised systems, and one which is becoming increasingly significant, is that of the security of the system.

It is sometimes assumed that the security implications of computers are not basically any different from those of normal manual practice. This is emphatically untrue.

From the standpoint of small business use, the biggest source of difficulty is the floppy disc; unlike documents on paper, which take time to copy, the entire contents of a floppy disc, amounting perhaps to several hundred pages, can be copied in a matter of seconds and *leave no trace of the copying having taken place.*

Various attempts have been made to improve security, and you should at least have an eye towards these when considering the purchase of new software.

The classical solution is **passwords,** combinations of letters and numbers without which it is impossible to gain access to confidential files.

Some sophisticated systems allow different levels of security, with different passwords for each level, so that a user may be able to see some records on a disc but not others — for example, it may be possible for payroll personnel to amend pay records of staff, but not to gain access to personal information of a confidential nature.

Passwords generally provide excellent security if they are properly used. However, as their value depends upon their secrecy, they can be rendered useless by people writing them down (to save forgetting them), or choosing easily-guessed words such as their own names — or the names of their nearest and dearest — as passwords. Password generator programs are available which will suggest secure and easy-to-remember combinations to avoid these problems.

Even if all due care is taken with choosing and using passwords, any user with a moderate level of experience of computing will probably be able to get at confidential information stored on a floppy disc.

Short of using various encryption techniques to 'scramble' data (and these are available), the best advice in any organisation bigger than a one-man-band is to enforce strict security standards when handling floppy discs, to keep them locked away when not in use and to restrict the number of staff who are permitted to handle them.

Payroll and accounts programs are particularly vulnerable to ingenious and dishonest tampering; and the very nature of the computer makes it less likely that an offender will be detected. There is now a fairly substantial literature about computer fraud, one of the effects of which has inevitably been to popularise it. Don't assume that it won't happen to you!

Equipment reliability.

Modern computing equipment is extremely reliable, and breakdowns are few and far between. However, they do happen from time to time.

The most vulnerable items are those which have a high proportion of mechanical parts, such as printers and disc drives. Short of providing actual physical back-ups for these (and a second disc-drive is certainly a very useful thing to have) it is worth considering that programs which give you the option of redirecting printer output to the screen can be a blessing if something does go wrong with a printer.

Obviously a word processor without a printer is practically useless (except in terms of preparing texts which can be printed out later), but many payroll and accounts programs can still be usefully run without a printer if the results are simply backed up onto a disc for printing later.

In this circumstance, there is a CP/M Utility program which may prove useful. This is the PUT.COM program, which is used as follows.

Enter the instruction

PUT PRINTER OUTPUT TO FILE *filename.filetype*

and everything that would have gone to the printer will instead be directed to a disc file with the file-name and –type specified.

To revert to normal output, enter

PUT PRINTER OUTPUT TO PRINTER

The PUT command has a number of forms beyond the two given here; full details of the others are given in the User Manual. However, the two forms listed are those which are likely to be found most generally useful.

When the printer is again operative, you can transfer the contents of the file which you produced with the PUT command onto the printer using our old friend PIP, thus:

P I P L S T : =*filename.filetype*

LST being CP/M shorthand for the LiSTing device, namely the printer.

Postscript.

In choosing application programs, points which should be borne in mind include being certain that the system will meet your own needs, that adequate support from the manufacturers is available in case you have problems and that the system is suitably secure for your own circumstances.

In starting with a new system, it is essential not to abandon the previous manual system immediately, but to run both side by side for a while. In this way, errors caused by lack of familiarity with the new system will be trapped, and difficulties caused by hardware or software failure will be eliminated.

Equipment failure can be guarded against to some extent by redirecting the output from the printer to disc files.

CHAPTER TEN

Spreadsheets — Supercalc2

Preview.

In this chapter the following topics will be introduced:

What is a spreadsheet?
SuperCalc2.
Starting out.
Loan repayments — a worked example.
Allocating column space.
Laying out the sheet.
Entering information.
Formatting numbers.
Saving and loading spreadsheets.
Printing spreadsheets
Hiding text.
An imprest spreadsheet.
Using IF commands.

What is a Spreadsheet?

Spreadsheets in the computer sense are directly derived from the manual spreadsheets used in some simple accounting systems; however, they are not limited to this type of work, but can be used in almost any application where calculations are required.

In its simplest form a spreadsheet consists of a number of compartments or **cells** arranged into vertical **columns** and horizontal **rows**, rather like the squares on a sheet of graph-paper.

Into each of these cells can be placed either some text – a title, perhaps, or instructions, or even a line drawn to divide one part of the spreadsheet from another – or numbers on which calculations can be performed, or formulae which will specify just what calculations will take place.

A spreadsheet typically contains a much greater number of cells than could be accommodated on a computer screen at one time; to get round this, the screen is treated as if it were a small **window** which can be put over any part of a large sheet, and which can be moved in any direction in order to reveal a different part of the sheet.

This facility resembles that of such word processors as LocoScript, which can handle lines too long to fit on the screen at one time; by using the cursor keys, the screen can be 'moved' to reveal a different part of the text.

The great advantage of a computerised spreadsheet over manual ways of calculating figures is that once the initial sheet has been laid out, any number of 'might be' options can be tried, and the answers will be immediately shown.

Although superficially spreadsheets and word processors are quite different sorts of program, there is actually a fairly close relationship between them. In particular, both need to have a fair amount of time spent in setting them up if you are to get the best out of them, and both benefit from the setting up of standard **templates** of the sort that we have already used in LocoScript.

There is one important word of caution that needs to be given here: most spreadsheets are highly complicated affairs, so until you are completely convinced that a particular sheet is working accurately – by a manual check, preferably – you should treat all its conclusions with suspicion.

The problem is not that the spreadsheet program itself will be inaccurate, but rather that you may yourself not have seen quite what interactions are taking place on the sheet. Additionally, errors can be caused by using inaccurate formulae, or even mistyping items of data.

The former problem can be overcome by using templates copied from books like this one; only vigilance can eliminate the latter one.

SuperCalc2.

Although there are nearly as many spreadsheet programs on the market as there are word processors, the number which have become well known is very small in both cases. SuperCalc2 has become established as an industry standard, and as a result there are several books devoted to it and its predecessor, SuperCalc.

Although much of the remainder of this chapter is specifically concerned with SuperCalc2, don't let that fact put you off reading it if you are using some other spreadsheet program; the various commands will differ somewhat from program to program, but most of what is covered here can be duplicated in one way or another with most spreadsheet programs, and it should therefore be relevant to your own situation.

Starting out.

In what follows we shall assume that you have read your SuperCalc2 manual carefully, and have grasped how the basic commands work. However, even if there are points there which you do not understand, you should be able to get acceptable results by following the procedures described.

In addition to the manual, there are a set of helpful files provided on the SuperCalc2 program disc. You can use these both to see how SuperCalc2 works and as a basis for developing your own spreadsheets. They are all capable of easy modification and expansion, and you will learn a good deal by entering new figures and formulae into them and seeing what happens.

If you run into problems with this, you will be able to get help from the program by typing ? – this usually works even when it is not specifically mentioned in the Status Bar at the foot of the screen that you can do it.

Assistance of this sort is often called a **Help Page**; SuperCalc2 calls it an **Answer Screen**, but its purpose is the same.

A worked example – loan repayments.

One of the most important uses for a spreadsheet program is to enable businesses to keep a closer check on details of their financial position than would normally be the case with manual methods.

Most spreadsheet users assume that the easiest place to start is with a simple income/expenditure table, with the months listed across the heads of the columns and various items of income or expenditure placed in the rows. Indeed, one such sheet is included on the SuperCalc2 program disc – it is called SAMPLE.CAL.

By a simple process of addition and subtraction, and transferring the total of one column (monthly surplus or deficit) to the head of the next column (cash or debit carried over), it is possible with this type of sheet to investigate cash-flow details for a given period.

Moving on from the ready-made templates on the program disc, our first example consists of a spreadsheet to work out the cost on any given date of making a lump sum repayment of a loan.

This may seem a fairly trivial calculation, but it is well worth following through because it is precisely this sort of analysis which can be very helpful in determining the best use of your resources when you have a surplus of ready cash at your disposal.

We have followed here the same procedure which we used with LocoScript, namely to adopt a fixed sequence of actions, whether they apply in any particular case or not. This can be dropped when you have acquired full familiarity with SuperCalc2, but until then it will help you to avoid leaving anything out.

Even when starting out to design a very simple sheet like this one, it is wise to begin by planning it on paper – graph paper is ideal. Where several columns of a sheet are basically identical – containing similar details for succeeding months, for example – you can save space by including these on the paper only two or three times.

Column sizes.

The first point to be taken into consideration when starting to lay out a new sheet is how much space will be required for each column. When SuperCalc2 is started, all the columns are preset to a width of 9 characters. If these 'switch-on' values need to be changed, it will be possible to set the new widths into the template with a /F (Format) command.

Column width is most likely to be determined by the numbers which will be fitted into the cells. In the particular case we are looking at, there should be no difficulties here, and so the switch-on values need not be changed.

The main divisions.

It is as well to begin by broadly dividing your sheet into several separate areas. How many you have will depend on the problem which you want to solve. In this first sheet there will be four areas – Headings, Instructions, Data and Conclusions. On big sheets, you may well decide you want an Index as well.

For a simple spreadsheet like this one, the first two of these areas may seem something of a luxury, but proper labelling of your work is a habit which it is worth getting into right from the start.

Most titles can easily be fitted into the top three rows – we favour giving over the top and third rows for some sort of rule character, such as = or *, and the second line for the actual title of the sheet, your name and the date of creation.

Instructions will be placed further down the sheet, and finding room for them will mean that you must make some guesses about how big the rest of the sheet is likely to be – work in pencil until you are sure. Somewhere around row 27 or below should leave ample room for the working section of the spreadsheet. Again, mark this point with some suitable rule.

Next, label row 6, or thereabouts, as DATA, and again rule it off top and bottom.

We are now ready to start thinking about fitting in the working part of the sheet. Its size will depend on how many rows of information (or input) are necessary.

In our case there will be five rows – the Principal Amount of the loan, the Annual rate of interest, the Term of the loan in months, the Number of payments already made and the Size of each monthly payment.

Begin each one of these headings some distance in from the left-hand edge of the sheet – Column B, perhaps – and enter each item in successive Rows, with the first item in Row 10 or so.

Next, leave some space clear underneath and write CONCLUSIONS, ruling it off top and bottom as before.

Exactly what we put here will depend on what we want out of the spreadsheet; we will assume that what we need is Total interest for the full-term loan, Sum of payments still to be made, the Rebate of interest due if the loan is paid off now and the Total lump-sum amount required to pay off the loan immediately. This information will require four Rows of text, starting at about Row 21.

Next, mark on your sheet those cells which will contain actual numbers – those which you will enter yourself as well as those which the program will calculate. These will appear in the same rows as the titles which refer to them, but one or two columns to the right – we suggest you use Column $\bar{\text{E}}$.

Finally you will need to enter onto your sheet the various formulae needed to compute the results. These will vary slightly, depending on how your Bank works out these charges. The formula which we have used is as follows:

$$\frac{(n-p+1) \times (n-p) \times i}{n^2 + n}$$

where

> n = the number of payments for the full term of the loan.

> p = the number of payments made when the loan is paid off, and

> i = the total interest cost for the loan.

Entering the sheet.

So far, we have not actually used SuperCalc2 at all – all our planning has been carried out on paper.

The importance of this method of preparing a spreadsheet cannot be overemphasised; trying to type in the information 'cold' will only result in wasted time and temper, and probably in inaccurate or misleading results as well.

You are now ready to load SuperCalc2 and to begin inserting the various headings and other information that will be required. What you are aiming at is something like Fig. 10.1 which represents the sheet with no figures or formulae yet entered.

If you are not yet familiar with making entries into a SuperCalc2 spreadsheet, the following observations may prove helpful.

Instructions always start with a Slash-character (/), and are followed by one of the letters which then appear in the Status Bar. If you are uncertain of which letter to enter for the effect you need, type a question mark after the /.

To remove a command in which you have made an error, it is generally easiest to use ^Z, which is the SuperCalc2 Abort command. (Z stands for Zap). On the PCW8256, the STOP key has the same effect as ^Z.

Information of all sorts is not entered directly into the cells of the spreadsheet, but into the window in the Status Bar at the bottom of the screen. When you press ENTER (either the big RETURN key or the little ENTER key will do), this information is checked to see if it matches the requirements of SuperCalc2.

If the form of the entry is correct, it is automatically placed into the cell occupied by the **cell cursor.** This can be moved from cell to cell either with the arrow keys or by giving a specific instruction to move it to a particular Row and Column – such an instruction consists of an equals sign followed by the letter and number of the destination – e.g. =A5.

```
 :  A  :: B  :: C  :: D  :: E  :: F  :: G  :: H  :: I  :
 1;-----------------------------------------------------------------------
 2;PAYING OFF A LOAN EARLY          J.HUGHES NOVEMBER 1985
 3;-----------------------------------------------------------------------
 4;
 5;-----------------------------------------------------------------------
 6;DATA
 7;-----------------------------------------------------------------------
 8;
 9;
10;       Principal amount
11;       Annual rate of interest
12;       Term of loan
13;       Number of payments made
14;       Size of monthly payment
15;
16;
17;-----------------------------------------------------------------------
18;CONCLUSIONS
19;-----------------------------------------------------------------------
20;
21;       Total interest for full-term loan
22;       Sum of payments to be made
23;       Rebate of interest
24;
25;       Total lump sum required
26;
27;-----------------------------------------------------------------------
28;INSTRUCTIONS
29;       Place relevant figures in DATA Section, Column E
30;       Force recalculation with !
31;       Read answer from CONCLUSIONS Section, Column E
32;
```

Fig. 10.1 The bare bones of the loan-payment spreadsheet. ‹ct›

In fact, most SuperCalc2 instructions and inputs are preceded by a symbol to declare what sort of input they are; these symbols can be inspected by pressing '?' when the spreadsheet is displayed on the screen.

For our present purposes, the two most useful symbols are ' and ", which precede repeated text and ordinary text respectively.

167

We shall need the first of these for a rule at the top of the sheet. With the locating cursor in Cell A1, press ' and a suitable rule symbol – we have used a hyphen for this, but an asterisk, an underline or an equals sign would all be suitable.

If you make an error in entering any item, you will not be able to correct it with the ←DEL key in the usual way; instead either press ^Z (or STOP), as mentioned above, to abort the entry completely, or use the ← key to move the writing cursor in the bottom window back over the incorrect character, and then overtype it with the correct character.

When you have entered a single hyphen, or whatever other character you have chosen to make up the rule, press RETURN; a sequence of hyphens, or whatever, will spread from A1 right across the screen.

Next, move the cell cursor down to the beginning of the second row and enter the title of the sheet. This will be ordinary (i.e. non-repeating) text, so declare it by starting with a ", then follow this with your chosen title text.

Although this text will only 'belong' to the cell in which the cell cursor is placed, it will actually appear spread out from that cell horizontally across the screen as far as is necessary. This is a useful feature of SuperCalc2 and many other sophisticated spreadsheets, and eliminates the need to set cell sizes large enough to accommodate long **strings** of text.

You can now proceed to fill in the text needed for the rest of the sheet, preceding each entry with one or other of the two symbols already introduced to show whether it is to be repeated or not.

If something seems to go wrong, make sure that you don't miss the error messages which are displayed towards the bottom of the screen – some of them are not terribly obvious.

Putting in the formulae.

Unlike text entries, formulae do not require any special introductory character, but are entered 'as is.' Assuming that you have set up your sheet with the various items as they appear in Fig. 10.1, and assuming also that you will wish to insert the actual data in Column E, the formulae you will need to enter in the various cells are as follows:

```
E21—(E14*E12)—E10
E22—(E12—E13)*E14
E23—((E12—E13+1)*(E12—E13))/((E12*E12)+E12)*E21
E25—E22—E23
```

As you enter the last two formulae, you will get an error message telling you that the formulae are incorrect. Provided you have made the entries correctly, and that they refer to the correct cells, this should not worry you – it happens merely because, as there are as yet no numbers in the cells, SuperCalc2 is attempting to carry out a division by zero. Once the various numbers have been inserted, everything should work properly.

Formatting numbers.

You could now go ahead and enter appropriate numbers into the various cells in the DATA section of Column E. However, before you do so, it will be as well to consider the way in which the numbers are to be displayed.

Your data will be entered in Pounds and Pence – that is, in a format which allows only two places after the decimal point. However, SuperCalc2 will expect to display the answers according to the format which 'fits best' into the cells, whatever that may be.

You can force the answers to follow the correct format by entering Format control (press **/ F**). To force all the numbers in the sheet to share the same format, select **G** for Global formatting and then press $ to show that the numbers are to be displayed with two figures after the decimal point.

(This approach has been suggested here because it is simple; to be more accurate, you should then change cells E12 and E13 to Integer Format, as otherwise they will display both the Term of the loan in months and the Number of payments made to two decimal places.)

Incidentally, SuperCalc2 may strike you as being a little inconsistent about which responses require the ENTER key to be pressed and which do not. For example, you will need to press it after entering the dollar sign, but not after the G for Global.

The usual rule is that if the command is an initial letter, then you will not need to press ENTER; otherwise you will. Or, more simply, if nothing seems to be happening after you have made a key-press, wait a few seconds and then press ENTER.

Using the $ format, even those numbers which might be entered as integers when the sheet is in use will appear on the sheet forced into the correct format, and with a double zero inserted after the decimal.

Saving and loading a sheet.

Before entering any numbers, it is always wise to save the sheet onto disc. Indeed, the same rule applies for spreadsheets as for word processing – save a lengthy piece of work at frequent intervals, in case of a power failure or some similar disaster.

Saving is done simply by pressing **/ S**, then providing SuperCalc2 with a filename, like **LOAN**. Unlike LocoScript, SuperCalc2 will not suggest any name of its own.

There is no need to enter a file-type, as SuperCalc2 will default all files to type CAL.

If SuperCalc2 finds another file with the same name on the disc, it will offer you the choice of overwriting it (thus obliterating the previous version), changing its name or setting its file-type to BAK.   This latter is a general CP/M convention to identify BACKup files, and we suggest that this is the course you follow.

You will notice after pressing **/ S** (and some other commands as well) that there is a slight delay before your command is accepted, and that the activity light on the disc drive will come on.

This is because the SuperCalc2 program is not all held in the PCW8256's memory at the same time. Instead, parts of it are **overlaid**; that is, they are kept on the program disc until they are needed, and then loaded automatically.

You will become most aware of overlays when using the Answer Sheet facilities and when Saving. In general, they are not a major source of delay.

When the drive stops, you will be asked whether you want to save All the sheet, the Values or only Part of the sheet. Here, as in many other instances, SuperCalc2 expects that you will type only the initial letter of your choice.

Type **A**, and the whole spreadsheet will be saved on the program disc. To save it on another disc, you could have asked for it to be saved on another drive – either type **M :** or **B :** before the filename, and your work will be automatically saved on that drive.

If you had typed **B :** in front of the file-name (the colon is vital), then the PCW8256 would have instructed you to put a new disc in Drive A, and then have proceeded to treat that as if it were Drive B, in the same way as it did earlier with PIP.

If you had chosen to save the sheet on Drive M, you would of course have to copy it from there onto a real disc before turning the machine off, or you would lose it.

Loading a new sheet from disc is carried out in a similar way; press / L, then enter the name of the sheet; there is no need to enter the file-type CAL.

Alternatively, if you are uncertain of the exact name of the file which you wish to input, press ENTER, and you will be shown a disc directory, either of the current disc or another disc as you wish.

When you have entered the name of the file you wish to load, stipulate that you want to load All of it by entering A; the file will then be loaded and displayed on the screen in the usual way.

Entering test data.

It is a general rule of computing that you should test a program by giving it questions to which you already know the answers. If everything works satisfactorily, then you can proceed to use real data; if not, you will at least know that things are not as they should be.

We suggest that you start by using the data provided in Fig. 10.2. Simply enter it into the appropriate cells in Column E, pressing ENTER after each number, and watch the appropriate answers appearing in the CONCLUSIONS section.

When you are getting the right answers with the test data, try some figures of your own; they will need to be reasonably consistent, of course, or the answers you receive will be meaningless. Indeed, there is an old computing maxim, usually quoted as GIGO, which stands for *Garbage In, Garbage Out!*

Printing the sheet.

The SuperCalc2 Print command offers various options to you when you want to output your work onto paper, but probably the one you will most often use involves simply reproducing the sheet, or a part of it, onto paper as it stands.

Press / and O (for Output), and then choose D, to Display the sheet as it appears. (You may also find the C option useful, especially when tracing formula errors; it simply produces a listing of the contents of every 'inhabited' cell, whether text, figures or formula).

You will next be asked for the **range** of cells which you wish to Output. The Range option enables you to specify Rows or Columns, or even individual cells. In its most common form, the addresses of the first and last cells in the Range are input, separated by a colon.

```
  :  A  ::  B  ::  C  ::  D  ::  E  ::  F  ::  G  ::  H  ::  I  :
 1:---------------------------------------------------------------------------
 2:PAYING OFF A LOAN EARLY        J.HUGHES NOVEMBER 1985
 3:---------------------------------------------------------------------------
 4:
 5:---------------------------------------------------------------------------
 6:DATA
 7:---------------------------------------------------------------------------
 8:
 9:
10:      Principal amount                 2000
11:      Annual rate of interest            11
12:      Term of loan                       24
13:      Number of payments made            7
14:      Size of monthly payment           97
15:
16:
17:---------------------------------------------------------------------------
18:CONCLUSIONS
19:---------------------------------------------------------------------------
20:
21:      Total interest for full-term loan    328
22:      Sum of payments to be made          1649
23:      Rebate of interest               167,28
24:
25:      Total lump sum required          1481,72
26:
27:---------------------------------------------------------------------------
28:INSTRUCTIONS
29:        Place relevant figures in DATA Section, Column E
30:        Force recalculation with !
31:        Read answer from CONCLUSIONS Section, Column E
32:
```

Fig. 10.2 Data for the loan-repayment spreadsheet

The Range command is one of the most powerful in SuperCalc2, and it will repay the time and trouble taken to learn how to use it. However, in its simplest form (as here) you can merely type **A**, and only that section of the worksheet which is actually inhabited will be printed.

The printing is carried out entirely under the control of SuperCalc2, and you cannot alter the print quality or the size of type used. To abandon printing in the middle, either press the PTR key or use the standard SuperCalc2 abort option (^Z).

Hiding text.

There are occasions when you may wish to prepare a spreadsheet for more than one purpose. For instance, you may wish to produce a business quotation, keeping one copy of it for your own records and sending another copy to your customer – indeed, you can actually use SuperCalc2 as a simple word processor for this purpose.

However, you would probably not want your customer to be aware of all the details which you would need to have for your own use. In particular, details of your mark-ups and costs of buying-in materials should not appear on his copy of the quotation.

SuperCalc2 offers you the ability to hide either individual cells or groups of them; this can be accomplished with the Range command mentioned above.

This is done through the Format command (**/ F**). After entering this command, select either the individual cells you wish to Hide, or name the Row, Column or other combination. Finally, press **H** to make them invisible.

The contents of cells hidden in this way can still be inspected by placing the cell cursor over them and looking at the window in the Status Bar; and any numbers or formulae contained in them will still affect the rest of the spreadsheet as usual. However, they will not appear in a printed copy of the sheet.

To make Hidden areas visible again, use any of the other Format commands, as appropriate – **$** for figures with two decimal places, I for integers, etc.

More advanced work – an imprest spreadsheet.

The simple spreadsheet on which we have been working so far displays barely a fraction of the power of SuperCalc2. We shall now look at a larger sheet which introduces some of the more powerful SuperCalc2 commands, and which at the same time can be directly adopted for small business accounting.

Where it is impractical or unnecessary for a business to keep a full set of account books, a very common and useful substitute is provided by the **imprest system.**

Essentially this requires all expenditure (or income) to be listed down the left-hand columns of a double-page spread. The various expenditures are then divided into categories on the right-hand pages depending on the classification into which the items fall.

Finally, all the columns and rows are totalled and the results compared, so that there is a complete check on all the accuracy of the sheet.

The computerised form of this spreadsheet is particularly attractive to those just getting to grips with office automation, as its close similarity to manual book-keeping arrangements ensures that it is easily understood. At the same time, it harnesses the precision of the computer to ensure correct results.

The actual form of the sheet is shown in Fig. 10.3. It will be seen that Cheque numbers are listed in Column A, their Dates in Column C, the Amount of each cheque in Column D, and details of the Payees, or whatever else you wish to include, in Column F.

Column E, which is headed 'Groups,' is intended to hold a classification number according to which of several groups each cheque falls into, and showing whether it represents the purchase of materials, postal charges, wages or whatever.

The various groups themselves are listed on the second page. At the bottom of each column there is a column total, and row totals are shown in Column Q. Finally, at the foot of Column Q are grand totals of both rows and columns, and these should naturally tally with each other.

Of course, the sheet illustrated in Fig. 10.3 is only intended as a guide for your own use; obviously you would wish to establish your own headings – perhaps many more than are listed in the example – and make room for more cheques as well.

On some computers, expanding the sheet in this way might present a problem, inasmuch as you might quickly run out of computer memory; however, on the PCW8256 there should be no such difficulty, and you should be able to expand the sheet to any reasonable size without trouble.

Formatting details.

The layout of a fairly large spreadsheet is very much a matter of trial and error. Work on paper, and when that is done satisfactorily and you are at the keyboard, remember to save your work to disc regularly. If something looks untidy, don't be afraid to go back and change it.

Column widths on this sheet are all set at the switch-on values, except for Column F; this needs to be made wide enough for whatever Payee or other

```
   ;  A  ::  B  ::  C  ::  D  ::  E  ::              F              ;
1;==================================================================================
2;IMPREST SPREADSHEET              Page 1              J HUGHES NOVEMBER 1985
3;==================================================================================
4;INSTRUCTIONS AT A35 ONWARDS
5;==================================================================================
6;Details of Cheques Paid
7;==================================================================================
8;
9;CHEQUE NUMBER        DATE    AMOUNT   GROUP          Details
10;==================================================================================
11;
12;    1000        8/11/85    150,27      2                   Brit,Telecom
13;    1001        8/11/85    425,60      4            Computer Supplies Ltd
14;    1002        9/11/85     22,50      3                   Smiths Garages
15;    1003        9/11/85    495,40      1                            Pay
16;    1004        9/11/85     32,87      4           James Stationery Shop
17;    1005        9/11/85     65,34      5              Postage Meters Ltd
18;    1006       10/11/85     27,52      3                    British Rail
19;    1007       10/11/85     19,50      4                 Mervin Software
20;    1008       11/11/85     26,76      5                        Datapost
21;    1009
22;    1010
23;    1011
24;    1012
25;    1013
26;    1014
27;    1015
28;    1016
29;    1017
30;    1018
31;
32;     Total of cheques;   1265,76                          Group totals;
33;
34;==================================================================================
35;INSTRUCTIONS     To enter a cheque, put Date in Column C, Amount in Column D,
36;                 Group in Column E and Payee in Column F
37;
38;                 To print page 1, Display A8;F34
39;                 To print page 2, Display G8;Q34
40;
41;                 Force recalculation with !
42;
```

Fig. 10.3 Page 1 of sample imprest spreadsheet.

```
    :  G  ::  H  ::  I  ::  J  ::  K  ::  L  ::  M  ::  N  ::  O  ::  P  ::  Q  :
 1;==============================================================================
 2;IMPREST SPREADSHEET                    Page 2                    NOVEMBER 1985
 3;==============================================================================
 4;
 5;==============================================================================
 6;Details of Payment Groups
 7;==============================================================================
 8;       1            2            3            4            5
 9; SALARIES       TELEPHONE      TRAVEL     MATERIALS     POSTAGE        TOTALS
10;==============================================================================
11;
12;       .00        150.27          .00          .00          .00        150.27
13;       .00           .00          .00        425.60         .00        425.60
14;       .00           .00        22.50          .00          .00         22.50
15;    495.40          .00          .00          .00          .00        495.40
16;       .00           .00          .00        32.87          .00         32.87
17;       .00           .00          .00          .00        65.34         65.34
18;       .00           .00        27.52          .00          .00         27.52
19;       .00           .00          .00        19.50          .00         19.50
20;       .00           .00          .00          .00        26.76         26.76
21;       .00           .00          .00          .00          .00          .00
22;       .00           .00          .00          .00          .00          .00
23;       .00           .00          .00          .00          .00          .00
24;       .00           .00          .00          .00          .00          .00
25;       .00           .00          .00          .00          .00          .00
26;       .00           .00          .00          .00          .00          .00
27;       .00           .00          .00          .00          .00          .00
28;       .00           .00          .00          .00          .00          .00
29;       .00           .00          .00          .00          .00          .00
30;       .00           .00          .00          .00          .00          .00
31;=========    =========    =========    =========    =========    =========
32;    495.40       150.27        50.02        477.97        92.10       1265.76
33;                                                                      1265.76
34;==============================================================================
35;
36;
37;
38;
39;
40;
41;
42;
```

Fig. 10.3 Page 2 of sample imprest spreadsheet.

details you may want to enter against each cheque – about 20 characters should be quite adequate.

It is a good idea when laying out a large sheet to keep an eye on its appearance when printed on paper. The example sheet has been arranged so that it divides into two halves, with the cheque details on one page and the various groups on the other.

Because it will be necessary to divide the sheet up for printing, the various title and other details should be repeated at the top of both 'pages' and page numbers should be included. Instructions and other matters which you do not want printed should be kept out of the way, below the lowest 'working' row of the sheet.

Most of the various text headings will appear neater if they are set at the right of the columns to which they refer. This is done with the / F (Format) command, entering TR to force text to the right-edge side of its cell.

Text entered in this way differs from ordinary text inasmuch as if it is too long to be fitted inside its cell, instead of running on across other cells it appears truncated at the *left-hand* cell boundary.

For this reason, you must make sure that the column headings you enter are no longer than the column widths – nine characters at switch on.

All financial calculations will need to appear in $ Format, with two digits after the decimal point.

Group header numbers on the other hand (in Row 8 at the head of each of Columns G to O) will need to be set to Integer format, as also will the cheque numbers and the group numbers entered in Column E.

When you have laid out the basic format and text content of the spreadsheet in a suitable manner, bearing in mind your own individual requirements, it will be time to start entering the formulae. As always, save a copy of your work so far – you have already done far too much to want to waste it!

We assume that you will use the sheet as follows: a blank template of the sheet, containing only text and formulae, will be kept on disc, and at set intervals – weekly or monthly, or whatever – this blank template will be loaded into the PCW8256.

The first item to be entered will be the number of the first of the period's cheques (into cell A12). Numbers of all the other cheques which might be drawn, as far as the bottom of the sheet, will then be calculated and appear automatically.

To accomplish this, enter the following formula into cell A13:

1 + A 1 2

This is then Replicated down as far as the last row reserved for cheques – A30 on the sample sheet – so that, for example, the formula in cell A18 would read 1 + A 1 7 .

Another formula which can be Replicated easily is used to calculate the column totals. This is first used at the foot of Column D, in cell D32 of the sample sheet, and reads

    SUM(D12:D30)

A similar formula is replicated at the foot of each of Columns G to Q – in Row 32 in every case except Column Q, where it is placed in Row 31.

The same technique can be used in Column Q to calculate the row totals. For example, the formula in cell Q12 reads:

    SUM(G12:O12)

This too can be Replicated to the bottom of the column, including to Cell Q32, where it is used to add up the various column totals previously obtained.

Making choices.

Formulae in the final group are not so easy to Replicate, so work carefully and check yout typing afterwards – this is the most likely place for errors to occur.

What we need SuperCalc2 to do is to check the Group number entered in Column E to see in which group the value of the cheque should be entered.

The formula which we shall need to enter into cell G12 is as follows:

    IF(E12=G8,D12)

This checks the group number typed in and compares it to the numbers in the column headings – i.e. in cells G8, I8, K8 and so on. If there is a match, then the value of the cheques (entered into Column D) will be copied across into the appropriate Group column.

In case that is a little unclear, it may be as well to give another couple of examples. The formula in cell G30 will read IF(E30=G8,D30) and the cell M15 will contain IF(E15=M8,D15).

When all the cells in the Group columns are filled, your imprest spreadsheet should be complete, so save your work again. This version will be the blank sheet which you will need to summon from disc at the beginning of every accounting period, so it will be as well to have a backup copy too.

178

Entering data.

Before you enter any data, there are a couple of points which you will need to watch.

First, much of the information will not be required for calculation at all – it will merely be what computer jargon refers to as **strings**– sets of characters which are not operated upon mathematically.

For example, the date on which a cheque is written might be entered as 12 / 3 / 86. Although this looks quite sensible to us humans, to a computer it looks like 12 divided by 3 divided by 86, as computers treat the slash symbol / as equivalent to ÷.

Items for Columns C and F (Dates and Payee details) will therefore always need to be entered as if they were text – that is preceded by a double quote, ". Everything else can be entered in the usual way.

When you have completed your test entries, double check that the results you have obtained are correct; the easiest way to do this is to input data which you have already processed through your manual system, to check whether there are any differences between the results of both.

Cursor movement.

When entering anything into the spreadsheet, it is worth noting the symbol which appears to the left of the current cell number in the Status Bar. This is either ↑ V→ or ←.

These symbols indicate the direction of the last movement of the cell cursor, and this is also the direction in which that cursor will be moved after the current entry has been made and the ENTER key pressed.

This is done to facilitate making entries which move consistently in the same direction across the spreadsheet; this is actually the way in which our imprest spreadsheet has been laid out.

One last point about the use of the sheet is that there will occasionally be cheques which do not belong in any one particular group. For example, it is possible at a Post Office or Bank to make payments with a single cheque to be applied to several separate accounts, and paid through the Post Office or Bank Giro systems.

The technique for entering these is as follows: enter the cheque total amount as usual in Column D, but leave the group number in Column E blank. Then move the cell cursor over to the appropriate columns and enter the due amounts manually into the appropriate cells.

It is here that the automatic checking of row– and column-totals becomes most useful. Provided that the formulae have been correctly entered when the spreadsheet was set up, discrepancies between the row and column totals are generally impossible. However, if you make an error in dividing a single cheque into its component groups, this will be signalled by an inconsistency between the row and column totals.

A different approach; using The Cracker.

So far our spreadsheet work has all been based on SuperCalc2, and the calculations which we have performed have been of a financial nature.

By way of illustrating the use of a different spreadsheet program, and at the same time showing how spreadsheets can be used for purposes completely different from those already introduced, we shall now take a brief look at The Cracker, a spreadsheet program from Software Technology Ltd., of Birmingham.

Like SuperCalc2, The Cracker operates in the usual spreadsheet manner of arranging data and formulae in columns and rows (although The Cracker calls them columns and lines).

Data can be represented in various formats, depending on the form of the data itself (text or numeric, for example) and the user's requirements.

Text can be right– or left-justified, or used as Headings; in the latter case, it is not confined to the width of the cell in which it originates.

Numbers can be in integer, exponent, decimal and financial formats; the last-named of these shows figures correct to two decimal places, and puts negative numbers in brackets.

Additionally, there is a Plot format, which fills cells with asterisks to the nearest integer value of the stored number.

Figure 10.5 shows a 'snapshot', or printout, of a spreadsheet screen produced by The Cracker; this replaces our more usual screen dump because although The Cracker's screens are perfectly legible and clear to use, they often have large areas of green which do not reproduce well in screen dump form; the snapshot facility is The Cracker's way around this difficulty. Data can additionally be passed on ('exported') to CP/M word processing or other applications programs.

```
A1     SECTION PROPERTIES OF T BEAM
       D17
T1       ABCDEFGIJLMNOPQRSTUVWXZ!+-\/>.('* arrows
       16828
Next:
       Auto.
                        A                    B              C           D

   1( SECTION PROPERTIES OF T BEAM

   2

   3 DATA INPUT SECTION

   4                   Width of top          150

   5                   Depth of top          15

   6                Overall depth            100

   7              Flange thickness           15

   8 WORK AREA

   9            Depth below table            85

  10               Area of table            2250

  11            Area below table             1275

  12 RESULTS

  13             Area of section             3525

  14         Depth of neutral axis           25.59

  15                                         'I'           'R'         'Z'

  16               xx direction        0.2844E+07        28.41       38224

  17               yy direction        0.4243E+07        34.69       56569
```

Fig. 10.5 A 'Snapshot' of a screen from The Cracker.

The top section of the printout represents the Status Bar at the top of The Cracker's screen; in this are listed the title of the sheet (Section Properties of T Beam), the size of the sheet, as shown by the 'rightmost' row and column (DF17), and a list of all the commands which are available from this part of the program (the letters ABCD, etc.)

The Cracker has 'dynamic prompts' – whenever a key is pressed, the Status Bar always changes to show what keypresses can be legitimately made next.

The Cracker is thus a **Command driven program**, rather than a **Menu driven program** ; however, pressing **?** will throw a Help Page onto the screen at any time.

Perhaps of more interest than the mechanics of creating and editing spreadsheets with The Cracker is the nature of the problem displayed in Fig. 10.5.

We must confess to almost no real knowledge of structural engineering, but it should be clear that spreadsheets can be used for a very large number of problems involving calculations and the inter-relationships between different cells; they are thus best considered as very powerful all-purpose mathematical and statistical tools, rather than just as simple financial calculators.

Postscript.

It has not been possible in the course of a single brief chapter to do more than outline a very few of the facilities offered by SuperCalc2 and The Cracker.

Creating templates for sophisticated spreadsheets is actually very close to fully-fledged computer programming, and for this reason you may prefer at first to limit yourself to the templates suggested in this chapter or supplied on the SuperCalc2 program disc.

Whether the spreadsheet program which you finally adopt is SuperCalc2, The Cracker or some other one, there are several points which ought to be carefully noted, and which will bear repetition.

First, be highly suspicious of the results of a newly-programmed spreadsheet, at least until you have had opportunity to check that it is working as it should. You will find quickly enough that programming of all sorts is an error-prone activity!

Second, when preparing a new spreadsheet, do as much as possible of the work on paper before you even load the spreadsheet program into the PCW8256. Even a fairly simple sheet may take several hours to plan and enter correctly, and sitting at the keyboard is emphatically *not* the best place to do it.

Third, save your development work onto disc at regular and frequent intervals, and keep proper backup copies not only of the spreadsheet program itself, but also of the various templates which you devise.

Finally, experiment! Spreadsheets have many uses beyond the obvious, and it will certainly pay you to ask whether a particular job can be done by a spreadsheet before you invest in some other accounting or statistical tool.

CHAPTER ELEVEN

Looking at Databases

Preview. This chapter will deal with the following topics:

What is a database?
Some important concepts.
Files, records and fields.
Key-fields and keys.
Types of database organisation.
Elementary work with Cambase.
Organising the data.
Loop fields.
Validation checks.
Designing the screen display.
Filename and record name.
Conditional fields.
Selection fields.
Entering file specifications.
Testing your work.
Initialising the disc.
Retrieving data.
More advanced processing.
Basics of Process programs.
Narratives.
Running Processes.
Using the imagination.
Databases large and small.

What is a database?

At its simplest, a **database** is no more than a collection of related information so ordered that it can easily be found when needed.

In this sense, databases are not necessarily limited to computers. A database which is familiar to everyone is a telephone directory. Like other databases, it contains information arranged according to a set of predetermined rules – in this case, alphabetical order of the subscribers' names.

Information can be found – **retrieved** is the usual computer term – by **searching** through the database. How easy it will be to carry out a search will depend on what you want to know and on how the database is organised.

For example, the only way in which it is usually practical to search for information in an ordinary telephone directory is by looking under the name of the subscriber.

Although there are many different sorts of information in a telephone directory, the design of the directory makes it very hard to extract some of it. Imagine how awkward it would be to have to search through the entire book looking for all the plumbers, or to find the name of the subscriber who has a particular telephone number!

To get around this problem, other directories are available which carry essentially the same information, but which arrange it differently – Yellow Pages, for example, or trade directories.

The examples which we have given so far have been of fairly large databases. In the same way, many computer databases are extremely large and sophisticated; an example of just how big they may grow is the giant BLAISE database run by the British Library which makes available bibliographical details of many of the holdings not only of the British Library but the U.S. Library of Congress as well.

However, the vast majority of databases are quite small; they may include lists of customers or club or church members; catalogues of books, records or slides; menus; items to be insured; and indeed almost anything else that will benefit from being organised in a logical way.

Furthermore, information stored in computer databases, unlike that in telephone directories or address books, can be manipulated in a variety of ways, and output according to a variety of different formats.

For example, a collector of antiques might wish to keep a database file listing the items in the collection together with such relevant details as the amount for which each item was insured.

He would then not only have a listing of all his collection, but one which could easily be updated both to accommodate new purchases and to remove items sold out. In addition, the entire list, or any part of it, could be printed out for insurance purposes, and the values of the individual items automatically adjusted to take account of any increase.

Some important concepts.

At this point, it will be useful to glance at some of the concepts associated with databases. None of them are difficult, but a grasp of them will be invaluable in understanding how a database works.

Files.

A collection of related items of the sort handled by a database is called a **file**. In this sense a computer file is very similar to an ordinary physical file of the sort which belongs in an office filing cabinet, with various items of related information contained in it.

The fact that all the information in any file is inter-related is an important one. For instance, a telephone directory is a file containing details of everyone who has a telephone (and who does not have an ex-directory number).

Other files might contain a list of all your customers, or a bibliography of books on goldfish, or whatever. But obviously a file which contained the names of some telephone subscribers together with details of books on goldfish and the addresses of a few of your customers would be pretty useless!

Records.

Inside a physical file-box there will usually be a number of separate **records**. In a file containing customer details, there would typically be one record per customer; a catalogue of paintings would normally allocate one record per painting, and so on.

Every one of these records would look pretty much like every other record, in the sense that they would all hold the same *kind* of information. For instance, a typical customer record might contain a name, an address, a list of purchases made, a credit limit and other similar information.

In the same way, records in a bibliographical file might contain details of particular books, one book per record, listing such details as author, title, publisher, date and place of publication and price.

Fields.

Just as a file is made up of a number of records, so each record is made up of one or more fields. A typical field would be a person's name, or his address, or his telephone number; in a different context, it might be an author's name, or a price, or a date.

When using a database, you almost always want to find out the details of individual records, and you look for them by searching for a particular field.

Using the telephone directory as an example, the search for an individual telephone number would go something like this: first, choose the correct telephone directory (the right file); next, find the correct record (by looking up the name field, which is how the records are organised); finally from within the correct record find the field which shows the telephone number.

Key-fields and keys.

An important aid to the accurate and rapid retrieval of information is to make sure that at least one field of each record is different from the same field of every other record. This field is called the **key field**.

Typical key-fields might contain membership or account numbers, or car registration numbers. The item which is contained in a key-field is called the **key** to that record.

It is often convenient to have more than one key per record – called primary and secondary keys – in order that a series of records can be searched according to more than one key.

Different database programs organise this in a variety of different ways, but generally it is possible to organise searches under either one field or several, depending on what information is required.

For example, a businessman might want to abstract from his records the names of all his customers who had not bought anything from him over the last six months, and who were in the retail stationery business. This would involve searching under two fields, one containing the dates of their purchases and one stating what business they were involved in.

Or he might want to retrieve from a bibliographical database a list of all the books on computing printed in Britain over the last ten years and written by someone called Jackson; this would involve a search on four fields – subject, author, place of publication and date.

Types of database organisation.

How easy a database is to use will depend very much on how it has been set up; therefore before you actually begin to type in any information at all, you will need to have a pretty clear idea of ways in which you (or others) are likely to want to take the information out again.

We have already suggested that one database program may well not work in quite the same way as another. This is partly because certain ways of organising a database are more suited to some types of information than others.

Some types of information, for example, tend to fall fairly naturally into 'family tree' relationships, with some items 'below' other items; in other cases no such obvious relationships exist. Naturally, different programs may expect data to follow different forms.

Another reason why database programs may work differently is that computerised databases are still so relatively new that techniques for handling them are still being developed; there is also the by now familiar choice between sophistication and user friendliness to be considered.

Despite this, there are certain general principles which apply to all databases. In this chapter we shall first be taking as an example a program called Cambase, which is a moderately sophisticated database program produced by Cambrian Software of Blaenau Ffestiniog.

Even if the program which you are using is superficially quite different from Cambase, you should find that underneath the surface differences, there will be many similarities at least in the ways in which data is stored and retrieved.

Elementary work with Cambase.

The fundamental purpose of a database is to hold organised information so that it can be easily recovered, either in whole or in part. Thus far, it can be thought of as no more than a highly-sophisticated address-book or customer accounts file.

The worked example which follows will take us through the creation of a simple name and address file of the sort which might be used for anything from the membership of a society or a church to a company mailing list.

Organising the data. As always, begin by planning your work on a sheet of paper. On it, make a list of the information fields that you expect you will have, and any additional information about those fields which may be helpful.

Cambase requires each field to be placed into one of four groups: Character, Numeric, Date and Yes/No.

Character fields are those upon which no arithmetical operations can be performed – what are often referred to in computing as **strings**. They might include names, addresses, telephone numbers and the like. Cambase character fields can be up to 60 characters in length.

Numeric fields are made up of numbers only, and all mathematical operations can be performed on them. Cambase represents numbers up to four decimal places.

Date fields have to be input in one standard format, i.e. **DD MMM YY**; this is the usual Camsoft format. For example, January 1st., 1987 would be shown as **Ø1 JAN 87**, and December 31st 1986 would appear as **31 DEC 86**. Date fields are automatically checked to see whether they represent possible dates (no February 29th, unless it is a leap year!).

Date fields are used for such purposes as working out interest payments, life-span, etc. This is done by working out the number of elapsed days since January 1st 1900.

Yes/No fields are for questions which have a Yes or No answer, such as 'Married?' or 'Retired?' The advantage of using them is that they need less storage space on the disc than would be the case if you typed in the whole word each time.

When you have some idea of the various fields that you will require for the information you will be inputting, check how long each character field will need to be.

Cambase works with 'fixed length fields,' so this is an important choice; if you decide to make the fields longer than they need to be, you will waste a lot of disc storage space; if you don't make them long enough, sooner or later you will find that someone's name or address won't fit into the allotted space.

Loop fields.

In the list of fields which you have drawn up, there will very possibly be some which will need to appear more than once. For example, although it would be possible to think of an address as consisting of one long field containing house number, street, post-town, county and post-code, it makes much more sense to treat it as a set of five address lines – it is easier to print it on labels that way, too.

Cambase allows you to stipulate such fields as **loop fields**; we shall see more of how they work in due course.

Validation checks. Probably everyone has heard stories, usually apocryphal, of people receiving electricity bills for £1,000,000.00 or some equally unlikely figure. Such errors (which, when they *do* occur are almost always due to an operator's slip rather than a real computer mistake) still occasionally happen; to make sure that they don't originate with you, you can prevent most of them with **data validation**.

This simply means checking data as it is input to see whether it makes sense. Obviously not all information can be checked in this way – personal names are a glaring example of something which it is almost impossible to validate, which is perhaps why they are so often mis-spelt – but incomes, dates, ages, and a few other items are easily checked.

We have already seen one validation procedure at work in the Cambase program, namely the check that the date which you have entered is not an impossible one. You can impose similar checks on the various items of information which will be input into the database you are creating.

In doing so you will need to be careful that you do not accidentally make real data illegal; it is not impossible for a person's age to be greater than 100, for example, although it cannot be less than 0. Look back through the fields you have already listed to see what validation checks might prove useful.

An additional point to consider is that what makes sense in data validation routines today may not always hold true in the future. For instance, you might decide that any credit limit must be set at less than £1,000.00, and build this figure into the database in such a way as to reject any higher value.

Although this may look very sensible now, you may find some considerable difficulty in altering the figure when an unforeseen change in your policy or a burst of inflation makes it necessary to raise the limit. Validation is meant to help you check your inputs, not to lock you into a straightjacket, so take care with the values you choose.

Designing the screen display.

An important point that needs to be considered in creating a database file is the way in which it will appear when it is output both to the screen and the printer.

Cambase allows the user to specify exactly where on the screen each field will be placed; when the data is output on the printer, the relative positions will be the same.

Where fields will appear is entirely up to you (provided that there is actually room on the screen for your wishes to be carried out), and you can stipulate any order in which you would like the items to be printed – you can place a name below the address or above it, just as you wish.

If you wish, you can even place more than one field in the same place, so that one overprints the other. The more complex the results which you want to achieve, the more important it is to experiment to see what is possible and what is not.

Filename and record name.

For the simple file which we are creating, only the name of the file and the name of the records still remain to be chosen.

The **filename** can be any combination of letters and numbers which you choose, up to a maximum of 16 characters. As with giving names to LocoScript files, it is good policy to choose names which will have some meaning to yourself and to others working with the system.

Conditional fields. Cambase allows the inclusion of certain fields to be conditional on the contents of other fields. This is because not all items of information are applicable to all records.

For example, a list of customers might include the previous address of those who had lived less than, say, three years at their present address. Thus whether or not information is sought about a previous address is *conditional* upon the length of residence at the current address.

Again, an organisation might provide a cheap admission season ticket to the unwaged, but charge everyone else at the door; a field would be needed to hold the serial number of a person's ticket, but whether or not this would be active in any given record would depend on a previous question about whether a person was at work or not.

Cambase can easily be set up to handle this and similar situations; the only requirement is that the conditional field must come *after* the field which establishes the condition.

Selection fields. When you are searching for certain records from within a file, not all fields will be of equal interest to you. For example, you might decide that you will never need to find all the people whose first name is *Jennifer*, or all the people living in a particular street or town.

With Cambase you must choose while drawing up the file specifications which fields you will need to search on later. Be careful in your choices here, as you may find too late that some particular field would have been useful for searching if you had only thought of it sooner.

Entering the file specifications.

So far we have not used the Cambase program at all; everything has been done on paper.

When you are satisfied that you know what information you want to store in your database, how you want it organised, and how you want it to appear on the screen, you will be ready to begin entering those details into the PCW8256.

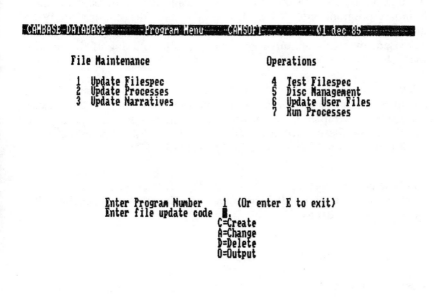

Fig. 11.1 The Cambase Main Menu

Loan and run the Cambase program by typing:

CAMBASE

when the CP/M **A >** prompt is showing. You will be asked to enter the date, using the **D D MMM Y Y** format mentioned earlier, and then the main menu, which is shown in Fig. 11.1, will be displayed.

From this menu choose Option 1, Update Filespec. You will next be asked whether you intend to Create, Change, Delete or Output the file. Choose C (to Create) and confirm this by pressing ENTER in response to the question Continue?(Y/N).

Like many other long programs, Cambase actually consists of several different programs which are loaded from disc as they are needed, and this causes some slight delays.

It would be possible to save this time by using PIP to transfer the entire Cambase program onto Drive M, except that on the standard PCW8256 there is insufficient space on Drive M to hold everything. If the memory is increased, then this option should speed up the running of the program somewhat.

When the appropriate overlay program is ready, you will be asked for a file specification number. These are analagous to LocoScript templates, except that Cambase templates are known by numbers rather than by name, and each Cambase filespec will hold only one data file, rather than the several which can be created by a LocoScript TEMPLATE.STD.

Cambase can support up to 9 different file specifications on one disc, and each one will control one database file. Enter the number 1, as this will be the first one to be Created.

You will then be offered the choice:

Copy from or RET?

This is because Cambase tries to save you the effort of setting up a new file by checking whether there is another one which it can use as a starting point. This too is similar to the way in which LocoScript offers an old template when you are designing a new one.

A similar offer is made at other times in Cambase, such as when you are setting up Processes for manipulating the data in your database files. In order to make the best use of the facility, it may be a good idea to keep a printout of each one of your filespecs and Processes for easy reference when creating new ones.

At the moment there are no old filespecs available, so press ENTER (or RETURN) to begin inputting the details of how your database file is to be organised.

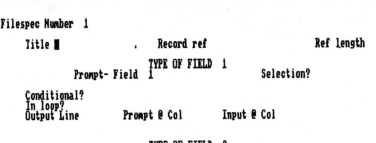

Filespec Number 1

    Title ■   .   Record ref   Ref length

                             TYPE OF FIELD 1
              Prompt- Field 1   Selection?

Conditional?
In loop?
Output Line   Prompt @ Col   Input @ Col

                             TYPE OF FIELD 2
              Prompt- Field 2   Selection?

Conditional?
In loop?
Output Line   Prompt @ Col   Input @ Col

                                          Drive is A:

Fig. 11.2 Creating Cambase File Specifications

The screen will now appear as in Fig. 11.2. Enter the Title (C u s t o m e r F i L e) , the Record Reference (A c c o u n t N u m b e r) , (i.e. the name of the Key-field) and the maximum length of any Reference (Key) – we will assume that all account numbers are 5 characters or less in length, so enter 5.

Only fairly primitive means of editing your entries are available; you can use the ←-DEL key to return to a mis-typed character as long as you have not pressed ENTER, but the cursor keys → and ← have no effect. Correcting errors once you have pressed ENTER is a little awkward, so be sure to check your work carefully as you go along.

However, if things go seriously awry you can simply hurry along to the end (by entering E where it is appropriate, and whatever other key will get you through quickly in other places) and then pressing N when asked whether you want to C o n t i n u e ? (Y / N) . This will have the effect of abandoning the creation of the new file specification and you will be able to start again from the beginning.

The remaining prompts can be grouped into three categories: they ask for information about the contents of each field (whether it is a number, a date, etc.); about what prompt should appear to remind the user what should be entered; and about where on the screen (as well as eventually on the printed page) the information should appear.

In our example, Field 1 will hold a customers's surname; this is a character field, so enter C against Type of Field. The appropriate prompt which we want to have displayed on screen when this field is to be input will be Surname, so enter this against Prompt-Field 1.

We shall not be using surnames as a basis for selecting records, so answer N to Selection.

Two new questions will now appear on the screen. The first of these is Character Count, and the information which it requires is the length of the longest item that the field will be required to hold. Enter 20, as all our customers' surnames should fit within that length.

The second question is Code Entry. This is used for those cases where character inputs are not to be read as words but as codes – M for Male, F for Female, C for child and the like. Names obviously do not fall into this category, so answer N.

A Y answer to this question means that Cambase will ask for up to 6 characters which would then be accepted as valid entries for this field: This is an important and useful way of checking the validity of coded data, and it should be used whenever appropriate.

Answer N also to the questions Conditional? and In Loop? – we shall see the purpose of both of these options shortly.

The final questions refer to the way in which the entries will appear on the screen when we are inputting or displaying data.

The Cambase screen is set at a width of 80 columns and a height of 18 lines. Any line number greater than 18 will clear the screen and force the next field onto a new screen 'page;' line 19 would thus be at the top of the second 'page,' line 37 at the top of the third and so on. The highest permissible line number is 120.

We can space the various fields out so that related items will appear close to one another; Field 1 (Surname) will be placed on Line 5, Field 2 (Forename(s)) on Line 6, then there will be a gap before the address starts on Line 8.

As we do not want the prompts and the inputs to be right 'on top' of one another, we will start all the prompts in Column 10 and all the inputs in Column 25.

The third field (Address) will be a little different from the first two, as it will be in a Loop. The purpose of this is to enable the same prompt to appear several times without needing to enter the various parameters such as field type, number of characters, etc., repeatedly for each one.

Proceed as for the first two fields (allowing a maximum length of 20 characters for each address line) until you reach the question In Loop? Answer this with Y.

You will then be asked at which field the loop is to begin, and then at which field it is to end. The answer to both of these questions is 3; in other words, you want Field 3 repeated a certain number of times, but no other field to be repeated with it.

This is one of those things which is easier to do than to explain; if it is unclear, try out different field numbers and watch the results, and all should be made plain.

How many times you want the loop to be repeated depends on how many lines of address you will need to input; we assume that the answer is 5.

The question Loops in Prompt? will now appear; if you answer Y to this, then each line of the prompt will be marked with an appropriate loop number – 1 for the first line, 2 for the second and so on.

This can be a useful facility, but as the loop number appears offset to the right of the prompts, it would necessitate moving the input from Column 25 to perhaps Column 30, which might spoil the appearance of the screen; so answer N.

Incidentally, if you do try to arrange the screen in an 'impossible' way, like putting an input on top of a prompt, Cambase will always warn you that an error has occurred. The first line of the address output should be 8, so enter this opposite Output Line; once again the prompt should be at Column 10 and the input at Column 25.

When you are using loop fields, an additional prompt appears here – Loop Adjust. This facility enables the successive lines of a loop to appear spread evenly across the screen in different locations.

We want the various lines of the address to appear immediately underneath one another, so enter 80; this means that each new loop field is entered 80 characters to the right of the previous one – i.e. one complete line, as there are 80 characters per line on the Cambase screen.

Field 4 will be a Y/N field, to determine whether a customer is a householder or not. This is the simplest of the fields to enter. Press Y to define the Type of Field, Y for Selection (as we shall use this as one of the ways we can select individual customers), and N to all the other questions.

The Output Line will be 14 (Address started at Line 8 and occupied a total of five lines, up to and including Line 12), and the Prompt and Input Columns will again be set at 10 and 25 respectively.

The last field will hold the customer's Credit Limit. This is a number, so enter a field type of N. We shall be using the Credit Limit as a way of sorting customers, so again answer Y to the question Selection?

Just as certain questions are only asked of Character field types – the number of characters, for example – so others are only asked if the field type is Numeric. The first of these is to ascertain how many decimal places will be required; answer 2

Because of the importance of avoiding errors with numeric data, Cambase then asks for Maximum and Minimum values for this field. This needs particular care because *you must include in your answer the numbers which would normally appear after the decimal point, though not the point itself.*

For example, to enter the value of 200 for a field with two decimal places, you should actually enter 20000 – the last two numbers are those which go to the right of the decimal point.

A further option available with numeric fields is that they can be entered as Zero Delete. A Y in this field means that a record cannot be deleted unless this field is set to zero. The object of this to stop stock records, for example, from being deleted before the number of items has been reduced to zero. When using this option, take great care to ensure that there is no conflict between this and the permissible values of the field as previously set by the Maximum and Minimum values; a mistake here might easily mean that a record could never be deleted.

We shall not be using the Zero Delete option, so answer N.

Since one of the features of our imaginary customer list is that credit is only extended to householders, we can make this field a Conditional one by answering Y to the question Conditional?

Cambase will then ask upon which field the condition depends; answer 4, the number of the previous field, which defines whether a customer is a householder.

To be precise, the condition is satisfied if Field 4 is answered with Yes. Consequently you will need to answer Y to the question Being? and Y again to the further question True?

This means that if it is True that Field 4 has been answered with a Y, then the condition will be fulfilled and the prompt Credit Limit will appear; if it is not True (i.e. it is False) that Field 4 was answered with Y, then the condition will not have been fulfilled and no Credit Limit prompt will appear.

Once again, this field is not in a loop; and like every other field, the prompt should appear in Column 10 and the input in Column 25.

When you have gone this far, you will have entered quite enough information to get the hang of how Cambase file specifications work. If everything is satisfactory, you should leave this part of the program by entering E to Exit; the file specification which we have been working on will then be Created on the disc.

Alternatively, if things have not gone well and you want to abandon everything that you have done so far, type N in answer to the question Continue? (Y/N) and everything will be wiped out. Be careful about this, as if you answer N in error, there will be no way of retrieving your lost work.

Testing your work.

When you think that the file specifications have been entered satisfactorily, it is well worth taking the time and trouble to check whether they do indeed work as you expect them to.

This is particularly important with Cambase as once you have started to input real data into the various records, it is not possible to go back and alter the file specification you have prepared without losing the data as well.

To proceed, choose Option 4, Test Filespec, from the main menu. As before, you will be asked which filespec you wish to check, so answer 1, and the name Customer File will be shown in confirmation.

A test file will then be initialised on the disc. During this process, any 'grammatical' errors which you may have made in setting up the file specification (such as making a field outside a loop conditional on a field inside a loop) will be detected, and a suitable error message displayed.

If you have followed the pattern suggested above, the initialisation should proceed without difficulty. Once the test file has been created on the disc, you will be able to create test records to fit into it.

These test records will not be kept when you carry out a full-scale initialisation of the file specification; they are merely used as dummy data to check that everything is working properly, so it makes sense to choose data which will thoroughly test the filespec which you have created.

Once the test file has been initialised, you will be asked whether you want to Exit to the main menu, Create, Change, Delete or Output a record or Reorganise the Index.

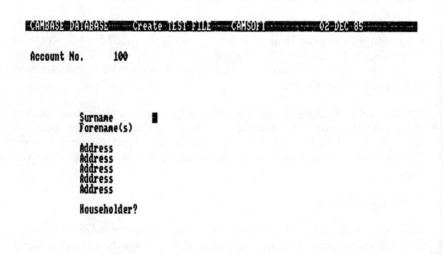

Fig. 11.3 Entering data in a test file.

The only option which is initially open is to Create a record, so select this by pressing C. You will be asked for an Account Number (that being

198

the key-field we had chosen earlier). When a suitable key has been entered, the screen will clear and show the display reproduced in Fig. 11.3.

You will notice that all the prompts which had been placed in the file specification have appeared on the screen exactly as we had specified, with the exception of Credit Limit; this was a Conditional field, and the prompt will only be displayed if the prompt Householder? is answered Y.

If you look closely you will notice that on the current line – the one with the cursor on it – the maximum permissible input length (which we had previously defined as a part of the filespec) is marked with a dot.

When each record has been completed, the familiar Continue?(Y/N) prompt will appear; press ENTER to confirm the record or N + ENTER to reject it and start it again.

Work through the process of inputting enough names and details for three or four records, checking that everything works properly. Then leave this part of the program by entering E at the start of the next record.

Initialising the disc.

One of the most pressing problems for the users of database programs concerns the amount of disc space which will be allocated to their files.

Put simply, as the only practical limit to the length of a database file is the total physical capacity of the disc on which it is stored, such files tend to grow, like Topsy, until further expansion is rudely stopped by lack of disc space.

Some database programs passively accept this state of affairs; indeed, under certain circumstances this rather crude approach can be quite adequate. If all your files are relatively small ones, and you are tolerably careful with your disc housekeeping, you may not encounter any difficulties with it at all.

Cambase however provides a rather more sophisticated approach to the situation. When you are quite happy that your file specification is working properly, select Option 5 (Disc Management) from the main menu and then pick the Initialise File option from the sub-menu which will appear.

What this does is to check how much free space is available on the disc, and work out how many records created according to the File Specification you have developed can be stored.

If more than one disc drive is active in the system, then you will be prompted for the drive on which the file initialisation should take place; otherwise, the file will be initialised on the same disc as the program (in Drive A).

When this has been done, the amount of free space available on the disc is reported, together with an assessment of how many records created according to your filespec can be accommodated on the disc.

```
CAMBASE DATABASE     Initialise file     CAMSOFT          02 DEC 85


              Filespec Number  1  Customer File

              The initialisation process will reserve space
              for a specific number of records for this file

                     Enter drive code for file A

              Available for new file is    63488 bytes

              Maximum number of records is   363

         Enter number of records required ▮    .(or zero to exit)




                                                   Drive is A:
```

Fig. 11.4 Initialising a file on disc.

Figure 11.4 illustrates the sort of report which Cambase will provide at this point. You can see that up to 363 such records could be stored on the disc in question. If this were done, all the free space on the disc would be reserved for the file; if some lesser number of records were chosen, then some free space would be left unreserved on the disc, and thus be available for other purposes.

The advantage of this technique is that the user can choose exactly how much room a file may need, and make sure that that space is not trespassed on by something else.

There are two disadvantages also. The first, and less serious one, is that at first users may under– or overestimate how much room should be allotted to a particular file, leading to either frustration later on (when the file needs to grow beyond the space reserved, but can't), or to disc space being unnecessarily wasted. Obviously the former of these is the greater nuisance, so be guided accordingly and reserve plenty of room for your files.

The second disadvantage is that reserving a fixed amount of space means that no room is left for backup files, although these are probably more important for databases than for many other applications. Always make sure therefore that you make a complete backup of your database files whenever you have made any modifications, however slight.

Returning to the process of disc initialisation, when you have picked a suitable number of records for your purposes and input it, the disc drive activity light will come on and the required amount of space will be reserved automatically.

Since we are still experimenting with the system at the moment, 20 or so records should be sufficient but for a 'real' system, you might well wish to reserve sufficient space for up to several hundred records.

Initialising the disc will obliterate the trial entries that have already been made on it. The file will then be ready to store the information which you need, and in the sections which follow we shall assume that this has been done.

Retrieving data.

The simplest way in which information stored in a Cambase file can be retrieved or altered is with main menu Option 6, Update User Files. Retrieved records can be directed either to the Screen (D, for Display), or to the printer.

Output to the printer is broadly similar to output to the screen, except that headings are printed Double Width and that lines left blank on the screen are omitted from the printout, in order to avoid wasting paper.

All Cambase printer output assumes the use of continuous form stationery with pages 11" in length, though this can be altered with the CP/M PAPER utility described earlier

Retrieving records almost always implies a certain amount of selection, although you can choose to output all the records if you so wish. The screen which controls this operation is shown in Fig. 11.5.

The first choice to be made is the range of records to be checked; either enter the record reference (key) of the first and last records you wish to output, or select the absolute first and last in the file by responding to both questions with the ENTER key.

```
CAMBASE DATABASE    Output USER-FILE 1 CAMSOFT          02 DEC 85

              Display(D) or Print(P)? D
First Account No.      100
 Last Account No.      105
Selection?(Y/N)  Y

Householder?      Y
Credit Limit       250.00                        Code ■.




RETURN for =, G for Greater or =, L for Less or =, R for Range from/to


                                                           Drive is A:
```

Fig. 11.5 Selecting records for retrieval.

The first and last records are not those that had been entered first and last, of course, but those whose keys are first and last in alphabetical or numeric sequence.

For example, if your records are organised by membership or account numbers ranging from say 100 to 250 and you subsequently create a record numbered 1, that record will be regarded as the first, although it was the last to be entered.

Because Cambase has to check the key field before outputting any of the records, it is helpful to make sure that the index has been properly `Reorganised` (input `R` at the Update User File screen) whenever any modification has been made to the file.

The `Selection?` prompt allows you to manipulate the output according to the Selection fields you defined when drawing up the file specification. In Fig. 11.5 you will see that this question has been answered `Y`, and that consequently the prompts for the two Selection fields have been offered.

Inputting a number causes Cambase to display an additional prompt, which can be seen at the bottom of Fig. 11.5; this asks whether you wish to select records with numbers which are equal to the number you have input, less or greater than it, or in a range starting or finishing at that number.

Date fields are selected in the same way, except that here a date which is 'greater' than another date is one which is more recent – i.e. one which has the greater number of elapsed days since January 1st 1900.

Finally you will be asked if the selected records are to be sorted, and if so on which field; if you accept a sort, then they will be sorted in ascending order of the chosen field.

This is straightforward enough with numeric fields; Yes/No fields are sorted with all the Noes first, date fields are sorted from the earliest to the most modern and character fields are sorted in alphabetical order.

There will then be a brief delay while the required information is retrieved from the disc. This only takes a few seconds; the precise time will depend on several factors, the most significant of which is the size and complexity of the file, both in terms of the number of records and the number of fields in each record.

When the information has been retrieved, the appropriate records will be displayed on the screen or the printer in the order and format you have chosen.

More advanced processing.

For most purposes, the sort of scanning through the file that we have carried out will be entirely adequate; with it you will be able to keep records, sort them, update them, delete them, and retrieve details of any or all of them whenever you wish.

All database programs can carry out this sort of work, and if you have some other program instead of Cambase you will still be able to perform much the same tasks, although the way in which files are set up may be a little different – in this regard, the less sophisticated programs are often a little easier to get started with, as they offer fewer options to choose between.

More sophisticated programs, however are able to carry out various forms of data processing as well as simple data retrieval.

With Cambase, all data manipulation (except simple record selection and sorting) is carried out by special **Processes**; these are, in effect, programs written and entered by the user.

Using these Processes, new data can be entered at the keyboard, existing entries can be altered according to user-developed formulae, items can be totalled and results can be output in a more flexible format than is otherwise possible.

Although Processes are not difficult either to enter or to understand, it is possible to make very destructive mistakes with them unless great care is taken to see that they work as they were intended to.

For this reason, it is best to begin with a few very simple experiments, preferably not on real data, and only to make real use of the facility when you are certain that everything is working as it should.

Unfortunately each Process is tailored to one particular filespec, so it is not practical to use a file of dummy data to test that a Process is working. However, if you include some dummy data in each of your real files, you can test your new Processes on that.

To give some idea of how simple Processes can be created and run, we shall develop one to make some straightforward alterations to the Customer File which we have already created; specifically, we shall want to increase all Credit Limits by a percentage which we shall enter at the keyboard when the process is run.

As a first step in preparing *any* Process, make a print-out of the actual data file which the Process will work on; the new Process will be tailored to match this, and a print-out will help you to avoid mistakes.

Next, make sure that you have a full back-up of the database file on another disc. We have already seen that Cambase does not support the automatic creation of backup files, and if a process goes wrong, all your data could be corrupted. **A backup is an essential safeguard against this possibility**.

When you have done all this, spend some time with a sheet of paper working out the details of the Process you are creating; it is even more important to do this with Processes than with File Specifications, because there is no option enabling you to test a Process before using it in the same way as you can test a filespec.

Creating new Processes is not very different from creating new file specifications. It is done by choosing `Option 2 (Update Processes)` from the main menu, and entering a number by which the Process will be known.

Up to 30 Processes may be created on one disc, but each one can only be applied to one filespec, though one filespec can be accessed by any number of Processes up to the maximum allowed.

When you have entered a name for the Process and the number of the filespec on which it will work, you will be able to start entering the actual Process 'program.'

The basics of Process programs.

Processes can be divided into four main components: Variables, Inputs, Derived Items and Outputs.

Variables are used to hold items of data while a Process is being run. Like Fields, they are divided into Character, Date, Yes/No and Numeric types.

Unlike Fields, however, the contents or values of Variables will be forgotten after the Process has been run, although the values of Variables – the data they hold – can be output as a part of the Process if you wish.

```
CAMBASE DATABASE    Create Processes    CAMSOFT         05 DEC 85   Page 1

Process Number   1

      Process Title Amend Credit Limit     Filespec Number 1

      Variable Type  1 N      Title Incr. Factor                    Dec Pls  2
      Variable Type  2 C      Title Full Names            Chars 40
      Variable Type  3 EN     Title
      Variable Type  4        Title
      Variable Type  5        Title
      Variable Type  6        Title
      Variable Type  7        Title
      Variable Type  8        Title
      Variable Type  9        Title
      Variable Type 10        Title
      Variable Type 11        Title
      Variable Type 12        Title
      Variable Type 13        Title
      Variable Type 14        Title
      Variable Type 15        Title




                                                          Drive is A:
```

Fig. 11.6 Entering Process Variables

Figure 11.6 shows the screen which is used to define the variables – a Process can include up to 15 different variables.

As with the Field definitions in the File Specifications section of Cambase, various additional questions are asked depending on whether a Variable has been defined as Numeric, Date, Character, etc.

To illustrate their workings, Variable 1 has here been defined as a Numeric field with two decimal places, and marked 'Incr. Factor.' We shall be using this when the Process is run to hold the figure by which present credit limits are to be multiplied in order to find the new limits.

Similarly we shall be using Variable 2 as a Character Variable to store the combined Forename(s) and Surnames of the customers – information which is held in Fields 1 and 2 of each individual Record, but which we shall join together into one item for convenience in printing the records.

The actual mechanics of these operations will be introduced later; for the moment, we are merely informing Cambase that we shall be using two Variables.

When you have defined as many Variables as you will need, move on to the next section by typing **E**. (All the screens in the Update Processes section are left in the same way.)

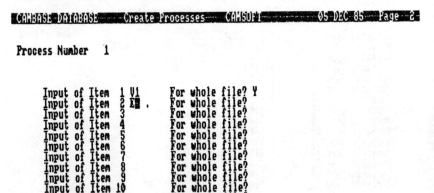

Process Number   1

Input of Item 1 V1   For whole file? Y
Input of Item 2 E2 .   For whole file?
Input of Item 3   For whole file?
Input of Item 4   For whole file?
Input of Item 5   For whole file?
Input of Item 6   For whole file?
Input of Item 7   For whole file?
Input of Item 8   For whole file?
Input of Item 9   For whole file?
Input of Item 10   For whole file?
Input of Item 11   For whole file?
Input of Item 12   For whole file?
Input of Item 13   For whole file?
Input of Item 14   For whole file?
Input of Item 15   For whole file?

Fig. 11.7 Inputting Process Items.

Input items are those which you will enter at the keyboard when the Process is running. For example, if you wished to change the details of whether a person was a householder or not in Field 4 then you would enter F 4 against Input of Item 1 – see Fig. 11.7.

The option For Whole File? allows a numeric value (or date, or Y/N choice, or set of characters, depending on the Field type) to be input, which will then be automatically placed in the named Field (or Variable) for every record.

For example, if we wanted to set every customer's credit limit to, say £200.0, we would only have to enter F 5 (which was the appropriate field in our sample file) against Input of Item 1 and Y against For Whole File?, and then type in 200.00 when prompted to do so during a run of the Process, and that value would be applied to every Record.

Alternatively, if we had answered N to IFor Whole File, we would be asked to input a new value to Field 5 for every record.

In our example, we shall be using Input of Item facility to enter the actual figure by which credit limits are to be altered; this value will then be stored as Variable 1. To do this, enter V 1 as the first Input of Item, and declare that it will be used for the whole file.

Derived Items are those which are created or modified by a Process while it is being run. Using these, new values can be assigned to any fields or variables. They are thus at the very heart of Process operations.

In our example we shall increase existing Credit Limits (Field 5) by multiplying each one by Variable 1 – i.e. the value input while the Process is running. Thus to increase all Credit Limits by 10%, we would input the value 1.1.

The new F5 for each record is then set equal to the old F5 multiplied by V1.

The four standard arithmetic operations can be used on Numeric Fields, as long as the formula which is used is not longer than 20 characters; the symbols used are the usual computing ones, $+, -, *$ (multiply) and $/$ (divide), but $\uparrow$ (raising to a power) is not available.

One oddity of Cambase is that the arithmetic operations are all performed from left to right; no attempt is made to carry out operations in the usual order of priority according to which multiplication and division are performed first and addition and subtraction afterwards. Nor can brackets be used to alter the order in which operations are performed.

Character fields can be set equal to other character fields; they can also be **concatenated** , or 'added' to one another, using + (but not **sliced** or subtracted).

For example, if in a particular filespec both Field 1 and Field 5 were Character Fields, and Field 1 contained "Good" and Field 5 contained "Morning", then setting F1 equal to F1+F5 would make it equal to "Good Morning" –the space between words will be supplied automatically.

We shall use this facility to join together the forenames and surnames of our customers into one field, by setting V2 equal to F2+F1. This will have no effect on the information in the actual fields themselves, but will make it easier to produce the final printout.

Process Outputs provides ways in which database file contents can be manipulated in a much more sophisticated way than is possible with the ordinary output option we used earlier.

The most useful option in this section – one indeed which you may well find useful even if you do not use the Cambase Processes for anything else – is Label Print.

This allows for printing addresses (or anything else, come to that) on continuous label stationery of any width. There is a series of prompts to enable the user to adjust the match output of the program to the size and format of the labels used.

Cambase also checks whether you want to P r i n t A s U p d a t e – in other words, whether the results of the Process should be printed or not. *Always answer* Y e s *to this question,* as this represents the only practical way of ensuring that the Process has worked as you wanted it to. In this way, if anything has gone wrong you will be made aware of the fact before any real harm has occurred, giving you an opportunity to restore your files from your previously prepared backups. Particularly when new, it is unwise to take the accuracy of your Processes for granted.

An American defence scientist was recently quoted as observing that the most complex program he had ever seen which had worked perfectly the first time was just five lines long. Moral – there is no shame in keeping a weather eye open for problems with your Processes!

Other options, shown in Fig. 11.8, allow for complete control of which Fields and Variables you want to have printed and where they should appear. There is no need for fields to be output in their normal numeric sequence, and the titles of the various fields will be omitted if no Column number is assigned to them.

Process Number   1

Label Print?   N
Print as update? Y   Print Controls   Print new page? N

```
Output Item   1  V2    Line  1    Title @ col  0    Data @ col 10
Output Item   2  F3    Line  2    Title @ col  0    Data @ col 10
Output Item   3  F4    Line  7    Title @ col  0    Data @ col 10
Output Item   4  F5    Line  8    Title @ col  0    Data @ col 10
Output Item   5  E█ .  Line                         Data @ col
Output Item   6       Line                         Data @ col
Output Item   7       Line                         Data @ col
Output Item   8       Line                         Data @ col
Output Item   9       Line                         Data @ col
Output Item  10       Line                         Data @ col
Output Item  11       Line                         Data @ col
Output Item  12       Line                         Data @ col
Output Item  13       Line                         Data @ col
Output Item  14       Line                         Data @ col
Output Item  15       Line                         Data @ col
```

Drive is A:

Fig. 11.8 Arranging record outputs

Process Number   1

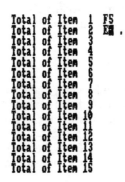
```
Total of Item  1  F5
Total of Item  2  E█ .
Total of Item  3
Total of Item  4
Total of Item  5
Total of Item  6
Total of Item  7
Total of Item  8
Total of Item  9
Total of Item 10
Total of Item 11
Total of Item 12
Total of Item 13
Total of Item 14
Total of Item 15
```

Drive is A:

Fig. 11.9 The Total of Items screen

In addition to printing out selected Fields and Variables, Cambase will also produce a series of final totals, if you so wish. This is done with the Total of Items screen, shown in Fig. 11.9.

As before, enter the names of various Fields or Variables you are interested in against the prompts; for example, to find out the total figure allowed for Credit Limits, you would type F5 against Item 1.

Totals can be provided for all types of field; Numeric fields produce true totals, character fields show the number of character fields encountered (not counting entirely blank fields), Y/N fields show how many Y's were found, and Dates show the total number of elapsed days since January 1 1900.

Averages are also provided for all except character fields – averages of Date fields appear as actual dates.

Narratives

Finally, Cambase offers a simple word processing option enabling straightforward messages, each up to 60 characters in length, to be inserted into Outputs. These messages are called **Narratives**, and up to 64 can be accommodated on any one disc, in addition to other files.

These Narratives can then be printed with the usual Process outputs, simply by inserting N and the appropriate identifying number into the required place in the Output Item screen.

A particular advantage of using Narratives is that they are maintained in a separate file, and are not linked to any particular filespec or Process; they can thus be applied to as many different Processes and File Specifications as you wish.

Running Processes.

When you are ready to run a Process, make sure that you have at least one backup copy of the file on which the Process will be carried out, and that you have taken a security printout of every record as well.

Run the Process with Option 7 from the main menu (Run Processes). As usual, you will be asked to confirm various steps along the way.

When the Process has finished running and been printed (ending with a display of the various Totals for which you had asked), advance the paper out of the printer with the Form Feed 'button' and then compare the results you have obtained with the figures on the security printout you had taken at the beginning.

If you come across any processing errors, immediately restore the database file to its previous condition, using the backup copy to do this.

If everything is in order, you should still keep a copy of the file as it was before the processing took place as a safeguard against future difficulties.

A glance at Flexifile.

So far, all the descriptions of database work have been based on the assumption that you are using the Cambase program.

However, the assertion that similar work can be carried out with other database programs is by no means an empty one; to illustrate this, and to show the diversity of programs which are already available for the PCW8256, we will now look briefly at some features of another database program, the Flexifile database produced by Saxon Computing of Beverley, North Humberside.

```
FLEXIFILE                    CREATE NEW DATABASE
```

```
Enter data disc (A/B)     ?A
Enter filename            ?address
Enter supervisor password ?rocana
Enter user password       ?balino ■
```

```
                                                    Drive is A:
```

Fig. 11.10 Creating passwords for a new Flexifile file.

Figure 11.10 shows the Flexifile screen as it appears when a new database file is about to be created.

Two levels of password have been prompted for, in order to safeguard the security of the completed file; users giving the Supervisor password are permitted to amend the file and add or delete records, etc, whereas those entering only the User password are able to access the file but not to change any of the data.

There are a couple of points to note about the words which have been entered as passwords. First, they are meaningless, which makes it unlikely that they could be guessed by an unauthorised user.

Second, both are based on a thrice-repeated consonant-vowel format, which is extremely easy to remember. Passwords which are difficult to recall are a positive security hazard, as users are prone to jot them down in case they forget them.

Fig. 11.11 Define Flexifile fields

The Define Fields screen – Fig. 11.11 – allows for the inputting of certain basic information about the various fields for the database.

This information includes the Type of field (TExt, NuMeric, a CAlculated value etc), a brief user-supplied identifier for the field (SNam represents SurName, for example), the length of the field, the number of decimal places for a numeric field, etc.

Up to four fields may be identified as Key Fields, and a complete index is maintained of all these, so that in effect Flexifile keeps track of your data in up to four different ways. Here we have entered ACno (Account Number) as the only Key Field.

```
FLEXIFILE                    DESIGN SCREEN LAYOUT                   COL=19 ROW=11

   Account No

   Surname
   Forename(s)
   Address
   Address
   Address
   Address

   Credit Limit █




 [ARROW] keys move the cursor around the screen - [f8] inserts a space
 [DEL] deletes character behind the cursor - [CLR] deletes a character
 [f2] deletes a line - [f3] inserts a line - [f4] clears the screen
 [f5] restores the screen to its original form - [f6] toggles draw on/off

 1ABORT   2DEL LINE   3INS LINE   4CLEAR   5RESTORE   6DRAW TGL   7ACCEPT


                                                                  Drive is A:
```

Fig. 11.12 'Painting' the field names

When the fields have been defined, they are 'painted' on the screen in a 'free-hand' manner, as Fig. 11.12 will show.

Here the various prompts have been put on the screen by simply locating the cursor key at a suitable place on the screen and then typing in whatever information you wish to appear. Additionally borders or rules can be placed on the screen using the 'Draw' option, which places asterisks at the chosen places.

The last stage in creating a file specification consists of locating the various field identifiers in the appropriate positions opposite their prompts, as shown in Fig. 11.13. When their locations have been fixed, they expand across the screen to indicate the amount of space which has been reserved for each field.

Account No   ACACAC

Surname   SNSNSNSNSNSNSNSNSNSN
Forename(s)   FNFNFNFNFNFNFNFNFN
Address   ADADADADADADADADADAD
Address   BDBDBDBDBDBDBDBDBD
Address   CDCDCDCDCDCDCDCDCD
Address   DDDDDDDDDDDDDDDDDDDD

Credit Limit   CRC.CR

[ARROW] keys move the cursor around the screen - [f3] positions a field
[f5] kills all marked fields - [f6] restores original field positions

To kill a field position overwrite the existing field position with NULL

1 ABORT   3 MARK FLD   5 KILL ALL   6 RESTORE   7 ACCEPT

Drive is A:

Fig. 11.13 Adding the field indentifiers

Account No   100

Surname   Jones
Forename(s)   Peter Alexander
Address   41 New Street
Address   Hamilton Gardens
Address   Parkway West
Address   Edgley

Credit Limit   500.00

Move the cursor around the screen with the [ARROW] keys.
Edit fields as required. NOTE: key fields should not be totally blank

1 ABORT   7 ACCEPT

Drive is A:

Fig. 11.14 A typical Flexifile record.

With Flexifile it is possible to amend the database file details at any time, and to add, delete or change field names.

Fig. 11.14 illustrates the sort of record which can be created with Flexifile. Although the route by which this was done was quite different from that employed by Cambase, the end results are, at least superficially, rather similar.

All Flexifile data is stored in ASCII format, and there are special options to enable information to be 'exported' into other CP/M applications programs or 'imported' from them. In particular, data can be exported to the Flexiwrite word processing program also produced by Saxon Computing.

Otherwise, information is output directly from Flexifile by means of **Reports**, which can themselves be stored on disc for future use or modification. A range of arithmetical operations can be performed in a Report, including Sums, Means, Standard Deviation, Variance, etc.

```
FlexiFile
      Page      1

Surname                  Forename(s)              Credit Limit
===========================================================================
Jones                    Peter Alexander               500.00
Jones                    Edward                        600.00
Jackson                  Glen                          750.00
                                                   **************
S                                                     1850.00
M                                                      616.67
                                                   **************

   3 Records printed,
```

Fig. 11.15 A short Flexifile Report

Figure 11.15 illustrates a typical brief Report on the contents of a Flexifile data file. Two calculations have been carried out here to produce the Sum and Mean of the Credit Limit figures, and these are displayed at the bottom of the right-hand column.

Using the imagination.

So far we have looked at databases as ways in which certain sorts of information – such as name and address records – can be stored and

215

retrieved. This approach, however, only uses a fraction of the power which is available in databases.

To make the best use of databases, consider that nearly *all* the organised information which you need to access can be stored in database files, and that the larger the file, and the more varied the Processes by which it can be accessed and modified, the more useful it will be.

Most individuals and organisations tend to store basically related information on several different files.

A voluntary organisation with several branches, for example, might well have a list of all its members and a different list of its branch officers; it might have another list again of those who are associate members and another of those whose subscriptions have lapsed.

Such diversity of files, although rational and probably essential for manual processing, actually carries some very severe dangers along with it.

First of all, the various files may not be consistent; information which is added to one file will very likely not be added to all the others, so that as time passes the various records will no longer 'keep in step' with each other.

Second, a multiplicity of files means that security is more of a problem than if there were only one file.

Third, when some new application needs to be set up, a laborious process is set in train to gather the required information either from the individuals themselves or from the various scattered files.

Finally, duplication of data is in itself an unnecessary evil; it is a throw-back to the 'put everything on a piece of paper and then try not to lose it' mentality which leads directly to the familiar phrase ' I had that information right here a minute ago, I wonder where it can have got to'.

When setting up database files, always consider the possibility that making them a little bigger and more complex than might seem necessary at first can actually save time and trouble by eliminating the need to keep a whole string of other files with broadly similar information on them.

Databases large and small.

Unlike word processing or spreadsheets, databases have an enormous public side. Indeed, one of the biggest growth areas in computing over the next few years may well turn out to be the increased use and further development of the various national and international databases which can be easily and quite cheaply accessed by anyone with a micro-computer and a telephone.

These big public databases differ from the smaller ones which you can create and retrieve on the PVW8256 in both size and complexity, but once you have acquired a familiarity with the functioning of Cambase or Flexifile, or any other reasonably sophisticated database program, you will be well equipped to handle these public files.

Postscript.

At first acquaintance, databases strike many people as being less obviously useful than, for example, word processing programs or spreadsheets. Worse, they often require a great deal of setting-up before they can be used, and this setting-up has to be done very carefully and accurately if the user is not to receive useless or misleading results.

Because of this there is a tendency either not to use databases at all or to skimp on the production of them, setting them up in the simplest (and quickest) possible way. After all, the information they contain is all in a file-box anyway....

However, when a database file has been carefully set up to allow for future expansion, and processes have been developed to make the fullest use of the information stored on the file, a database can save a great deal of data duplication and lead to more accurate and secure record keeping.

CHAPTER TWELVE

Other Programming Possibilities

Preview. Topics discussed in this chapter are as follows:

Expanding operations
The Camsoft payroll program.
The Sagesoft Accounts program
The NewWord word processor.

Expanding operations.

In this book so far all the operations and programs that have been discussed have in common the fact that they are equally practical for personal use, home-based businesses and for larger concerns.

In this chapter we shall be taking a brief look at some operations which are frankly more at home in companies which employ perhaps a dozen people or more, or which need full-scale accounts or payroll of a sort which cannot be produced with a spreadsheet program as shown earlier.

This is not to suggest that they may be unsuitable for smaller concerns, rather that their full benefits will only be experienced where turn-over or other requirements necessitate their use.

In such circumstances, it can be assumed that the PCW8256 –or perhaps several of them working independently – are being used fairly heavily by staff who are generally familiar with them.

In expanding your use of the machine, it is therefore particularly important that you should take careful stock of the availability of the machine and the experience of the operator in deciding both which jobs to automate and which programs to buy.

For example, in most companies above the very smallest, word processing and accounting are everyday activities which require a great deal of machine time; because the programs are used so much, the operators rapidly acquire a high degree of familiarity with them.

Payroll, on the other hand, is almost never done more than once a week, and often only once a fortnight or once a month. As a result, payroll automation provides a useful way of exploiting the accuracy of the computer in a new application without taking up a lot of time on an already heavily-used machine.

However, the fact that payroll is only performed infrequently means that it is unlikely that the users will acquire the same degree of familiarity with a payroll program as they will perforce with a word processor. The result is that although *all* programs should be user-friendly, this is particularly important if the program itself will not be used often.

Camsoft payroll

The payroll program which we shall discuss here is produced by Cambrian Software Works (Camsoft) of Blaenau Ffestiniog, Gwynedd, The program runs on the PCW8256 without any installation being needed, and can accommodate up to 600 employees, although the optimum number which it can handle is probably substantially less.

The program is password-protected, with password creation and change governed by the user's licence number. This is intended to dissuade users from distributing illegitimate copies of the program to other people.

```
Camsoft Payroll        Program Menu    DEALER DEMO ONLY  05 DEC 85

     File Maintenance                      Operations

     1 Update Employees                    4 Run Payroll
     2 Update Constants                    5 End of Period
     3 Update Narratives




         Enter Program Number  █ . (Or enter E to exit)

                                                      Drive is A:
```

Fig. 12.1 The Camsoft Payroll Program Menu.

220

The program is entirely menu-driven, and Fig. 12.1 shows the main menu. From this it should be clear that the program can be used to actually produce the payroll (on a weekly, two-weekly or monthly basis), to produce Month End or Year End Statistics, or to update the tax or personnel data which the program required.

When the program is run for the first time, various **initialisation** procedures are necessary. These are carried out through, in order, Options 3, 2 and 1 from the File Maintenance side of the main menu.

When using the program, you will observe that every menu option which you choose is checked by C o n t i n u e ? (Y / N) appearing at the bottom of the screen. To confirm a choice, either type Y and press E N T E R or merely press E N T E R on its own; to abort an option, press N and E N T E R.

The initialisation procedure mentioned above creates or updates three of these files. Working through these in the order in which they should be set up. **Narratives** are items used for your company's own regular pre-tax additions or post-tax deductions (such as savings schemes, bonuses, deduction of union dues and the like). A total of up to 15 Narratives can be accommodated in the Narratives file.

Perhaps a little awkwardly, once you have started to create a Narratives file, there is no way to leave it until you have specified all 15 items, and whether they are Additions or Deductions. Get around this by entering dummy items (blanks), and specifying them either as Additions or Deductions. However, there are no such problems when Amending an existing Narratives file. Here, you are merely asked which Field No. you want to modify (i.e. whether it is the name of an item or whether it is an Addition or Deduction), and then asked to specify exactly which of the items (here called Sub Records) you wish to change.

Finally, when you are ready to leave any file after making Alterations to it, you are asked, as usual, whether you wish to continue. If you answer this with N, then the changes which you have made will not take effect, and the original version of the file will be preserved. This can be a very useful feature when you find that you have made some serious error in your work.

Moving on through the initialisation procedure, **Constants** are features which when once fixed are not likely to be changed frequently. They include the company name (for a heading on the payslip), a choice as to whether one or two copies of each payslip should be printed, information about percentage tax-rates and the width of tax-bands, and other data about National Insurance contribution rates, etc.

The program is supplied with current information already provided on the Constants file ready for use; unless tax-rates, etc., have been changed since your copy of the program was produced, you should only need to update this file in response to such changes.

Update Employees.

The final File Maintenance option, is the one which will probably need amending most frequently. It will be used not only when employees enter or leave the company's service, but also when they change departments within the company as well as when there are changes to the way in which they are paid (Hourly, Weekly or Monthly), the rate at which they are paid, their PAYE Code, whether they are eligible for SSP, etc.

With all the File Maintenance options it is possible to **C r e a t e** a new file (though only if no old file exists), to **C h a n g e** an existing file, to **D e l e t e** an existing file or to **O u t p u t** the contents of a file either to the screen or the printer.

Running the payroll.

Different payroll programs adopt different approaches to the actual running of the payroll itself.

On some systems, once the relevant data has been input, everything else is done automatically, and the operator is not involved unless there has been some physical problem with the system, such as the printer jamming.

The Camsoft Payroll approach is different. First some general information is required as to which employees are to be paid – the program ascertains the tax period for which pay is being made, and offers the choice of performing payroll for either Monthly, Weekly or Hourly paid employees, as well as for individual staff, individual departments or everyone.

Once this has been done, the program searches through the employee file to find an employee who matches the specifications. If the employee file is large and the number of people to be paid is a small one, this search procedure may take a little while.

From the point where an employee has been identified for paying, the program proceeds to display certain details on the screen and to check whether they are correct. There are also various manual overrides to the automatic tax and SSP rates, etc.

Only when all the details have been identified and checked does the program offer to print the payslip; if required, an additional message of up to 40 characters may be added to the payslip at this time.

```
********************************************************************************
     Payslip      SMITH-JONES  CO

  Ref        Name         Week    Date    Tax Code  NI Code  Dept, ·No.Weeks  Code
  J42    Jackson Peter      10   05 dec 85   h432      A        0      10      T

  Hours   Rate   Pay                      Bonus                   Gross Pay
  42,00   2,25   94,50                    12 80                    107,30

           Tax     NI                                       Deductions
          23,44   0,00                                         23,44

       Tax YTD  NI YTD  Gross YTD    Ers NI                      Net Pay
        23,44    0,00    227,30       0,00     Paid by Cash       83,86

       Join the Staff Saving Plan
                                                    Copy Payslip
********************************************************************************
```

Fig. 12.2 A Camsoft Payroll Payslip

The actual payslips are printed not on special preprinted payslip forms, but on standard continuous stationery, 3 slips per 11" page. Figure 12.2 shows a typical payslip produced by this program.

After each slip has been printed, there is a final check that everything is in order before the program moves on to the next employee; if there has been a paper-jam, or if any errors are spotted at this stage, the program returns to the position it was at before any of that employee's details had been entered, and the various accounting details which the program keeps are not updated until a correct payslip is produced.

Final Analyses.

When all employees have been paid, full details of all pay totals are displayed and printed.

In addition, a coin and note analysis is produced covering all employees paid in cash; this will facilitate the collection of money from the Bank and the making up of pay packets.

End of Month and End of Year Routines.

The final operations of the Camsoft Payroll Program cover the production of month-end reports and clear and year-end clear.

Month-end reports provide statistics for the completed month and for the year to date; the information provided is that required for the usual monthly PAYE tax returns.

After these statistics have been printed, they can be reset and cleared for the following month.

The year-end clear provides no new statistics, as these should be taken from the final month-end report. As the year-end clear involves wiping out all the year's accumulated results, including the last month-end statistics, it is important that the year-end clear should not take place until the final month-end details have been taken.

Another step which must be taken before the year-end clear is taking a printout of the employee file. This is because, in addition to resetting the various year-to-date totals, the year-end clear also checks through the employee file for those who have left during the year and removes their details.

Appreciation of Camsoft Payroll.

The Camsoft Payroll program is in effect a computerised version of good manual payroll practice.

It allows pay to be calculated for up to 600 people, either on an individual, department or all-employee basis, with pay calculated by the hour, the week or the month, and paid weekly, two-weekly or monthly.

The program works **interactively**; that is, it requires the operator to input certain information about one individual at a time; it then uses this, in conjunction with other information stored on disc files, to produce the payroll for that individual.

(The alternative to interactive processing is **batch** processing, whereby a whole series of cheques and payslips is produced in one 'batch' from information supplied previously.)

This has the effect of making the program easier to use, at the expense of needing to input details at the time the payroll is actually produced. This should not be a major problem in a small company.

Apart from the increased accuracy which the use of a payroll program makes possible, the other major savings it offers are in the field of quicker and easier accounting, particularly for PAYE and SSP purposes.

Full accounts.

As we have already seen, there are various ways in which a smallish business can avoid keeping full accounts – the simplest way is by using the facilities of a spreadsheet, such as SuperCalc2, to produce imprest spreadsheets on which all income and expenditure can be entered quite straightforwardly.

On the other hand, there are occasions when fuller accounting programs, offering such facilities as automatic printing of statements and the production of lists of aged debtors are very useful.

Several such programs are available to run under CP/M on the PCW8256; the one which we shall discuss here is the Popular Accounts Program produced by Sagesoft plc of Gosforth, Newcastle upon Tyne.

Sagesoft Popular Accounts.

It should be noted that this particular program forms part of a complete accounting system; for example, statements are automatically produced to a particular format to match pre-printed computer stationery which is also supplied by Sagesoft. The company also offer 90 day 'hotline support' and long term program maintenance for a fee.

Users of the program will be directly concerned with only two CP/M COMmand files on the program disc, namely INSTALL.COM and ACCOUNTS.COM. (There are actually several other COM files on the disc as well, but they are called up automatically when needed, and the user is generally unaware of them.)

The INSTALL.COM program is an extremely simple installation routine which must be run before the ACCOUNT.COM program is used **the first time**; there is no need to use it on subsequent occaisions.

The only question which it asks is whether the program will be run on the PCW8256 or Amstrad 128 computer; no further installation is required at this level.

The main program is started by typing ACCOUNTS. Before the main menu appears – the program is entirely menu-driven – the serial number of the program and the name and address of the registered user are displayed, as a deterrent to unauthorised copying.

Some of these details also appear on certain of the documents which are printed by the program – such as the customer statements – so that a pirated version would lose a great deal of its usefulness.

The main menu is shown in Fig. 12.3 and there are several points which need to be made about it.

The various options are selected from this and the various sub-menus by pressing a suitable number; Ø is consistently used to return either to the main

No. of Entries : 2

1) Create Ledgers   4) Sales/Purchase Ledger Reports

2) Posting Routines   5) Nominal Ledger Reports

3) Utility Routines   6) Statement Routines

                         0) Exit from Program

Which Option :▮

Drive is A:

Fig. 12.3 The Sage Popular Accounts Menu

menu or to one of the sub-menus; if the latter, then a further 0 will take you back to the main menu. There are several overlays in this program, involving a substantial amount of swapping around between the ledgers disc and the program disc.

Program setup.

Although most initialisation is done automatically when you respond to the single question asked by the INSTALL.COM program, it is necessary when the program is being used for the first time to carry out certain initialisation routines.

This is done through the Utility Routines option from the main menu. Enter 3 to select Utility Routines, then when the appropriate sub-menu appears, select option 1, (Initialisation) to inform the program of how many Purchase, Sales and Nominal accounts you will need.

It is important to choose a sufficiently large number to allow for future development, especially bearing in mind that as all accounts are referenced numerically, you will need a sufficient number of 'empty' account numbers to enable future accounts to be slotted in in more or less their correct alphabetical position.

Numerically, you should allot the first 'run' of numbers to Purchase Accounts and the following 'run' to Sales Accounts –for example, Purchase Accounts might be numbered 1 – 200 and Sales Accounts numbered 210 – 400.

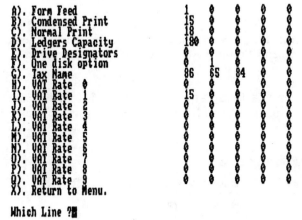

```
Option 4: Installation Parameters

A). Form Feed              1    0    0    0    0
B). Condensed Print        15   0    0    0    0
C). Normal Print           18   0    0    0    0
D). Ledgers Capacity       180  0    0    0    0
E). Drive Designators      0    0    0    0    0
F). One disk option        0    1    0    0    0
G). Tax Name               86   65   84   0    0
H). VAT Rate 0             0    0    0    0    0
I). VAT Rate 1             15   0    0    0    0
J). VAT Rate 2             0    0    0    0    0
K). VAT Rate 3             0    0    0    0    0
L). VAT Rate 4             0    0    0    0    0
M). VAT Rate 5             0    0    0    0    0
N). VAT Rate 6             0    0    0    0    0
O). VAT Rate 7             0    0    0    0    0
P). VAT Rate 8             0    0    0    0    0
Q). VAT Rate 9             0    0    0    0    0
X). Return to Menu.

Which Line ?
                                        Drive is A:
```

Fig. 12.4 The Installation Parameters

Another important function of the Utility Routines menu is to change various Installation Parameters; those which can be modified are shown in Fig. 12.4.

Several of these alterations are designed to change the print style used, as well as to enable the program to be used with other types of printer than the one supplied with the PCW8256.

It is also possible to alter the preset VAT rates. The program allows for up to ten different rates of VAT to be charged; the program is supplied with VAT Rate 1 set to 15%, which is the current rate at the time of writing, and all the others set to zero, but any or all of these rates can easily be changed.

The numbers opposite Items B and C refer to the code used to select different print styles with the PCW8256 printer (and many others as well). The code 15 sets the printer to Condensed type, at about 17 characters per inch, and code 18 sets it to Pica Type, at 10 cpi.

It is unlikely that you will need to change any other items on this page. One curious feature, however, is Item G, which allows you to change the name of the sales tax from VAT to something else; the numbers 86, 65 and 84 which appear in Row G under Columns 1, 2 and 3 represent the ASCII codes for the letters V, A and T respectively, and changing these numbers would change the tax name too.

Initialising accounts.

When setting up to operate the Sagesoft accounts system, you will first need to create Purchase, Sales and Nominal Accounts, and allocate numbers to each one.

This is done with the Create Ledgers menu (Option 1 from the main menu); from within this menu you will need to select 1 again, to create Purchase Accounts.

```
Option :  1  Allocate Purchase Accounts

A/C  Existing Account Name      New Account Name        Credit Limit
----  ----------------------     ----------------        ------------
2    UNUSED ACCOUNT             Butterfly Software            2,000
6    UNUSED ACCOUNT             Cat's Whisker                     0
46   Post Office                █------------------------


Press 'ESC' for the menu

                                                        Drive is A:
```

Fig. 12.5 Setting up new accounts

The basic routine for creating and renaming all types of account is broadly similar; you will be asked for the account number, and when this has been entered the current account name will be displayed. Of course when setting up accounts for the first time none of the accounts will be named, so the words UNUSED ACCOUNT will be shown instead; Fig. 12.5 shows how a Purchase Account looks when being set up in this way.

When you have entered the appropriate name, you will then be able to enter the credit limit applied to the account, or E N T E R if it is zero.

```
Option :  2  Allocate Sales Accounts

          Account No.  :     130

          Name         :  ()Friendly Software
          Address      :    Valley Farn Road
            "          :    Holbrook
            "          :    Yorkshire
          Credit Limit :    2000




          Press 'ESC' to store details.

)▮                        (


                                              Drive is A:
```

Fig. 12.6 Entering Sales Accounts.

Sales Accounts are created in a broadly similar way, through Option 2 of the Create Accounts menu. Here, as you will see from Fig. 12.6, fuller details are required, including the customer address, but broadly the procedure is similar to the creation of Purchase Accounts described earlier.

Finally, you should create your Nominal Accounts in the same way as the Purchase and Sales Accounts; however, Nominal Accounts are kept separately from purchase and sales accounts, and the account numbers can share the same range as those already used.

Five Nominal Account numbers are already allocated, as follows:

    38 – Debtors' Control
    65 – Creditors' Control
    69 – VAT
    88 – Petty Cash
    89 – Bank Account

The balance of Nominal Accounts will be made up to suit your own accounting system.

These accounts are then entered from the Create Accounts menu, Option 3, in the same way as Purchase Accounts, except that instead of a Credit Limit you will be asked to enter a budget figure, if appropriate.

Other aspects of setting up the accounting system (and in particular the various elements of the Balance Sheet) are best done in consultation with your accountants. The mechanics of the actual entries are straightforward enough, and broadly follow the pattern familiar from creating the Purchase and Sales Accounts, but – particularly if you have not previously used a full accounting system – you will need expert guidance if you are to get your accounts to balance properly.

Day to day use of the system.

Once the system has been set up, it can be used without further specialist help by anyone familiar with invoicing and payment routines. These are reached through the Postings Routines, Option 2 of the main menu.

Both payments and invoices are handled by a **batch** sytem; the details of invoices to be sent or payments to be made are entered first (by choosing the appropriate options from the Posting menu), and when they have been entered, all the invoices or payments are processed automatically.

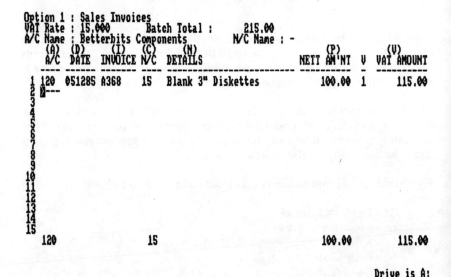

Fig. 12.7 Entering details for a sales invoice.

230

For example, if you choose Sales Invoices, which are reached through Option 1 of the Postings menu, you will be shown the screen reproduced in Fig. 12.7.

Account numbers can be entered in any order. As they are entered, they are automatically checked to see whether they are valid. Next, the date is entered and a code number for the invoice, up to 6 characters in length.

Next, the number of the appropriate Nominal Account is entered followed by the nett amount of the invoice.

Finally, the VAT rate is entered; this consists of a figure between 0 and 9, referring to the rates which are reached through the Utilities option described above. The program is produced with 15% pre-coded as 1. Then press > and the correct VAT amount is automatically calculated and entered.

An alternative is to enter < when asked for the VAT amount; this assumes that the sum entered in the Nett column is actually Gross; the appropriate nett amount and VAT are automatically calculated and shown on the screen.

It is also possible to enter the actual VAT amount manually; this may be necessary if VAT is only to be charged on a portion of the invoice.

When all the invoice entries have been made and checked – there is an editing facility for correcting any errors which are spotted after an entry has been made – the ledgers are updated ready for the invoices to be printed.

Payments and credit notes are processed in the same way as invoices; facilities are provided for dealing with part payments.

Statements Routine.

1). Print Address List.

2). Print Statements.

3). Print Labels.

4). Enter Company Address.

0). Return to Accounts Menu.

Which Option : 1-

Drive is A:

Fig. 12.8 The Statements Menu.

Statements.

Statements are produced by selecting Option 6 (Statement Routines) from the main menu. This reveals the Statements Menu shown in Fig. 12.8.

Option 1 from this menu allows you to produce a listing of the names of all your customers. This listing is designed to fit onto standard continuous stationery, and a copy should normally be taken whenever new account numbers have been allocated. The empty spaces allow you to write in the names of new accounts before they are entered into the disc files.

```
JOHN M HUGHES                    SALES ACCOUNTS                   Page :  1
                                                                 Date :  06/12/85

                              Credit                                       Credit
A/C  Account Name             Limit     A/C  Account Name                  Limit
---  ------------             -----     ---  ------------                  -----
101                                     102
103                                     104
105                                     106
107                                     108
109                                     110  Amazing Software              1,300
111                                     112
113                                     114
115                                     116
117                                     118
119                                     120  Betterbits Components         2,400
121                                     122
123                                     124
125                                     126
127                                     128
129                                     130  Friendly Software             2,000
131                                     132
133                                     134
135                                     136
137                                     138
139                                     140
141                                     142
143                                     144
145                                     146
147                                     148
149                                     150
151
```

Fig. 12.9 A listing of Sales Accounts.

A sample listing is shown in Fig 12.9. Any errors in this listing can be corrected by going back through the Allocated Accounts routine described earlier.

A useful facility is offered when producing statements, or indeed printing any information which has to appear in a precise format to fit the stationery. The program offers to print a test pattern, and will continue to do this until you are satisfied that everything is lined up correctly.

When printing actual statements, the program asks for the lowest and highest account numbers to be processed; if these are the same, only one statement will be produced.

An important option available from this menu allows you to print address labels as well as statements; this will be useful in cases where window envelopes are not used.

Once again, a test pattern is offered to enable the user to align the printing pattern precisely with the paper, and only when this is satisfactory are the various details for the labels checked; the details required are the same as those for the production of invoices, making it very easy to produce labels and statements in one session.

Reports.

The Sagesoft Accounts program produces a full range of reports, based on the updating of the ledgers which takes place automatically when entries are posted.

For example, the Utility Routines menu offers a complete Accounting Trail, with every item which has been posted listed on it in order.

Other reports are created through the Nominal Ledger Reports option of the main menu. These include a VAT analysis which provides the necessary information for making up the regular VAT returns to H.M. Customs and Excise as well as a list of all transactions in the appropriate period, month-to-date and year-to-date accounts and a budget report.

Appreciation of Sagesoft Accounts.

For businesses which need to maintain full accounts, the Sagesoft Popular Accounts program provides a framework for a practical automated system, which is however not so far removed from manual practice as to cause difficulties for new users.

233

A full accounting trail is maintained, and full reports for VAT, Profit and Loss, Bank Reconciliation etc. are supprted. Invoicing procedures ensure that billing procedures are carried out rapidly and efficiently.

Compact Accounts.

There are, of course, other accounting programs available in addition to Sagesoft Popular Accounts.

A particularly interesting example is the Daybook program produced by Compact Systems, of Romsey, Hampshire. This program makes full use of some of the special file-handling characteristics built into the PCW8256, leading to very efficient storage and retrieval of data at the cost of slightly increased loading time.

Like several of the other applications programs we have examined in this book, Daybook has been designed with first-time computer users very much in mind; accordingly, it offers close computer parallels to the usual manual account books which Daybook users will already be familiar with.

We have already seen several ways in which programs can make their data files available to different programs using the CP/M Operating System, in order to import or export data. Obviously this has considerable value in reducing or even eliminating the need to enter text or numbers twice, or to manually transfer the results of a statistical program to a word processed document.

Daybook reveals a slightly different way in which files can be made accessible to other programs beside the originating one; Daybook files are **upwardly compatible.**

In computer terms, compatability means that programs, data files, and even hardware, can be used on other equipment than that for which they were originally created; upward compatibility means specifically that when you upgrade (improve) your old system, elements of it can still be used.

Compact Systems produce a range of accounting software rather more sophisticated than the Daybook program; indeed, for all its sophistication, Daybook can be looked at simply as an 'Entry level' system, designed to make the transfer from a manual system to a computerised one as painless as possible for those with little previous computing experience.

Files created with Daybook are, as we noted above, upwardly compatible with such other Compact Systems programs as Invoicing and Sales Ledger; thus if you do outgrow your present system of accounts and need to change to a more sophisticated system, you will find that all your Daybook files can still be used just as before.

Moving on from LocoScript.

Although the LocoScript word processing program which comes 'bundled' with the PCW8256 is easy to use and generally quite efficient, there are certain reasons why users of the machine may prefer to purchase and use a different package.

These reasons include the fact that some aspects of LocoScript are rather slow – especially when ending an edit – that the files which LocoScript produces are not in ASCII format, and that some useful commands are not available from within LocoScript, at least in its earlier versions – there is no mail merge facility, for example, no **print part text** command and no way of arranging for the printer to stop at some pre-determined place in the text.

(This latter is not really necessary with the printer provided, but if you substitute a daisy-wheel printer, you may need to stop printing at certain times in order to replace one wheel with another, to change to italic type, for instance.)

The fact that LocoScript is not a CP/M program means that the files it produces cannot be accessed by other CP/M programs, such as envelope addressers, spelling checkers and the like.

Furthermore, users may come to the PCW8256 already familiar with some other word processing program, and not wish to devote time to learning how to use LocoScript.

Alternatively, in educational establishments there are substantial advantages in teaching word processing with an industry-standard program, so that the pupils will not then need to learn another program when taking up a job.

Probably the most popular word processing program which has ever been produced is Word Star. A derivative of this, called NewWord, is available for the PCW8256, and although the inclusion of LocoScript makes it less than a necessity to invest in another word processor, NewWord might well appear attractive as a 'step up', for the reasons given above.

The NewWord word processor.

New Word is available for both the PCW8256 and the Amstrad 6128; the PCW8256 version includes a SUBMIT file which resets the keyboard to take some advantage of the additional keys available.

It would obviously not be possible to provide a full introduction to NewWord in such a short space as is available here; indeed, the NewWord manual is an extremely detailed and lengthy document, and is absolutely indispensible to using the program.

There are, however, certain points to which it may be beneficial to draw the reader's attention, in particular as regards the more important differences between NewWord and LocoScript.

Commands and Menus.

We have seen that LocoScript is driven by a range of pull-down menus, but that the more experienced user can dispense with their help to a greater or lesser degree.

Something of the sort is also true with NewWord, though matters have been handled somewhat differently.

NewWord offers a choice of four **help levels.** At level 3, a list of menus and prompts is always displayed in the upper section of the screen; Level 2 displays only prompts, and at Level 1, page, line and column counts are removed as well. Finally, in Level 0 not even safety nets of the Are you sure? variety are displayed.

At all levels, the Edit menu can be called up with the command ˆJ .

Because NewWord was designed for smaller keyboards than the PCW8256's, several commands take the form CONTROL+**key** (ALT+**key** on the PCW8256), and represented as ˆ**key** in many manuals.

The key redefinition part of the SUBMIT file makes it possible to carry out several of these commands with single key-presses, but despite this the great majority of the commands are still of the ˆ**key** variety. Indeed, many of them actually require **two** keys to be pressed in addition to the ALT key.

As a time-saver, and to help a new user learn the various commands, the Edit menu (which is always displayed in Help level 3) lists the **first** key that needs to be pressed for a particular action. If pressing the first key is not followed within a couple of seconds by pressing the second key, a complete new menu is displayed to show what possibilities are available.

For example, ˆK on its own will call up the **blocking and saving** menu; however, there is no need to wait for the menu to be displayed if you are already familiar enough with the commands to be able to type ˆKD (to save a document) or ˆKQ (to abandon one).

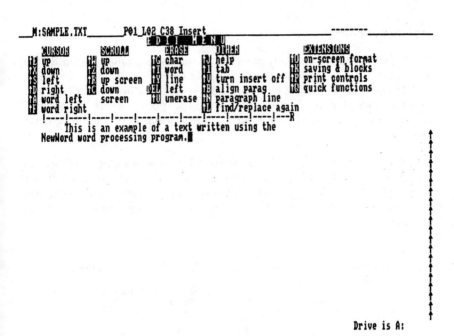

Fig. 12.10 Composing text with NewWord.

A typical screen (with the Help Level set at 3) would look something like that shown in Fig. 12.10. The Edit menu is displayed, occupying almost the top third of the screen; above this is shown the Status Line, giving the title of the document, the current page, line and column number.

Towards the right-hand end of the status Line, a 'barometer' (the hyphens) is shown as a guide to what percentage of the computer's memory is still available – as it fills up, the hyphens change to equals signs.

Margins and tabs are shown under the menu, in the form of hyphens (spaces) and exclamation marks (tabs), ranged between L and R, representing the Right and Left margins respectively. (In Fig. 12.10, the L is hidden by the Tab Stop.)

An interesting feature of this is that a new page format is created simply by typing in a new rule composed of whatever combination of hyphens and exclamation marks are required, enclosed between L and R, and instructing NewWord to conform to this rule. This feature makes rearrangements of margins extremely straightforward.

237

Mail-merging files.

NewWord offers an extremely powerful facility for mail-merging files. This means that it is possible to create a single letter, for example, in which certain features, such as the name and address of the addressee, are left out. Instead, special items are included at those places where names and addresses would normally be placed, and enclosed between ampersands (**&**).

When those ampersands are encountered during printing, the text in between them is not printed; instead, it is replaced by text from a previously prepared file. In this way, it is possible to produce a large number of letters all individually addressed and each one looking as though it is a unique document.

```
. op
. df FORM. DAT
. rv NAME1, NAME2, ADDRESS1, ADDRESS2, ADDRESS3, ADDRESS4


                              14 New Street,
                              Belton,
                              Gloucester


                              March 21, 1985

     &NAME1& &NAME2&
     &ADDRESS1&
     &ADDRESS2&
     &ADDRESS3&
     &ADDRESS4&

     Dear &NAME1&,

          I just had to write and thank you for the lovely
     pair of socks you sent me for my birthday -- green with
     yellow stripes! They certainly make a unique and much-
     appreciated gift!


                              Lots of love,


                              Bill
. pa
```

Fig. 12.11 An example of a Mail-Merge Document

An example of a mail-merge document is shown in Fig. 12.11. At the top of the document are a series of **dot commands**. In order, these are instructions to NewWord to Omit Page Numbers (**. op**), to look for names and addresses in a datafile called FORM.DAT (.df FORM.DAT) and to Read the Variables in that file when it sees an ampersand (.rv).

At the foot of the letter there is another dot command (.pa), which forces the printer to the top of a new page.

```
Ada,Smith,The Laurels,Tregarrick,Ponteglos,Cornwall
Paul,Jackson,Newton House,Station Street,Wanton Abbot,Whimshire
```

Fig. 12.12 Data ready to be merged into a letter.

To provide the letter with a set of appropriate names and addresses, it will be necessary to produce a data-file called FORM.DAT, with the various necessary details on it. A typical example is shown in Fig. 12.12.

When the original letter is merge-printed, all the items inside the ampersands are duly replaced by items taken from the data file. As the data file can hold up to 99,999 lines, it is obvious that you can now write individual letters to a substantial number of people! Fig. 12.13 shows two letters produced using the files mentioned.

Nor are the merged items necessarily limited to the address section of the letter; if you wish, you can include further personal references in the body of the letter, and NewWord will automatically reformat the text around this as the letter is printed.

Producing ASCII files.

NewWord can be used to produce document files in ASCII format, suitable for making up CP/M SUBMIT files, for example.

Normal NewWord files are actually stored in a slightly different format, in which every word is stored as ASCII except for the final character. For the benefit of those interested in computing, this last character has the **parity bit** set, and if you TYPE a NewWord document you will observe that this has some rather curious effects.

Although NewWord itself offers a way to store documents in ASCII format, it is probably easiest to proceed by creating an ordinary NewWord document and then copying it to Drive M with PIP. To do this, you will need to use the special PIP option [Z] which strips the parity bit off a file; to copy a NewWord document called SAMPLE.TXT from Drive A to Drive M, and to simultaneously convert it to straightforward ASCII, you should type:

```
                              14 New Street,
                              Belton,
                              Gloucester

                              March 21, 1985

Paul Jackson
Newton House
Station Street
Wanton Abbot
Whimshire

Dear Paul,

     I just had to write and thank you for the lovely
pair of socks you sent me for my birthday -- green with
yellow stripes! They certainly make a unique and much-
appreciated gift!

                              Lots of love,


                              Bill



                              14 New Street,
                              Belton,
                              Gloucester

                              March 21, 1985

Ada Smith
The Laurels
Tregarrick
Ponteglos
Cornwall

Dear Ada,

     I just had to write and thank you for the lovely
pair of socks you sent me for my birthday -- green with
yellow stripes! They certainly make a unique and much-
appreciated gift!

                              Lots of love,


                              Bill
```

Fig. 12.13 A letter produced by merging the two files.

```
PIP M:=SAMPLE.TXT[Z]
```

and everything else will happen automatically.

Using the dictionary.

Supplied with the NewWord program are a set of eleven extension programs under the general title of The Word.

These programs are centered around a 45,000 word main dictionary which is included on the disc, and offer a range of useful accessories when using the NewWords program, although they are not limited to using NewWord files.

Probably the most important of these programs is the Spelling Checker. This can be used to read through NewWord or ASCII file to see whether any words have been mis-spelt.

There are clear limitations to such programs, the most obvious of which is that they can only check whether the words you have entered actually exist in the dictionary, and not whether you have actually chosen the correct word. For example, a spelling checker would find the mistake in **He came here yeterday**, as **yeterday** is not an English word; but it would not find anything wrong with **He come here yesterday** as all the words are individually correct.

A second problem is that even a 45,000 word dictionary will not include all the words you are likely to use – obviously words such as **Amstrad** and **LocoScript** would not be included. However, special additional dictionaries can be set up to accommodate new words if this proves necessary.

Despite these minor problems, a spelling checker program is a great help in locating and correcting errors arising from the sort of mis-typing that most people are prone to from time to time. In addition to checking through an actual written document, the dictionary can be used in various other ways.

If you know yourself to be a shaky speller, for example, you might wish to use the LOOKUP facility, which allows you to enter a word whose spelling you are uncertain of; the program will then check to see whether it can find anything else similar to it by applying a set of spelling 'rules' to what you have entered.

If you are interested in cheating at crosswords, you may find the FIND and ANAGRAM programs helpful; the latter, as its name suggests, finds from the dictionary any other words which have the same letters as those you input, while the former allows you to input the letters of which you are certain and then suggests all possible words which would fit.

For example, if you needed a word of seven letters, of which you knew only the third (A) and fourth (C) you would type:

FIND??AC???

and after due deliberation while it consulted the dictionary, NewWord would come up with a list of 61 words ranging from APACHES to WRACKED by way of CLACKED, JOACHIM and TEACART

Other facilities provided include ways to count how long a document is (a word-count), what the frequency is of individual words (if you are interested in lexicographic analysis) and ways of sorting out homonyms and homophones.

Appreciation of NewWord.

NewWord is not as friendly to use as LocoScript because a large number of the commands involve one– or two–letter combinations and the ALT key.

Additionally, when you are using Help level 3 about a third of the screen is occupied by the Editing menu. This can be removed by using Lower Help Levels, at the price of a few moments, delay while the disc drive operates and loads the appropriate information if you need it at any time.

The advantages of NewWord are that it offers some important facilities not yet available with LocoScript, in particular the spelling checker and its associated dictionary, and the ability to create ASCII files.

NewWord is a CP/M program, and its files are also fully compatible with Word Star, so that they can be read and modified by that program as well. Additionally, it can use the various auxiliary programs produced to work in conjunction with Word Star.

Because of its close affinity to Word Star it may already be familiar to some users, and may have value as a teaching tool for others. The problems of a slight lack of friendliness will obviously become less important as users become more familiar with it, and for those users who need its particular strengths, NewWord may prove very valuable.

Postscript.

This chapter has not set out to do more than suggest a few ways in which a user may find it helpful to expand his PCW8256 system, and to look at some of the programs which are available to do this.

The programs have been chosen because they represent good modern programming practice, and because they represent the sort of direction in which many new users are interested in moving once they have become generally familiar with the machine.

POSTSCRIPT
Looking Back.

By the time you reach here (unless you are one of those people who read books from the back forwards) you should have a pretty fair idea of the sort of thing which the PCW8256 is capable of doing.

In effect, you will have repeated the journey of dicovery which we made when one of the early machines was delivered to us. Indeed, it was on this machine that almost the whole of the book was written, using the LocoScript word processor.

Several thousand words after that first encounter, there are a few extra lessons which we have learned about the PCW8256, and which it may be useful to pass on to you.

First, LocoScript itself has proved very acceptable, with only three minor problems showing – though 'problems' may be too strong a word.

The first of these is the inherent slowness of LocoScript when moving from one part of a document to another or when Exiting from an edit when the cursor is well away from the end of the text.

The second problem is the awkwardness of the procedure used to print a short section out of a larger text. As LocoScript currently lacks a 'print part text' facility, the only practical way to do this is to Copy the required passage into a new file. This file will lack a header, so you will then have to Insert the text into a new file specially Created for the purpose, and Print that.

We have also found very occasional problems with LocoScript 'locking up' when Pasting in a text fragment which has been moved from another place in a document. The cure for this appears to be to always begin a Paste with the cursor located in the left hand margin, and then to Relay the text afterwards.

Not to end on a negative note, LocoScript has many positive advantages. It has done everything we have asked of it, has generally been extremely reliable and easy to use, and the basics were easily and quickly learned. In terms both of ease of use and sophistication, it is certainly better than nearly every other word processing program we have ever used on a micro-computer.

As far as the other parts of the system are concerned, there have been no problems at all. The disc drive, the printer and the keyboard have all stood up manfully to the very heavy demands made on them, and have given not a moment's cause for concern. The screen, too, has been a delight to work from.

In conclusion, it is fair to say that the PCW 8256 has proved a positive pleasure to work with. We hope that your own experience will be as good.

Converting LocoScript files to ASCII

Much stress has been laid in the body of this book on the fact that LocoScript files are not stored according to strict ASCII rules, and that furthermore there are dangers in mixing LocoScript and CP/M files on the same disc.

Despite this, if you have some familiarity with programming in BASIC, it *is* possible to convert LocoScript files to ASCII format, provided you are prepared to go to a little trouble.

The advantages of this are that you will then be able to export LocoScript files to other programs, including spelling-checker programs. You will also be able to use LocoScript-generated documents in CP/M SUBMIT files and the like.

The work is not difficult, but it does require a little care, especially in entering the BASIC conversion program listed below. This program – which is written in the Mallard BASIC provided on Side Two of the CP/M+ Master Disc – should then be saved on an appropriate disc.

Preparing the LocoScript file.

The first task is to strip the LocoScript file of its header. The simplest way to do this is to create a new, headerless document with the Block Save option entered through *f*8.

This new Block – which LocoScript would regard as 'Not a LocoScript Document' – must then be saved in Group 0; the procedure outlined here will not work if any other Group is chosen.

Preparing CP/M.

Next, exit from LocoScript, reset the computer and start CP/M in the usual way, Load Mallard BASIC from the CP/M disc, and then load and run the BASIC conversion program which you have previously saved.

The program will ask you for the name and drive of the Source File (the LocoScript text which you have saved in Group 0) and then for the name and drive of the Object File (that is the ASCII file which you are creating).

Both items of information are entered according to the standard CP/M rules, with the name of the Disc Drive (A, B or M) coming before the name of the file, and separated from it by the usual colon. If either file is on Drive A, the name of the Drive can be omitted.

The program will then proceed to convert the file to ASCII format and save it under the new name. In doing so it will strip the first section of the file, which is used by LocoScript, as well as the LocoScript end-of-text marker.

'Hard' carriage returns in the original file are represented in the new file by both Carriage Return (CR) and Line Feed (LF); 'soft' returns are not inserted, and the new lines are regarded as of infinite length, so that when the new file is displayed on the screen, words may appear broken at the right-hand edge.

The BASIC Program.

The program which follows is BASIC in more senses than one; individual users may wish to amend it to ensure, for example, that the Source File and the Object File do not share the same name.

```
10 CLS$=CHR$(27)+"E"+CHR$(27)+"H":PRINT CLS$
20 INPUT "Input DRIVE:SOURCE FILE"; S$
30 INPUT "Input DRIVE:OBJECT FILE"; O$
40 OPEN "O",2,O$
50 OPEN "I",1,S$
60 FOR A=1 TO 128:A$=INPUT$(1,#1):NEXT
70 WHILE NOT(EOF(1))
80 A$=INPUT$(1,#1)
90 IF A$=CHR$(&H81) THEN A$=" "
100 IF A$=CHR$(&H88) THEN A$=INPUT$(1,#1):A$=CHR$(13)+CHR$(10)
110 IF A$<>CHR$(&H80) THEN PRINT #2,A$;
120 WEND
130 CLOSE
140 PRINT "Job Completed"
150 END
```

INDEX